The Writer's Craft

Sue Harper

Patricia Westerhof

Harcourt
Canada

Harcourt Canada

Orlando Austin New York San Diego Toronto London

National Library of Canada Cataloguing in Publication Data
Harper, Sue, 1952–
          The writer's craft / Sue Harper.

For use in Grade 12.
ISBN 0-7747-1607-X

          1. English language—Rhetoric—Textbooks. I. Title.

PE1408.H3443 2003   808'.042   C2003-901168-2

AUTHORS
Sue Harper, Cross-curricular Literacy Head, John Fraser Secondary School, Mississauga, ON, and Developer for the Ontario Secondary School Grade 10 Literary Test

Patricia Westerhof, English Teacher, St. Clement's School, Toronto, ON

REVIEWERS
The authors and publisher gratefully acknowledge these reviewers for their contribution to the development of this project:

Nick Maiese, Former Journalist, Graduate of the Medill School of Journalism, Northwestern University

Bruce Sainchuk, English Department Head, Archbishop O'Leary High School, Edmonton Catholic District School Board, Edmonton, AB

Karen Wason, Program Team Leader, Communications, and Head of English, Earl Haig Secondary School, Toronto District School Board, Toronto, ON

Heather Wheatland, English Teacher, Bishop Carroll High School, Calgary Catholic District School Board, Calgary, AB

Project Manager: Su Mei Ku
Production Editor: Tricia Carmichael
Copy Editors: Emily Ferguson, Susan Till
Production Coordinator: Cheri Westra
Permissions Editor: Karen Becker
Cover Design: Sharon Foster Design
Interior Design: Sharon Foster Design
Page Composition: Heidy Lawrance Associates
Cover Photograph/Illustration: "Chair and Window" by Vincent McIndoe/Stock Illustration Source
Printing and Binding: Transcontinental Printing Inc.

∞ Printed in Canada.

1 2 3 4 5   07 06 05 04 03

Contents

TO THE STUDENT

Welcome to *The Writer's Craft*. The purpose of this text is to help you consolidate what you already know about writing and to further develop your ability to write in a variety of forms. In addition, this text provides the following:

- It encourages you to explore a workshop approach to writing. The workshop approach will challenge your skills of critical and creative thinking, planning, developing, critiquing, revising, and editing.

- It offers you a wide range of activities and tools. With these, you can begin to build your writing portfolio in preparation for publication, post-secondary education, and job applications, or just for the love of writing.

- It provides you with the opportunity to begin thinking about writing and writing-related careers. A chart at the back of the book (on the inside back cover) lists some of the careers that you might investigate.

What Is Expected of You?

If you have chosen to take a writing course, there is an expectation that you will have acquired the following skills and attitudes:

- Equity: You recognize, accept, and respect the diverse communities that contribute to the power of writing and the voice of writers in Canada and around the world.

- Writing process: You understand the stages of the writing process and use them.

- Perseverance: When faced with a challenge, you accept it and find ways to make progress and accomplish the task.

- Ethics: You understand the seriousness of plagiarism and the consequences that accompany plagiarizing anyone else's work.

- Technology: You understand and use computer applications that are available to you and that assist you to do research, organize information, revise and edit your written work, and enhance your written and oral presentations.

What Can You Expect from This Book?

You can expect this book to be a rich resource. In Chapter 1, many myths about writing are dispelled. You will learn about participating in a community of writers, publishing your work, and building a portfolio. Each of the next five chapters focuses on a form of writing: creative nonfiction (Chapter 2), story (Chapter 3), script (Chapter 4), poetry (Chapter 5), and business writing (Chapter 6). The final unit focuses on writers reflecting on and writing about their craft.

In Chapters 2 to 6, you will find a number of useful elements and tools.

- Learning Goals: what you can expect to learn in the chapter

- the definition of the type of writing

- The Writer's Warm-Ups: activities to help you loosen up your mind and your creativity

- The Writer's Toolkit: technical aspects of each of the types of writing and the tools that writers use

- Applications: activities that help reinforce specific techniques you have learned

- The Writer's Projects: independent and small-group projects that are divided into research activities (Investigating the Writer's Craft) and writing activities (Practising the Writer's Craft)

- The Writer's Reading List: a bibliography of books about the specific types of writing discussed in the chapters and books exemplifying those types of writing

We hope you enjoy this book and find it useful, stimulating, and fun.

Sue Harper
Patricia Westerhof

What Is the Writer's Craft?

Writing is a craft. You have to take your apprenticeship in it like anything else.

KATHERINE ANNE PORTER[1]

Chapter 1: As You Begin

Appendix A: Sentences and Clichés

As You Begin

You clear a space for the writing voice, hacking away at the others with machetes, and you begin to compose sentences. You begin to string words together like beads to tell a story.... But you cannot will this to happen. It is a matter of persistence and faith and hard work. So you might as well just go ahead and get started.

ANNE LAMOTT[2]

LEARNING GOALS

▶ demonstrate an understanding of the writer's craft
▶ reflect on one's own experiences in writing
▶ develop an appreciation for and begin to use a workshop approach to produce a range of writing
▶ understand the value of using group skills effectively during the production and assessment of written work
▶ understand and apply the steps of the writing process
▶ produce thoughtful, effective publications and prepare them for distribution to wider audiences
▶ develop and maintain a writing portfolio

WHAT IS THE WRITER'S CRAFT?

"Creative" writing is often interpreted to mean poetry, fiction, and plays. Business letters, essays, and thank-you notes are, in contrast, considered "functional" writing. While not all forms of writing are works of art, anyone who has written a cover letter for a job application, a personal essay for application to a university or college, or even a personal note to include with a greeting card, knows that most kinds of writing require imagination and careful crafting of words.

For most students, writing is a daily activity. From course assignments to e-mail exchanges with friends, students write frequently, and for various reasons. Perhaps you write to communicate information or ideas, to share opinions and express feelings, or to entertain others. Perhaps you write for more personal reasons—in a journal, to figure something out by writing your way to understanding or to a solution. Or perhaps you write to exercise your imagination, to find an outlet for your creative impulses and ideas. Whatever the reason, you're reading this book because you want to improve your writing skills. You're likely already a very good writer, and you understand that there's a difference between *competent* writing—writing that is clear and appropriate for its purpose and audience—and *memorable* writing—writing that is not only appropriate for its purpose and audience but is vibrant, energetic, and satisfying to read. We focus on the latter kind in this book, and the instructions, examples, and activities throughout will help you to hone your abilities to create clear, appropriate, and lively writing in various genres.

MYTHS ABOUT WRITING

Writing, like all acts of creativity, has a mystical side to it: We can't pin the process down; we can't reduce it to step-by-step instructions. Because of our inability to name fully what happens in the creative process, myths about writers and writing abound. Since believing the myths can be discouraging and even debilitating to writers, let's examine some of these popular beliefs.

Writing Is All About Talent

▶▶ WRITING TIP
Develop a goal for writing daily outside of class. Choose a specific time of day and a specific amount of time, and stick to it.

Talent definitely helps. However, a natural ability is not enough. Writing is mostly about hard work. Someone may have a natural "ear" for music, but that doesn't make him or her a concert pianist. Only through practice and hard work does a musician master his or her instrument. Likewise you must master your craft through learning everything you can about writing and through practising regularly. Stephen Leacock once said, "I am a great believer in luck, and I find the harder I work, the more I have of it." So it is with talent: The harder you work, the more talent you'll seem to have. Jack Heffron in *The Writer's Idea Book*[3] contends,

> Showing up is the main thing. Get to the desk regularly.... The writers we admire—or envy—might be geniuses whose talent dwarfs ours, but more often they're people who show up, with those seven-hundred-page novels they've been rising at five to write every morning for the past year.

Writers Should Wait for Inspiration

Most writers who wait for the muse rarely finish their drafts. Waiting for divine or mystical inspiration is merely a form of procrastination. Granted, just as it may work better for you to tackle your algebra problems in a quiet room first thing in the morning, writing may come more easily in a certain place at a certain time of day as well. Furthermore, on some days, you will find writing easier than other days, and on some days you may write very little that will make it into your final manuscript, but it is the discipline of writing regularly that will lead to complete pieces. Alberto Moravia[4] explains his method: "When I sit at my table to write, I never know what it's going to be till I'm under way. I trust in inspiration, which sometimes comes and sometimes doesn't. But I don't sit back waiting for it. I work *every* day." Toni Morrison[5] states, "I don't wait to be struck by lightning and don't need certain slants of light in order to write."

Rather than wait for inspiration, many writers practise free writing. There are variations of this technique, but essentially it involves putting pen to paper (or fingers to keyboard) and writing whatever comes to mind, without stopping to think, without stopping to revise. Some writers use this technique as a warm-up—they begin their writing sessions by pouring out distracting thoughts on paper, a process which then frees them to tackle the writing project at hand. Other writers use free writing as a way to turn off the self-critical voices in their heads and get a very rough draft of a piece down on paper. Free writing is a method of finding inspiration *through* writing.

Canadian novelist and poet Michael Ondaatje[6] points out that inspiration does not happen in the composing stage of writing alone. In an interview with poet David O'Meara, Ondaatje explains:

> [The] process of editing, shaping, rewriting ... is where a lot of inspiration also happens.... Inspiration doesn't only happen in the first draft of writing; it happens when you're rewriting. Where you see that in fact the alliteration is over the top in this poem, or that you need to slow down the pace in some way, or add a couple of beats of air in there when you feel the line going too fast.

You Need a Lot of Life Experience to Be a Good Writer

This myth comes in several versions: a common one is that all good writers had bad childhoods. While we all can name several famous "tortured artists," misery is not a prerequisite for writing well. Nor

▶▶ WRITING TIP

As you practise the discipline of writing every day, take note of when and where you get your best ideas, when and where the words seem to flow from your fingers, and when and where you feel uncreative, slowed down, or blocked. Experiment with free writing. Work at discovering more about your writing process in order to develop writing habits that keep you sharp and disciplined.

do you need years of experience from which to draw. According to American author Willa Cather,[7] "Most of the basic material a writer works with is acquired before the age of fifteen." Margaret Laurence, in an autobiographical piece titled "Where the World Began," describes the influence of her childhood setting on her life's work. She points out that tiny prairie towns like the one in which she grew up have been described as "dull, bleak, flat, uninteresting"—hardly a promising place for gaining sensational life experience. Yet Laurence[8] expresses the emotional draw of the place for her, explaining, "Because that settlement and that land were my first and for many years my only real knowledge of the planet, in some profound way they remain my world, my way of viewing. My eyes were formed there." Wherever and however your own way of viewing has been formed, your point of view is unique. What you need to bring to your writing is not years of exotic or devastating experiences, but, in Laurence's phrase,[9] "the sight of [your] own particular eyes."

▸▸ **WRITING TIP**
In your notebook, do some autobiographical writing. What has influenced your view of the world? What makes your perspective unique?

You Can Write Only About What You Know

While you want to write about yourself, your experience, your unique perspective of the world, and what you know, you don't have to limit yourself to your own life experience. Imagination allows both writer and reader to put themselves in other people's shoes, to envision worlds, characters, and events that have not happened to them personally. As Mark Twain put it, "Fiction is obliged to stick to possibilities. Truth isn't." "A writer's material is what he cares about," says John Gardner.[10] It is your job to find out what you care about and then use your imagination and all the skills you have mastered to make the subject come alive on the page. Tracy Kidder[11] maintains, "You can write about *anything*, and if you write well enough, even the reader with no intrinsic interest in the subject will become involved."

If you're writing fiction, however, you must be cautious about using settings you've never been to or types of people you have no firsthand knowledge of. William Arthur Deacon's hilarious essay "What a Canadian Has Done for Canada" shows how absurd fiction can be when the author doesn't use accurate details about the climate, terrain, wildlife, and so on, of the setting he or she is using. The essay describes the far-fetched plot of a Canadian novel published in 1924, pointing out its many flaws, such as the hero catching "two fish with his hands—one a five pound maskalonge, not native to that section of the country" and digging cedar roots, "though no cedars grow that far north." Later, the hero attacks a bull moose, who "strikes the man with its 'forepaws.'" Deacon comments, "An ordinary moose with hard, sharp hoofs would certainly have killed him; but this one, doubtless because equipped by the author with 'paws,' only succeeds in giving him 'a bruise or two' which cause him no trouble."[12]

Including characters from cultures or subcultures that you know little about can also be tricky, often leading to stereotyping. So, if you choose unfamiliar settings and character types, research care-fully and find reliable peer editors to help you with accuracy and authenticity.

Only "Literary" Writing Is Good Writing

Snobbery abounds in the world of art and literature. While it is true that you likely won't win the Nobel Prize for Literature if you write a popular detective novel, you will have many readers. As you write, you need to discover your voice and the genres it works best in. For example, if your voice is naturally comic and you love writing humour, then you should hone those skills. There are many, many forms of writing, all with merit. Don't dismiss certain types of writing because they are not considered high art. We need journalists, song-writers, travel writers, business writers, writers of "beach reads." Furthermore, don't limit your definition of *creative* writing to fiction. You can bring your creativity to many different forms of writing, both fiction and nonfiction.

AN AUDIENCE OF MORE THAN ONE

Chances are that you are using this book as part of a creative writing class. Let's talk for a moment about that class, because it is likely quite different from other classes you have taken. In a writing class, your teacher and classmates take on various roles. As occasion demands, they will be your cheerleaders, taskmasters, editors, and audience. If you can build a community of writers in your class, you will end up with a comfortable environment where you can safely share your works-in-progress and exchange both encouragement and constructive criticism. This type of environment is so important that some class time must be devoted to getting to know one another. The following section provides suggestions on how to begin to discover the qualities, interests, and concerns that you and your classmates have as *writers*.

Forming a Community of Writers

One way to get to know your classmates is to create and share a writing autobiography, a story of yourself as a writer. (See this assignment on page 8.) Another way is simply to have a discussion in which class members share their experiences with writing and their goals for the class. For your discussion, you may want to consider some of these issues or come up with topics as a group:

- your style of writing or favourite genre

- positive and negative writing experiences

- fears about writing

- favourite authors

- the qualities of good writing

- what you think a writing class can do for you

- what you can provide for others in the class

If your class is too large to have a discussion that involves everyone, you could interview a partner about some of the topics above, and either present your findings orally or write a profile on your partner to be shared with the class.

Functioning as a Community

Sharing Your Writing

In a writing course you will be expected to share your work or work-in-progress with others. You can read a piece to the whole class, or you can try the following methods:

- With a partner, silently read each other's work-in-progress, then give oral feedback.

- Work in a group of three. Each writer reads his or her work aloud (or asks another group member to read it aloud), and group members give feedback.

- The teacher or a classmate reads a class member's work aloud; the class gives written or oral feedback.

Reflect on your experiences with writing. Some of you may already be serious writers and have perhaps experienced considerable success with your writing attempts in the past. Others of you may be less secure about your talent and skills, but know that you want to write. The autobiography is a place for you to describe your feelings about and experiences with writing to better understand yourself and to introduce yourself as a writer to the class. Here are some questions to get you started:

- Do you remember learning to write?
- How did you experience writing in your early years?
- How is writing viewed or valued by your family/friends?
- What were some significant early school experiences you had with writing?
- What were some significant middle and/or secondary school experiences with writing?
- Do you keep samples of your past writing? How did you feel about them at the time you wrote them? How do you feel now?
- How did/does your family respond to your writing?
- Do you write for personal (non-school-related) reasons? When? How? Why?
- Do you keep a journal? What type of journal do you use? How often do you write in it? What do you use it for?
- What victories and/or failures have you had as a writer?
- How do you see yourself as a writer? How do you think you formed this view of yourself?
- How would you like to see yourself as a writer?

Use these questions to help you remember and reflect on your experiences. When you begin your draft, however, you will want to narrow your focus. Don't try to cover every detail in your final product; instead, tell an interesting story about your experiences with writing.

It's up to you how to frame that story. You may, for instance, begin from the beginning, from your first memory of holding a pencil in your hand. Or you may begin with your most painful experience and move on from there. Feel free to include excerpts of pieces you have written and other relevant artifacts.

Models to examine:
Margaret Atwood, "How I Became a Poet"
Anne Lamott, *Bird by Bird*, Chapter One

Audience: your teacher and classmates
Length: approximately 1000 words[13]

Much of the joy and satisfaction of writing comes from the knowledge that you have communicated with others. By sharing your drafts with your writing community, you can find out if the writing resonates for them in the way that it resonates for you. American writer Anne Lamott[14] says that she always shows her work to at least one trusted person before sending it to her editor or agent.

> Feedback from someone I'm close to gives me confidence, or at least it gives me time to improve. Imagine that you are getting ready for a party and there is a person at your house who can check you out and assure you that you look wonderful or, conversely, that you actually do look a little tiny tiny tiny bit heavier than usual in this one particular dress or suit or that red makes you look just a bit like you have sarcoptic mange. Of course you are disappointed for a moment, but then you are grateful that you are still in the privacy of your own home and there is time to change.

Sharing your work in your writing class will provide you with valuable feedback on your own work. You will also find that you will gain writing skills through the process of examining your peers' writing.

Analyzing Your Peers' Writing

Whether or not you have experience with peer editing, you do have qualifications and tools to respond to a classmate's work. You, as an editor, can respond first as a *reader*. How does the piece affect you? What do you like about it? Is anything confusing—are there any gaps? What parts make you laugh? What parts move you? These kinds of observations are invaluable to the writer.

Second, you can respond as a student of literature and of other kinds of writing. In previous English classes, you acquired tools to help you to look at writing more critically. The categories you use to analyze writing in other courses are the same ones you will use now; concepts such as point of view, word choice, characterization, and verisimilitude—along with the many other terms you've learned—can be brought to the discussions of writing you have in your meetings.

Third, you can approach your peers' works as a fellow writer. William Safire and Leonard Safir[15] explain:

> When writers read, they read with narrowed eyes, knowing that their emotions or thought processes are being manipulated and subtly directed by a fellow member of the scribe trade.... [Writers] take an active part in a textual exchange, inwardly commenting "Good," or

"Wrong," or "Why?" and lubricating or challenging the prose by mentally larding in personal experience in support or refutation. Reading writers are never mere receptacles.

As you gain experience with the craft of writing, you can apply your knowledge and skills as a writer to other people's writing as well. You will, for example, recognize techniques that the writer is using, and you will be able to comment on how effectively the technique is working. You will also be able to give suggestions from your own experience of writing. For instance, you might recognize a spot in a short story that is not working well, and know from your own experience that changing the narration to dialogue in such a spot will perk up the pace or re-engage you as the reader.

These three ways of responding to your peers will overlap considerably. Regardless of what you focus on, your comments as a peer editor must be phrased sensitively and positively. Avoid a combative approach.

THE WIDER COMMUNITY OF WRITERS

While your classmates are your immediate community of writers, there is also a wider community of writers—and readers—outside your classroom. Whether you live in a city, a town, or the country, you can access this community. Try one or more of the following:

- Check your local newspaper, nearest bookstore, or library for advertisements of readings by contemporary authors. Often the readings are free, and they provide opportunities for you to hear contemporary writing and to meet authors and other people interested in writing.

- Ask your teacher about writing contests that you can enter, as well as other publication opportunities. Many newspapers, arts magazines, and organizations have annual contests.

- Ask your teacher whether you could invite an author to speak to your class. Many authors are willing to read their work and answer questions, some for free, and others for a modest fee or an honorarium.

- Check out the many writers' groups and publishing opportunities on the Web. However, be cautious and discerning about what you join and where you submit your work. Get a second opinion from a parent or your teacher before you join a Web group, and avoid sites that charge you fees to publish your work.

- If your class has access to computers, network with a creative writing class in another school in order to read and comment on each other's work.

- Share your work with your school in the school newspaper, yearbook, or other publications.

- Most importantly, read, read, read. Read books and magazines about writing; read fiction and nonfiction. In the words of William Faulkner,[16] "Read everything—trash, classics, good and bad, and see how they do it. Just like a carpenter who works as an apprentice and studies the master. Read! You'll absorb it. Then write. If it is good, you'll find out. If it's not, throw it out the window."

THE WRITING PROCESS

Gathering Ideas

The Notebook

Many writers keep a notebook with them at all times so that they can write down ideas when they occur. This notebook can be a beautiful leather-bound journal; it can also be a plain spiral notebook, or even a pad of sticky notes that you keep with you. A notebook is a place to record ideas for stories, provocative conversations you've overheard, intriguing anecdotes people tell you, things you read or see that are interesting, words you like, and lists. Keeping such a notebook will help you to see the world through a writer's eyes, and will give you a source book when you are writing a piece.

The Exercise Book

As well as a portable notebook, you will need a place to try on different voices and to do writing activities as you work through this book. Again, this exercise book can take many different forms, but it should hold a collection of work securely, so that you can find previous pieces when you need them. The exercise book will likely contain the starting points for your polished pieces.

The Word Processor

If you have access to a word processor, use it as early as possible in your writing process. Many writers are able to compose only with pen and paper, and if you are one of them, you will probably spend hours transcribing your work. However, if you use the word processor, you can streamline the process. Remember to save your drafts. Use the Save As feature and name your drafts with numbers to identify them.

Drafting and Revising

Although the stages of drafting and revising comprise the bulk of your writing work, there are no step-by-step instructions that work for every writer. Professional writers vary their approach according to the genre they are writing and according to the personal style they have developed. Some writers work from detailed outlines; others discover what they want to say as they go. Many writers and teachers of writing advocate that you write freely and quickly as you compose your first draft, not stopping to reread or make changes until you are finished. They claim that revising too soon in the process will curtail your creative energy and flow of ideas. Other writers, however, revise as they write. You will have to experiment with different methods of drafting and find out which works best for you. Many novice writers prefer to separate the steps and focus first on letting their imaginations roam. Later, when they return to the draft, they can look at it with a critical eye, bringing to it the objectivity that some distance from it can provide.

Revising and Editing with Your Classmates

Revising and editing can often be done on your own. But why not take advantage of your writing peers and ask them to read your work and provide feedback? They can help improve your writing by bringing some objectivity and providing useful suggestions that you may otherwise not have thought of.

Using Peer Editors

Once you have a completed draft that you have revised, share it with your peer editors. To make the most of the editing session, you need some distance from your draft. If you just finished your rough draft at 2:00 A.M. that day, you are too close to it (and too exhausted) to have a clear perspective on it yet. When you have more distance and objectivity, you will feel more ready to receive comments from your peers.

Remember, the onus is on you to make the editing session useful. This means you must come prepared. Consider the following suggestions.

List specific strengths and weaknesses

When you complete your rough draft, make a list of areas that you feel are successful and areas that need work. These areas can be specific sections of your text (for example, a line in a poem, a piece of dialogue in a short story, and so on) or specific elements of the work (for example, setting or imagery). Naming these areas prepares you for the editing session, because it helps you to step into the reader's shoes in looking at your draft.

Let your editors read your work and respond to it

If your draft is long, hand out copies to your editing group in advance. If it is short, you may give it to your group on the day of editing, but provide time for them to read it and reflect for a few minutes before you begin discussing. Let your work speak for itself—don't launch into explanations immediately after reading it to the group. Remember, your job is not to explain or defend your work, but to gather information about it.

Listen and ask questions

Let your editors talk, and take notes on their reactions. If necessary, ask questions to clarify their comments. For instance, if an editor states that the ending is confusing, ask where he or she got confused, and what, exactly, he or she didn't understand.

If your editors are not forthcoming, ask specific questions about your draft. For example, you can ask the following:

- What did you feel when you finished reading the piece?

- Why do you think I included _____ (a particular incident, image, sentence, or word)?

- What does the title make you think about?

- Did you feel a sense of resolution at the end? Why or why not?

Inform your editors of your intentions

Sometimes you may wish to inform your editors of some of your intentions in the piece you wrote. For example, if they do not comment on a pattern of imagery or a theme that you wove in, point it out and ask about its impact. Perhaps it is too subtle—or perhaps they were not reading carefully. When you point out your intentions in the piece or the impact you were hoping to have on the reader, ask your editors how effective you've been and what you can do to be more effective.

Save all drafts of your writing

Save the different versions of your draft as you compose and revise. You may even want to bring two different versions to a peer editing session with the changes highlighted for your editors. Ask your editors which version is most effective and why.

If you find yourself feeling defensive during the editing session, remember that you are the author and that you have the final say. Occasionally, you may find yourself at the receiving end of unhelpful or even conflicting recommendations. As H.G. Wells once said,[17] "No passion in the world is equal to the passion to alter someone else's draft." Even when the group is unanimous in their recommendations for improvements on your draft, you don't have to change a thing. However, if your editors feel strongly that something in the work needs attention, you should at least consult with another trusted reader for a second opinion before you submit the piece for evaluation or for publication.

Copy Editing

Before you submit a work for evaluation or for publication, you must ensure that it is free of errors in grammar, usage, punctuation, and spelling. If you cannot spot these errors yourself, find a meticulous proofreader to help you. If you are serious about being a writer, hone your language skills. A good writer's handbook is an essential tool.

Evaluation

When we talk about what makes a good piece of writing good, for the most part, we are talking about craft. Good pieces of writing have in common certain qualities such as clarity of purpose, logic, effective use of detail, and strong voice. The writing scales, rubrics, or lists of criteria that your teacher uses to evaluate your work are based on the characteristics of good writing. Though writing scales and rubrics have limitations, they are helpful in that they clearly indicate the qualities you need to strive for in your writing, and they inform you of the specific strengths and weaknesses of your piece of writing. When a piece isn't working as well as it should, identifiable problems are usually responsible. For example, the lead may be weak, the focus may be unclear, the dialogue may sound unbelievable, or the prose may rely on clichés. When you receive a piece back from your teacher, read the comments and suggestions carefully. Waiting a week or two and then revisiting your piece and the teacher's comments on it may help you to see the piece and the comments more objectively, and you will be more likely to apply the suggestions to new pieces of writing.

As you gain experience as a writer, not only will your ability to write improve but your ability to assess the quality of your own writing will develop as well. Some writing classes use a portfolio approach to evaluation, which allows students, in consultation with the teacher, to choose their best pieces for evaluation. Some teachers include self-evaluation in the calculation of marks or include student input when developing the specific criteria for evaluation. Developing an ability to judge your own writing is a worthwhile skill regardless of whether your judgement counts toward the final mark.

Cover Letter

One way to develop an ability to assess your own work and to have input into the evaluation process is to write a cover letter to accompany a piece of writing that you submit for evaluation. This letter should explain your intentions in the piece. Point out the deliberate choices you made, such as a pattern of imagery, the structure of the piece, the type of lead, the speech patterns of a character, and so on. You can also point out what sections or what elements of the piece you are pleased with and which you would work on more if you had more time. The purpose of writing such a cover letter is, first, to give your evaluator a guided tour of the work, and, second, to show your growing awareness of the craft involved in good writing.

Subjectivity

Some people claim that evaluation of writing—or any kind of art, for that matter—is a subjective process. However, think about the writing you have read. Likely, you would feel quite confident separating the good from the not so good. As you read earlier, good writing shares certain qualities, and while it is harder to identify what makes a good essay than what makes a good oven cleaner or a good winter boot, most readers can spot writing that doesn't communicate well, writing that is competent, and writing that sparkles and sings.

Occasionally, however, you may write a piece that is technically sound but doesn't receive the rave reviews you expected. Even when a piece is well written, it may not resonate with every reader. No doubt you've had the experience of reading a novel that was enthusiastically recommended to you, and finding that the book does nothing for you. Reading is an interactive activity: Readers bring themselves to the work—their gender, class, culture, attitudes, experiences, opinions, interests, expectations, and feelings. Because of all these variables, the same piece of writing can change one person's life or put another person to sleep. This is one reason why many fine pieces of writing that are rejected by a magazine editor or book publisher are later picked up by another editor or publisher. Thus, while we can identify the qualities of good writing, we can't apply them entirely objectively to any one piece of writing. (John Ciardi calls this relationship between writer and reader "the sympathetic contract." See Chapter 5, page 185, for more discussion of this issue.) If you are convinced that your piece of writing has unrecognized merit, keep it in your files and revisit it in six months or a year. If you still love the piece, you can always seek out a wider audience for it through "real life" publishing opportunities.

PUBLICATION

When you are ready to publish your work, you must first decide how wide an audience you want. Consider the following suggestions:

- Many beginning writers start with "in-house" publications such as a school newspaper, yearbook, or even a class-produced booklet. If you belong to clubs or organizations that print a newsletter, they may be interested in articles you write on topics relevant to them.

- Your local newspaper is another possibility. Some newspapers have a weekly column reserved for guest editorials or a section for student work.

- The Internet is another great source for publishing opportunities. Many sites accept articles, poetry, short stories, and plays from students; some will provide opportunities for the readers of the work to write their reactions to a piece, which then are posted on a Web site. The quality of Web sites that publish creative writing varies widely, as do the contributions to the sites. Research a site by reading the writing posted on the site and by carefully reading the guidelines for submitting your work. Don't submit work to a site that charges you fees to publish your work, a site devoted to questionable political views or causes, or a site that publishes work that condones or celebrates illegal activity. If you are unsure about the quality or trustworthiness of a site, ask your teacher to look at it with you.

- Writing contests are another avenue for publication, although you should beware of contests that charge you large fees to enter. Many local libraries, school boards, newspapers, and writers' organizations offer annual contests that are free to enter. Some organizations, such as the League of Canadian Poets, publish an anthology of winning entries to their writing contests each year.

- Finally, you should consider "little magazines"—small-press publications that come in many varieties and that usually accept unsolicited manuscripts. *The Canadian Writer's Market* is an invaluable resource. It is published annually in the fall, and lists thousands of places to send your work. You may, of course, start by submitting your work to mass-circulation magazines or international publishing companies, but, while you are yet unknown, you are more likely to get published if you pursue another path first.

Guidelines for Submitting a Manuscript

Before you submit your work for publication, be aware of the requirements for submission, otherwise you may receive more rejection letters than acceptances. Following are some guidelines to keep in mind:

- Read the magazine, newspaper, or Web site that you're submitting your work to. Does your piece match the style, tone, and slant of the publication? Does your writing have the same intended audience? Matching the subject and style of your work to the subject and style of the publication is often the key to getting published.

- When appropriate, write a query letter to the editor of the publication to inquire whether he or she is interested in your idea or topic. Often, especially in the case of poetry or fiction, editors will have to see the finished piece before they can make a decision. But in the case of a feature article, the editor may be able to tell you clearly ahead of time what the publication is or is not looking for.

- E-mail, phone, or write to the publication in order to obtain its submission guidelines. Follow the guidelines *exactly* when you send in your work.

- If you can't get submission guidelines, a good rule of thumb is to key your name, address, phone number, and e-mail address in the upper left-hand corner of the title page. In the top right-hand margin, type the word count. Type your last name, title of the piece, and page number on all subsequent pages.

- Your manuscript must be word-processed, double-spaced on white 8½" x 11" paper, in a basic 12-point font (like Times New Roman), and have one-inch margins, unless the publication's manuscript guidelines ask for something different.

- Include a brief cover letter. If you just won a writing contest or got a piece published somewhere else, you may mention those facts to establish your credibility. Don't, however, explain or justify the piece of writing you are sending.

- Enclose a self-addressed, stamped envelope (SASE), large enough to contain your manuscript. The SASE is used to return your manuscript to you (don't expect the publisher to pay for postage). Note that if you're submitting a work to a publication in another country (the United States, for example) you must stamp your enclosed envelope with the postage of that country or use an international reply coupon, available at the post office.

- Keep a copy of your manuscript and a record of when and where you sent it.

- Don't submit a piece of writing to two places at once. Most editors take your submission of the work as permission to publish, and would take offense at having the piece come out from two different publications at the same time. If you don't hear back from an editor within three months of submitting a piece, you may write to him or her and ask about your manuscript. If you still don't receive a reply, you should write again and say that you are assuming that they are not interested and that you will be submitting the work elsewhere. Keep a copy of all your correspondence.

The scope of this book does not allow for an in-depth discussion of the rights of writers. However, if you get a piece accepted for publication, you should ask specific questions about payment for the work (if any), and ownership rights. For example, the publication may have all rights, meaning they now own your manuscript; or they may have one-time rights, meaning they can publish it once, and you can sell it again. It is important for you to find out what kind of contract you have entered into. For more in-depth discussion of the rights of writers, refer to *The Canadian Writer's Marketplace*.

THE WRITING PORTFOLIO

Whether or not you choose to publish your work, you should keep a portfolio or a collection of your work. A writing portfolio will help you meet course requirements, add to your post-secondary school applications and interviews, and enhance your job applications and interviews. It is better to put together a customized portfolio rather than a generic one for all purposes and audiences. Just like a résumé, you need to revise and rearrange your portfolio for different purposes and audiences. You will want to have all your writing filed, either in hard copy or on a disk, where it can be accessed easily. Keep everything! The piece of writing you throw out will always be the one that you wish you had kept. When submitting a portfolio (except perhaps for a secondary school course), do not include your originals. Use photocopies instead, or print a second copy, just in case they get misplaced.

Keeping a Portfolio for an English or a Writer's Craft Course

While you may want to put everything you write in your writer's portfolio, set some goals for your writing and include samples that show you working toward those goals. Try to include some of the following in your portfolio:

- exercises or experiments in which you attempt or demonstrate a particular writing skill

- a piece of writing that did not achieve the effect you were trying to get but that demonstrated a variety of approaches or techniques

- one or more successful finished pieces with all their process

- a page of possible ideas for stories, poems, articles, and so on

- two pieces of writing with the same purpose (one weaker than the other) that show evidence of growth

- a variety of types of writing to show versatility

- an exercise or experimental piece of writing that was prompted by an interview with a published author, or by an article written about or by a published author (include, as well, the piece of writing that prompted your writing)

Create a table of contents and keep your portfolio in a binder or folder that can be handled easily by your teacher or by you and your teacher in a writing conference.

Each piece of writing or group of writing should be accompanied by a critical reflection. Here are some things you should include in your reflections:

- the purpose of the piece(s) of writing

- what you were trying to achieve with the piece(s)

- the strengths of the piece(s)

- the areas that you think you could improve

- how the writing reflects your growth as a writer

Below are some prompts from Schools Achieving Excellence that you can use to help you write your reflections:

- I learned …

- I feel good about …

- My next goal is …

Tell briefly how you approached a problem. What were the strategies and/or techniques that you used to get started?

- How did you solve the problem?

- Where did you show the most improvement?

- If I were to do this assignment again, I would …

- This piece of work shows my growth as a _____ because …

Reflect on and explain briefly why you chose a particular piece for your portfolio, what you learned from it, and why it is important to you. Here are some prompts:

- I chose this piece of work for my portfolio because …

- I'm most proud of _____ because …

- Some things I do well are ...

- Some things I'm working on are ...

- The best thing about this piece is ...

- It would be even better if ...

- When I finished this work I felt ...

- I want to practise ...

- What I like about this work is ...

- Next term, I want to know more about ...

- What I found especially meaningful was ...

- Something I wrote that pushed my own thinking was ...

- I learned it is important for me to ...[18]

Creating a Portfolio for an Interview or an Application for a School of Writing

The portfolio you create for a school of writing depends entirely on the requirements of that school. Many writing schools do not want to see a portfolio, but will give you a writing assignment to complete and submit with your application.

Before you assemble your portfolio, carefully read the school's requirements. The application committee knows exactly how much it can read in the time it has. Including more than the specified requirement or additional pieces not required will not ensure entry. Take, for instance, the requirement for Humber College/Guelph University's School for Writers for the fall of 2003:[19]

> To assess your ability, we require that you submit a sample (no more than 15 pages) of your writing by November 15, 2002. The manuscript must be submitted in duplicate and prepared according to professional standards: double-spaced, typed on one side only, and with your name, title, and page number on each page. Samples of writing will not be returned.

The University of British Columbia's writing admission requirement for its school of journalism (2003) is very specific.[20]

Manuscript Submission

Process

All work must be typed in English and double-spaced. Please do not send cassettes, discs, videos or handwritten material and do not send us your original and only copy of your work.

Once we have received your manuscript, and all requested supporting documentation, this will be forwarded to the Admissions Committee for review. Be sure to include two self-addressed, stamped envelopes for Canada or international reply coupons if you are out of the country.

You should also include a covering letter noting the particulars of your educational background or life experiences which are relevant to your writing and the Programme, as well as a short description of your goals as a journalist.

Content

The submission can be about any subject of your choosing that you think would be interesting to the readers of a daily broadsheet newspaper. It should be no more than 15 double-spaced typewritten pages and should be intended for the Saturday Review section of a paper such as *The Globe and Mail, The Vancouver Sun,* or *The New York Times.*

It can be analytical but not opinionated. Facts and sources are most important so that we can judge your ability to research and organize material. It should be written in a journalistic style. Consideration will be given to the fact that those required to submit manuscripts lack journalistic experience.

The Victoria School of Writing in Victoria, BC, is one of many schools that offer summer writing courses. In order to place registrants in appropriate classes they require the following:[21] "Attendee's Qualifications: 3–10 pages of recent writing in any genre."

If you are in doubt about exactly what to include, call the university or college registrar or e-mail the contact listed with the course requirements. It's better to be sure of what a school wants than to submit a portfolio that does not meet its expectations.

Preparing a Job Portfolio

Since individual jobs require different types of writing, it is difficult to generalize about the content of your job portfolio. There are some general guidelines for presentation, however.

- The carrying case or presentation folder should be in good shape.

- The contents of your portfolio should be neat and organized.

- Your portfolio should include pieces that best demonstrate the types of writing you will be doing on the job.

- It should also have a variety of writing samples to show your talents.

- You should prepare some interesting things to say about each of your samples.

Once again, if in doubt, call the human resources officer or director to ask for specific guidelines.

THE WRITER'S READING LIST

Atchity, Kenneth. *A Writer's Time*. New York: W.W. Norton, 1995.

Goldberg, Bonnie. *Room to Write: Daily Invitations to a Writer's Life*. New York: Penguin/Putnam, 1996.

Goldberg, Natalie. *Wild Mild*. New York: Bantam Books, 1990.

Goldberg, Natalie. *Writing Down the Bones*. Boston: Shambhala, 1986.

Haines, Dawn Denham, Susan Newcomer, and Jacqueline Raphael. *Writing Together: How to Transform Your Writing in a Writing Group*. New York: Perigree/Berkley, 1997.

Heffron, Jack. *The Writer's Idea Book*. Cincinnati, OH: Writer's Digest Books, 2000.

Kirkpatrick, Betty. *Dictionary of Clichés*. London: Bloomsbury, 1996.

Klauser, Heriette Anne. *Writing on Both Sides of the Brain: Breakthrough Techniques for People Who Write*. San Francisco: HarperCollins, 1987.

Lamott, Anne. *Bird by Bird: Some Instructions on Writing and Life*. New York: Anchor, 1994.

Safire, William and Leonard Safir. *Good Advice on Writing: Great Quotations from Writers Past and Present on How to Write Well*. New York: Simon and Schuster, 1992.

Schneider, Pat. *The Writer As an Artist: A New Approach to Writing Alone and With Others*. Los Angeles: Lowell House, 1994.

Endnotes and Credits

CHAPTER 1

1 Katherine Anne Porter, quoted in Safire, *Good Advice on Writing*, 13.

2 Anne Lamott, *Bird by Bird*. New York: Anchor/Random House, 1995, 7.

3 Jack Heffron, *The Writer's Idea Book*. Cincinnati, Ohio: Writer's Digest Books, 2000, 7.

4 Alberto Moravia, quoted in Jon Winokur, *Writers on Writing*. Philadelphia: Running Press, 1990, 142.

5 Toni Morrison, quoted in Winokur, *Writers on Writing*, 143.

6 Michael Ondaatje, interviewed by David O'Meara in "The Company of Great Thieves." *Where the Words Come From: Canadian Poets in Conversation*, ed. Tim Bowling. Roberts Creek, BC: Nightwood Editions, 2002, 36.

7 Willa Cather, quoted in Winokur, *Writers on Writing*, 153.

8 Margaret Laurence, "Where the World Began." *Heart of a Stranger*. Toronto: McClelland and Stewart, 1976, 23.

9 Laurence, "Where the World Began," 28.

10 John Gardner, quoted in Winokur, *Writers on Writing*, 152.

11 Tracy Kidder, quoted in Winokur, *Writers on Writing*, 158.

12 William Arthur Deacon, "What a Canadian Has Done for Canada." *Poeteen*. Ottawa: Graphic Publishers, 1926. (This essay has also been reprinted in Thomas S. Kane, and others, *Writing Prose: Techniques and Purposes*. Toronto: Oxford University Press, 1987, 612–615.)

13 Adapted from Dr. Mary Kooy's Literacy Autobiography Assignment. Reprinted by permission of Dr. Mary Kooy.

14 Lamott, *Bird by Bird*, 164–165.

15 William Safire and Leonard Safir, Preface to *Good Advice on Writing: Great Quotations from Writers Past and Present on How to Write Well*. New York: Simon and Schuster, 1992, 13.

16 William Faulkner, quoted in Winokur, *Writers on Writing*, 7.

17 H.G. Wells, quoted in Winokur, *Writers on Writing*, 115.

18 Portfolio Prompts, from Schools Achieving Excellence—Reprinted by permission of Data Based Directions Inc.

19 Humber College, The Humber School for Writers Web site. Correspondence Program in Creative Writing. www.humberc.on.ca/~writers/correspondence/.

20 Manuscript submission: University of British Columbia, School of Journalism Web site—Reprinted by permission of School of Journalism, University of British Columbia.

21 Victoria School of Writing Web site, www.writing.shawguides.com/VictoriaSchoolofWriting/.

Sentences and Clichés

You have to find the key, the clue. In language all you have are those 26 letters, some punctuation and some paper.

Toni Morrison[1]

ABOUT SENTENCES

Before you read on to examine how to write specific genres of writing, we need a word or two about sentences. Sentences are the building blocks of all writing, and a carefully written sentence can be a work of art in itself. The well-wrought sentence is usually grammatical (though you may choose to tamper with traditional syntax and grammar for a specific effect, especially in your writing of poetry and dialogue). Good writers do more than craft "correct" sentences, however. What separates competent writing from memorable writing is not just a splashy plot or clever ideas but a creative use of language. There is no "wonder formula" for shaping your sentences; however, some understanding about types of sentences is helpful, since you then can experiment with varying your sentence structure to achieve effects such as a shift in tone or a pleasing rhythm.

Sentence Types

Examine the following types of sentences.
A *simple sentence* has one principal clause with a subject and predicate.

> Example: The sun was a faint smear on the horizon.

A *compound sentence* has two or more principal clauses that need connecting words.

> Example: Shadows were growing longer, and the sun was a faint smear on the horizon.

A *complex sentence* has one principal clause and one or more subordinate clauses. A connecting word is used to relate the subordinate clause(s) to the principal clause.

> Example: As I crept down the pathway, the sun was a faint smear on the horizon.

"The sun was a faint smear on the horizon" is the principal clause and "as I crept down the pathway" is the subordinate clause; "as" is the connecting word.

A *compound-complex* sentence combines two principal clauses and at least one subordinate clause. This is the most difficult sentence structure to use correctly; it requires a sophisticated control of language and ideas.

> Example: As I crept down the pathway, the sun was a faint smear on the horizon and shadows were growing longer.

"The sun was a faint smear on the horizon" and "the shadows were growing longer" are both principal clauses; "as I crept down the pathway" is a subordinate clause.

Sentence Order

We can also group sentences by the order of the subject and predicate, or by the order of the grammatical elements in the sentence.

A *natural order* places the subject before the predicate.

> Example: She sipped ginseng tea.

An *inverted order* places the predicate before the subject.

> Example: Before him stood an awesome figure.

A *split order* places part of the predicate before the subject (or between the subject and the verb) for emphasis or effect.

> Example: The man, when he saw the shadow, trembled with fear.

A *balanced sentence* gives two or more ideas parallel importance by using identical grammatical constructions.

> Example: Finish your homework; do your chores.

A *loose sentence* begins with the main idea, then states the subordinate material.

> Example: You may go to the concert when you finish your homework and do your chores.

A *periodic sentence* begins with the subordinate material, and concludes with the main idea. Periodic sentences build to a climax.

> Example: When you finish your homework and do your chores, you may go to the concert.

Verb Voice

One other concept that you should review is verb voice. Verbs can be active or passive.

Active voice expresses an action that is done by the subject.

> Example: Mariah threw the baseball.

Passive voice expresses an action that is done *to* its subject.

> Example: The baseball was thrown by Mariah.

Sometimes the passive voice is necessary when the doer of the action is unknown: "The 'for sale' notice was posted on the bulletin board" (you don't know who posted the notice; thus, the doer of the action is unknown). Sentences that use active voice tend to be more forceful and hard-hitting. While passive voice has its functions, overusing it can make your writing sluggish.

Most writers use a variety of sentence types and sentence orders in their writing. Informative prose, such as business memos, front-page news stories and how-to manuals, favours the clear and direct style that is the result of using natural sentence order and the first three types of sentence structures (simple, compound, complex). Creative writing—both fiction and nonfiction—lends itself to more complicated structures and unusual syntax. While you never want your sentences to become wordy or unnecessarily convoluted, you do want to experiment with length, order, and structure, so that your use of language sparkles. Through the structure of your sentences, you can emphasize ideas, create tone, control the rhythm, and suggest subtle shades of meaning in your writing. Try these activities:

1. Examine two or three descriptive paragraphs written by a published author whom you admire. In a list, identify the sentence structure and sentence order of each sentence in those paragraphs. Check your analysis of the paragraphs with a partner for accuracy. Then, write your own descriptive paragraph with the same structure (for example, beginning with a compound, balanced sentence, followed by a simple sentence in split order, and so on). Share your paragraph with a partner.

2. Go through a page of your writing and identify the sentence structure and the sentence order for each sentence. What patterns do you use most? Share your findings with a peer. Rewrite five or six of your sentences, changing the structure or style. How do the revised sentences affect the tone and impact of your piece? Share your changes with a peer and get his or her comments on the effects of your revised sentences.

3. As a writing exercise, craft a paragraph using only simple sentences in natural order. Then rewrite the paragraph, experimenting with sentence structure and order. Change as few words as possible in your revision.

As you experiment with sentences, you will develop your writing style. Creative writing, unlike most academic writing or instructional writing, allows you the freedom to break rules or deviate from standard patterns in your use of language. Even in journalism, the style today allows for greater artistic freedom and creativity. Your writing can be formal, informal, or even completely colloquial, depending on the effect you wish to achieve. In general, your verbs will be more vivid and vigorous and your nouns more concrete and specific than in the academic writing you've often done in high school. You may use more adjectives and adverbs, figures of speech, and other literary devices. What will make your sentences effective will depend on their context, and only through practise and careful reading will you learn when it's best to write a short, snappy sentence, when you need a meandering structure, or when you might need a fragment or a single word.

ABOUT CLICHÉS

The clichés we're tired of today were once fresh and new. It is only through overuse that these expressions have become the pariahs of good writing. Many students don't recognize clichés because the expressions are new to them. A dictionary like Betty Kirkpatrick's *Dictionary of Clichés* can help you to become familiar with expressions you shouldn't overuse as well as provide you with expressions you can twist purposely to create certain effects. Kirkpatrick[2] classifies clichés into several categories, as follows:

- *Simile clichés* use "as" or "like" ("cool as a cucumber," "deaf as a post," "like a breath of fresh air," "like two peas in a pod").

- *Foreign clichés* are foreign phrases used in English, most of which are from French (*"cause célèbre," "coup de grâce," "de rigueur"*), and a few from Latin (*"terra firma," "deus ex machina"*).

- *Proverb clichés* were originally proverbs or sayings, but have now become clichés (for example, "the early bird catches the worm," "make hay while the sun shines," "one good turn deserves another").

- *Allusion clichés* are proverbs and sayings that appear only in part as clichés ("a bird in the hand"—an allusion to "a bird in the hand is worth two in the bush"; "birds of a feather"—an allusion to "birds of a feather flock together"), that refer to partial quotations ("the best-laid schemes"—alludes to two lines in Robert Burns's poem "To a Mouse"), that allude to myths and biblical stories ("the Midas touch"—to the Greek myth of King Midas whose touch turns things to gold; "the forbidden fruit"—the apple in the biblical story of Adam and Eve).

- *Quotation clichés* are full quotations from literature ("for this relief much thanks" from Shakespeare's *Hamlet*; "for better or worse" from *The Book of Common Prayer*) and misquotations ("a little knowledge is a dangerous thing"—a misquotation of "a little learning is a dangerous thing" from Pope's *An Essay on Criticism*; "money is the root of all evil"—a misquotation of "the love of money is the root of all evil" from the Bible).

- *Doublet clichés* contain synonyms, near synonyms, and associated ideas ("bits and pieces," "leaps and bounds," "odds and ends," "safe and sound," "the dim and distant past").

- *Euphemistic clichés* are mild phrases that mask the harshness of reality ("economical with the truth," "kick the bucket").

- *Idiomatic clichés* are expressions and metaphors ("the light at the end of the tunnel," "make waves," "take the bull by the horns").

- *Catchphrase clichés* originate from the media—advertisements, movies, and television shows ("don't call us, we'll call you," "a man's gotta do what a man's gotta do," "tell that to the marines," "you can't take it with you").

- *Vogue clichés* are buzz words and phrases ("the bottom line," "the generation gap," "the name of the game").

- *Filler clichés* fill up space in sentences, often in informal speech ("the thing is," "just between you and me," "you know what I mean," "believe it or not," "needless to say"), and sometimes in formal speech ("unaccustomed as I am to public speaking," "at this moment in time").

Endnotes and Credits

Appendix A

1 Toni Morrison, quoted in Caryn Mirriam-Goldberg, *Write Where You Are: How to Use Writing to Make Sense of Your Life—A Guide for Teens*. Minneapolis, MN: Free Spirit, 26.

2 Taken from *Dictionary of Clichés* by Betty Kirkpartrick. (Bloomsbury, 2001).

Nonfiction

Read a lot and hit the streets. A writer who doesn't keep up with what's out there ain't gonna be out there.

TONI CADE BAMBARA[1]

Chapter 2: Creative Nonfiction

Appendix B: Society of Professional Journalists, Code of Ethics

Creative Nonfiction

The best stories are often the ones that surprise you.

JOHN TIERNEY[2]

LEARNING GOALS

▸ organize information and ideas effectively to suit the form, purpose, and intended audience of nonfiction writing

▸ select appropriate techniques, diction, voice, and style and use them effectively to communicate ideas and experiences in nonfiction writing

▸ assess the content, organization, style, and impact of drafts and final versions of work produced by peers, providing objective and constructive suggestions

▸ revise drafts to produce effective written work by refining content, form, technique, diction, voice, and style

▸ produce thoughtful, effective publications and prepare them for distribution to wider audiences

WHAT IS CREATIVE NONFICTION?

Creative nonfiction is the name for the type of journalistic writing that we use widely today. This style began about thirty years ago in a movement named "new journalism."

The word *jour*, as in "journal" or "journalism," comes from the French, meaning "one day." The word "journal" then, according to the *Oxford English Dictionary*, means "a daily record of events or occurrences kept for private or official use." The word "journalist" is "one who earns his [her] living by editing or writing for a public journal."[3]

Traditionally, journalists wrote only for newspapers or "penny-a-liners," as they were called in England.[4] But today, journalists write for many media including newspapers, magazines, radio, and television.

Many students think of journalism as unbiased, objective reporting that appears on the front pages of the national newspaper or that headlines the six o'clock news. This type of journalism doesn't—and never really did—exist. Creativity has always been a part of journalism—from which facts are chosen, to how the facts are arranged. The media have always shown us the news through filters: political, socioeconomic, cultural, religious, and so on.

In the 1970s some journalists purposely started to add literary elements to their nonfiction writing. Some of these literary elements include literary voice (for example, direct address or first-person observer); story narration; characterization; place/scene/setting; personal engagement with the story by the author; and artistic, instinctual writing (not necessarily following the traditional structures of journalistic pieces).[5]

While these "new journalists" included elements of fiction, they still thoroughly researched their topics, reported the facts, and wrote in essay or nonfiction form. One of the most popular examples of "new journalism" from the 1970s in the United States was Truman Capote's *In Cold Blood*, the true story of a family brutally murdered. Capote wrote the book in a narrative style, resembling fiction, but based it on six years of researched facts (see also "Creative Nonfiction" by Pegi Taylor, pages 326 to 331). In Canada, Bill Trent wrote *The Steven Truscott Story*, which detailed the arrest and conviction of teenager Steven Truscott for the rape and murder of a young girl.

These, among many other breakthrough journalistic pieces, started a trend that continues today under the name "creative nonfiction." Many of the examples you will read in this book are examples of creative nonfiction, since this is the current trend.

What Do Journalists Write?

Journalists write about science, technology, medicine, sports, food, travel, teenagers, senior citizens, animals, religion, disabilities, and politics—among a myriad of other topics. They research behind the scenes, report in front of the cameras, write in tiny columns without a byline, and edit behind desks. Donald Murray,[6] a writer, editor, and writing coach, says about journalists:

> The reader depends on writers to make sense of their world, to provide at least what Robert Frost described as a "momentary stay against confusion." The reader needs writers who reveal, explain, persuade, and, most of all, articulate readers' own feelings and thoughts…. The writer reveals the world to those living in it … and in doing so we [the writers] enjoy the gift of first sight, the glimpse of pattern that explains our world to us. In using language to define our

world we practice a craft that should give us many gifts—the gift of concentration, the gift of making, the gift of play.

Journalists write analyses, columns, reports, articles, feature stories, editorials, profiles, and reviews. In this chapter, we will focus on the latter five types of writing plus a specific genre of journalism—travel writing.

Audience

Before writing anything, it is essential to consider your audience. More than anything else, your audience controls what you write and how you write it. Consider the characteristics of your audience (see the diagram below) and ask yourself these questions:

- Who am I writing for and what effect am I trying to have on my audience?

- What does my audience expect of me?

- How do I want my readers to feel about me?

- What do I want this piece of writing to do for my readers?

- What do I want my readers to do as a result of reading my writing?

Knowing your audience will have an impact on the level of language, style, tone, sentence structure, vocabulary, and content of your writing.

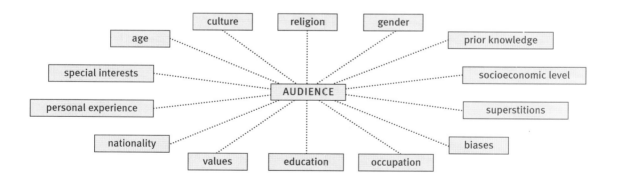

Tone and Purpose

Your use of language will change with the purpose and the audience of your writing. The language you choose for a piece of writing helps create the tone in your writing. Tone is created partly by the level of language you use, which can range from very formal to informal. The following table shows the characteristics of three levels of language: formal, moderate, and informal. Depending on the purpose of your writing, you may choose the form and the level of language that is most suitable.

LEVEL OF LANGUAGE			
	Formal	*Moderate*	*Informal*
vocabulary	• longer, less common words • few colloquialisms or popular phrases • little slang • few or no contractions • no personal pronouns (*you* and *I*)	• large and small words • more popular language • some contractions • occasional use of the pronouns *you* and *I*	• shorter, simpler, everyday words • some slang, more popular words and phrases • contractions • use of the pronouns *you* and *I* is common
sentence and paragraph structure	• longer and more complex sentences and paragraphs	• combination of simple, compound, and complex sentences; average-length sentences and paragraphs	• shorter, simpler sentences and paragraphs
tone	• academic and impersonal, often instructional	• varies, depending on purpose and audience	• conversational and casual—sounds like everyday speech

Tone can also convey a mood. Just like a speaking voice, a writing voice can convey anger, humour, earnestness, sincerity, enthusiasm, dry wit—or any other emotion or mood. As with the level of language, adjust the mood to suit your audience and purpose. Your letter to the editor pleading for more recycling initiatives in your town may use a serious, urgent tone, while your review of the latest Hollywood blockbuster may use an enthusiastic tone.

To improve your awareness of tone in writing, read articles of the type you want to write from a variety of magazines that cater to different audiences. Determine the audience by the title of the publication, the advertisements in the publication, and the types of articles that are accepted. Take notes on the tone. Or try your own experiments with tone by writing two short pieces on the same topic, one aimed at adults and one aimed at teens or at children.

If you are going to submit an article to a magazine or newspaper, study several issues of that publication. You should also request the publication's submissions guidelines. Sometimes they can be found on the publisher's Web site, but more often you will have to write or phone to ask for a copy.

Voice

Related to tone is *voice*. Voice in writing refers to the unique way in which you use language. A voice gives the reader a sense of the person behind the words. Some writers have such distinctive voices that you can identify a piece of work as theirs by reading just the first few sentences. A distinctive voice is discouraged in some kinds of writing, such as hard news stories or some academic essays. However, in creative nonfiction, you are encouraged to develop your own distinct style. Journalist David Mehegan[7] says, "We ought to remember that we are storytellers, not just researchers, and every storyteller must develop a voice. When people say of one of my stories, 'I would have known that was you, even if it hadn't had your name on it,' I feel that I am succeeding."

A voice is based on many choices you make—both consciously and instinctively—as you write a piece. Here are some choices:

- Your angle of vision. Are you approaching the piece of writing as someone personally affected by the topic or as someone recording the facts you've researched? How close or distant are you from the topic? What, exactly, is your focus? The answers to these questions will affect your voice.

- Your word choice. What level of language are you using? (See the chart on tone on page 35.) How precise are your words and what connotations do they have? Refer to page 196 (Chapter 5) for more about word choice.

- The way you order your ideas. What words or ideas will you emphasize through your sequencing? How fast will the piece move? How will you shift from idea to idea?

- The sound—the melody, the beat, the mood—of the piece. What tone will you employ? What rhythm will you use?[8]

Note that your voice in writing will change somewhat depending on your purpose and audience for each piece. However, some features in your use of language will be consistent from piece to piece, because your voice reflects who you are—your personality, values, level of education, cultural background, and other factors that make you unique.

The more you read, the more familiar you will become with variations in voice. The more you write and analyze what you have written, the more you will become aware of your own voice. You will also see how you have created it through the choices you make in angle of vision, word choice, sequencing and pace, tone, and rhythm.

The Lead

What does all journalistic writing have in common? The lead. The opening lines, paragraph, or paragraphs constitute the lead of your article.

- Like a thesis statement of an academic essay, a lead tells the readers what the article is about (makes a promise).

- The lead tells the readers why they should care about the topic.

- The lead grabs the readers' attention; it invites or even lures the readers in.

- The lead sets the tone or the attitude the writer will take toward the topic.

You should be able to identify your promise to the reader and, at the end of your article, you should be able to say, "Yes, I have kept my promise." It is important that in writing an attention-grabbing lead, you don't promise something that the article does not deliver. If you can't keep the promise implied in your lead, rewrite it.

Richard Saltus,[9] a reporter, has this to say about leads:

> The most important thing in the first lead I settle on is that it have the tone (or voice, if you prefer) that I'm aiming for. That's more important than the right content or the right idea, even. It has to evoke the effect I want the story to have—formal, conversational, dramatic, technical, skeptical, humorous, flippant, apocalyptic, heart-rending, whatever. That may come through an appropriate quote, a summing-up, or a set-up for suspense. Many times a visual image is where I start, whether it's the ambience of a laboratory, the main subject's gesture, or the look of a piece of technology.
>
> More often than not, though, the lead I come up with this way doesn't survive revision, especially if it's a long complex story, because by the time I get to the end the lead isn't right anymore.

Types of Leads

Most writers agree that leads fall into the following general categories.

Summary or News Lead

A *summary* or *news lead* provides just the facts: the who, what, where, and when of the topic. It is used for hard news or wire service stories (which are generally shorter and to the point). This type of lead might be as short as three- to five-*column* lines long.[10] Take a look at the following lead from a *Canadian Press*[11] article:

> Vancouver police had to break up a riot Thursday night by angry rock fans after the last-minute cancellation of a Guns N' Roses concert.
> Thousands of rock fans flew into a rage at GM Place last night after the no-show by lead singer Axl Rose.

You can clearly see the what, where, when, who, and even the why in this two-sentence lead.

Quotation Lead

A *quotation lead* contains a quotation, which may be from anyone—a famous person or a person on the street. For this to be an effective lead, the writer must choose a quotation that captures the essence of the article while encouraging the reader to read on. The quotation can give authority to an article, as well as bring a new voice to the article.

This following article in *The Globe and Mail*[12] is about a journal donated to a Canadian aviation museum by a Canadian pilot who served in World War II. The pilot had written the journal, which contains a record of a prisoner-of-war-camp escape. The article does not start with information about the donation, but with an excerpt from the journal itself. The few short sentences are stark without embellishment.

> I awoke about 5:15 AM to learn that the tunnel had been found. Two goons were in the hut with their dogs. I burned all my papers, etc., and threw all my chocolate and food out the window.... 76 POWs had got out before it was discovered.

The quotation from the actual diary adds interest, verisimilitude, and poignancy—three qualities that make a reader want to read on.

Anecdote Lead

An *anecdote lead* uses a brief story to introduce the topic and draw the reader's interest. The anecdote can add interest to subjects that might initially appear uninteresting, as well as add a personal voice to the article. Examine the following lead from an article in *The Toronto Star*:[13]

> Nero, that most musical of ancient Roman emperors, certainly knew the meaning of applause. In order to assure a favourable reception for his own performances in the vast, open-air theatre at Naples, his incendiary majesty saw to it that 5000 brawny young men were specially trained in the fine art of clapping their hands together.

This lead is not only attention getting, it also has a tinge of humour. It carries an unstated promise that this article will look at the history of applause—and it does.

Direct Address Lead

In a *direct address lead*, the writer speaks directly to the reader, using the pronoun "you" or simply implying the "you," creating an informal personal tone. As examples, take the following two leads:[14]

So you like waiting for that morning coffee even though it might take you more than 10 minutes to finally motor through the drive-thru line.

Betcha don't realize that $2 coffee is costing you a lot more than you ever realized.

ALL RIGHT, no whining.

If the educated guesses are correct and Tiger Woods will skip this year's Bell Canadian Open at Angus Glen—as yet unconfirmed, either way, officially—it sure won't be the end of the world.

In the first example, the writer addresses the reader directly using "you." In the second, the writer intimates the "you" by using a command, in which "you" is understood. Later in the article, he uses "we," which is more inclusive. In both cases, the tone is very personal and casual.

Sometimes the direct address lead may be used to intentionally sound accusative or scolding. Such a technique may be ineffective if the tone is too strong.

Narrative Lead

A *narrative lead* sounds a little like the beginning of a short story or novel. It places the reader in the scene of the event about which the author is writing. This helps to involve the reader. Examine the following lead from a magazine article:

There was a little girl on the ground in purple rubber boots, not breathing. A crowd was forming around her, which was what drew Darryl King's attention in the first place. The corporal was on routine duty, closing up his peacekeeping tour in Kosovo, with Canadian Forces 15 Combat Engineers, when he saw civilians running towards a car that had stopped near his position in Pristina. It was early December 1999.[15]

The article is about post-traumatic stress disorder (PTSD). The narrative beginning is an interesting and fitting introduction to this topic, relaying a key event that affected Darryl King and which causes his PTSD. This opening could be the beginning of a novel or short story. It has suspense, description, characterization, and the beginnings of a plot.

Descriptive Lead

A *descriptive lead* describes a person or setting, bringing the person or setting into focus for the reader. Read the following example:[16]

> I noticed Carl Bixby's 40-year-old hands first, a strange focus for me since I usually find myself immediately drawn to a patient's eyes: the downward gaze of depression, the frenetic glances of mania, the hypervigilance of psychosis. But these hands, erupting from the red flannel sleeves of his shirt, commanded my attention. They were too big for the rest of the man, even though he was big himself. Thick calluses stood out like cat's pads amid webs of crevices edged with grease. Dried blood lined new scratches, and numerous scars marked the old. They were strong hands, I thought to myself — well-worn rather than worn-out. They were the kind of hands you'd pray would reach for you if you were drowning. Nothing fragile about them. Grab on as hard as you like. Just as I convinced myself to search the man's face, he dragged my attention back to his wonderful mitts, slapping them on his knees twice to herald what he was about to say.

This vivid description, about a man who loves to repair train engines, brings the subject alive for the reader. The descriptive lead compels the reader to read on and find out more about the rest of this man.

Question Lead

A *question lead* works only if the question has an answer. It must involve the reader in the issue of the story. Take a look at the following example:[17]

> Is the 2003 Volvo XC90 an SUV?
> It looks to me like a tall wagon.
> Now, Volvo is well known for its wagons and would be happy to sell you one. But Volvo says the XC90 is an SUV, not a wagon.

The writer answers the question both at the beginning of the article and at the end: Volvo thinks its new vehicle is an SUV but the reporter doesn't, even though he loves the vehicle. Throughout, he gives all the technical statistics on the car, providing enough information for the readers to answer the question for themselves.

Note: A question lead should be used carefully because it can mislead the reader. Question leads have become overused and have thus become less effective than they were in the past.

Twisted Cliché Lead

In a *twisted cliché lead*, the writer uses a cliché and then changes or twists the words so they have a new meaning in the context of the article. For example, a negative review for a baseball movie may start, "Take me out to the ball game ... take me anywhere but to this movie!"

Choosing a Lead

So how do you decide what type of lead to use? Ask yourself the following questions:

• What is the story really about?

• How can I make this story interesting for the readers?

APPLICATION

1. Read several articles from a daily newspaper (either hard copy or on-line). Cut out, print, photocopy, or write out the different types of leads you found effective. Annotate the leads so you remember what drew your attention to them.

2. Buy three papers on the same day or access them on-line. Read stories on the same events or topics in different papers. Compare the leads and explain the differences in them, focusing on the audience and on what the story is really about.

3. **a)** Skim through a social science or history textbook and choose an event or person about whom you would like to write. Write a lead for an article about that person or event.

   b) Read your lead aloud to two or more classmates and have them tell you what they expect from the rest of the article.

4. As a class, choose a topic to write about. Make sure you all know enough about the topic to be able to write something credible without research. Choose the purpose and audience for your article and create several leads for that same topic. Compare your leads to those of your classmates. Discuss what makes your leads work. As well, discuss the promise made in the lead and where the article would go from that lead.

- Will it appeal to my audience?

- Is the voice or tone the one I want to use for the rest of the article?

- Does it sound fresh?

- Is the lead clearly written?

Try different leads for the same story.

The Body: Patterns of Organization

In previous years of your school career, you learned to use various organizational patterns to structure your writing, particularly in essays. All types of creative nonfiction use these same organizational patterns. As a refresher, here are descriptions of some of the patterns you may choose for the overall structure or for developing individual arguments. Remember that using more than one approach in a piece of writing is always an option.

Analogy

Analogy compares two different subjects by focusing on something similar between the two that are otherwise not the same. Analogy is often used to explain the unfamiliar (or things that are complex) in terms that are familiar.

Cause and Effect

Cause and effect tells why something happens. Some questions for cause and effect are listed below:

- What has caused it?

- Where has it come from and where is it going?

- What will happen to it?

- What is it used for?

- How does it fit into the larger scheme of things?

- What could happen if it didn't exist?

- Why does it exist?

- Could it be changed?

When organizing your cause-and-effect paragraphs, you can start with a cause and show or try to predict its effect (for example, "if handgun ownership is not regulated, more handgun-related deaths will occur"). You can also start with an effect and try to explain its cause (for example, "fewer secondary schools offer auto mechanics because of the expense of the program").

Be careful, however. Just because one event follows another, the first event is not necessarily the cause of the second. For example, "I wore my red socks when I won my first tennis match": wearing those red socks did not cause the win. As another example, "I wrote two exams with the same pen and got over 80 percent on both exams": using that pen did not cause the success.

Chronology

Chronology is the order in which a series of events takes place. For example, in a feature story or a review, you might relay a series of events leading up to an election or the outbreak of war. But keep in mind that using a chronological approach when writing about a novel or a movie may lead to retelling the story instead of examining the various aspects of the story that are important to the key arguments in the piece.

Classification

Classification is used to show how a subject fits into, or how it differs from, other elements in a category. The following are some questions you might ask yourself:

- What other things are like it?

- What kinds of it are there?

- What is it part of?

- What goes along with it?

- How does it differ from others like it?

- What connects it to all the other things in the category?

If you are developing an entire piece using classification, make sure you have an adequate and accurate definition for the category. Ask yourself why it is important to look at the subject as part of a category. Include both similarities to and differences from the category to create more interest. As well, make sure a connection exists between your subject and the categories you create. Finally, if the category is a literary genre, you must research that genre for accurate information.

Comparison/Contrast

Comparisons show how two or more people, places, animals, or objects are similar; *contrasts* show how they differ. Some questions you can ask yourself to help define similarities and differences for your writing are the following:

- What is it like?

- What is it not like?

- Is it like or unlike several other objects?

You can use both comparison and contrast in your writing, but be careful. Trying to compare and contrast two objects that are extremely dissimilar will result in a feature story or editorial that has little purpose (although some writers may compare or contrast two very dissimilar things for humour). Remember, the reason for comparing or contrasting is to *clarify* an idea. Here are other points to keep in mind:

- Select relevant details or ideas to compare or contrast.

- Choose the major commonalities and differences.

- Use strong transitions to move coherently and logically from point to point.

- Choose the best order for your ideas by using one of two choices of organizational pattern: (a) comparing feature by feature or (b) presenting the objects of comparison one at a time.

Definition

Developing a piece of writing by *definition* is the process of explaining what is meant by a particular term, idea, or object. When developing a definition, start with a general statement: "A hero performs acts that put the welfare of others before himself or herself."

If you were writing a short piece on modern-day alienation, for instance, you would need to find examples of alienation that fit your definition. Having found the example, you would have to explain how the example fits your definition. With each new example, start a new paragraph.

Example

Examples are used to clarify and support a generalization. When developing an idea using examples, you can use one example and discuss it fully or use a few examples and refer to them more briefly.

Some questions you can ask yourself to help create examples for your writing are listed below. Substitute your topic (for example, "irony," "poetry," or "television") in each question.

- What does it do?

- What does it mean to me?

- What has been said, done, thought about it?

- What experience have I had with it?

Problem/Solution

Many writers use *problem/solution* as a pattern of organizing. This type of organization is particularly effective when you are writing about a problem that may have a solution (for example, the shortage of summer jobs for students, young children finding inappropriate Web sites on the Internet, or violence on television).

Similar to cause-and-effect organization, this pattern poses a problem, discusses its history or background, and proposes a solution. When several solutions are offered, the benefits and drawbacks of each should be explained.

When offering possible solutions, a writer must mention a solution's negative points, since readers will often have already considered what the writer is proposing and will know the strengths and weaknesses of the arguments beforehand. The writer loses credibility if he or she does not acknowledge these weaknesses. It is up to the writer, then, to prove that the strengths far outnumber the drawbacks.

APPLICATION

Find expositions that use each of the above organizational patterns. You can look at Internet sites with feature articles, magazines, newspapers, or essays you have written for other courses. Explain which characteristics of the pattern led to your classification.

The Closing

Like your opening, your closing should make a strong impression on the reader. You can connect your ending to the lead, to the objective of the story, or to the ideas in the previous paragraphs.[18] "Your article must have a theme, make a point of some kind, drive toward a conclusion," author Max Gunther[19] advises. "It must lift the reader up, carry him along, and set him down with a satisfying thump—and he must end with a strong sense of having arrived somewhere, of being in a different place from the place where he started."

The following are some types of closings:[20]

- the proximity close, which connects to content in previous paragraph(s)

- the restatement of purpose

- the play on words

- the quotation close

- the anecdotal close

- the summary close

- the word of advice

Which type of closing you choose will depend on the topic, your purpose, your audience, and your tone. Analyze the endings of articles you read to identify the type of closing each uses and to determine for yourself how effective each closing is. Experiment with different types of closings in your own writing and ask peer editors to help you determine which works best for each piece. (For more on closing, see pages 332 to 339 in Unit 5.)

APPLICATION

Find an article—one you have written or one from a magazine or Web site. Write three new endings for the piece, using a different type of closing in each. Share all four endings (the original and your new ones) with a small group and discuss which works best and why.

Titles

If you are writing for a newspaper, chances are someone else may title your article for you. If you are a freelance writer, you can ask for your own title to be used. If you are writing for a magazine or a book, you will probably be creating your own title. Don't become too attached to it, however, because an editor might change it to "fit" better with other pieces in the publication. For classroom writing, assume that you are required to invent your own titles. It's a good idea to think of a title after you have written the article; you will know exactly what the article is about and won't waste time thinking up a title that you may eventually throw away. Sometimes inventing a title before completing the article can limit the scope of the article, and the surprise or the unknown is never allowed to creep in. When you write the title, think of it as part of the lead, since its function is similar. Here are some tips for creating a title:

- It's usually best to keep it short.

- Use the title to suggest what the article is about (there's nothing worse than a catchy title that has little to do with the content of the article).

- Make it interesting — some people read only the titles and then decide whether or not to read the actual article.

- Make it reflect the tone of the article.

Here's a list of various kinds of titles that you could use:[21]

- shock titles
- command titles
- punch-line titles
- statement titles
- place titles
- sad titles
- happy titles
- short titles

- surprise titles
- question titles
- alliterative titles
- dramatic titles
- trick titles (e.g., double entendres)
- catch-phrase titles
- VIP-name titles
- long titles

1. Choose an article from a newspaper or magazine and create several alternative titles for it.

2. Examine all the article titles in one publication. Note the effectiveness of those titles in attracting people who read only the titles.

3. Examine the "Readings" section of *Harper's* magazine. Make a list of titles that caught your attention. For each, explain why it caught your attention.

Profiles

WHAT IS A PROFILE?

A profile is a nonfiction story that describes a person or, occasionally, an institution or company. Though a profile is less comprehensive than a biography, a profile usually reveals some aspect of the character of its subject and highlights his or her accomplishments.

THE WRITER'S WARM-UPS

1. To hone your skills of observation, try this exercise: With the sound muted, watch a TV show (preferably a reality TV show or a documentary so that you are not watching actors). In your notebook, carefully describe two or three people you see—their clothing, hairstyle, features, expressions, gestures, posture, gait. Alternatively, observe your own family members and write about them in a way that will enable someone who doesn't know them to picture them.

2. Listen with your eyes: find a TV show that you have not seen before. It must include dialogue between two or more charac-

ters/people. Mute the sound and focus on two people talking. Try to figure out what they are talking about. What is the emotional tone of the conversation? How do you know? Hone your skills of observation by repeating this exercise often.

3. Watch with your ears: in a public place, without looking at them, listen to two people talking. Try to determine as much as you can about them—age, appearance, relationship, what each is doing, body language, and so on. Hone your skills of observation by repeating this exercise often.

 ## THE WRITER'S TOOLKIT

Finding a Subject for Your Profile

While a good writer can make just about anyone sound fascinating, certain types of people make better subjects for profiles than others. In general, the subject must be—or appear to be—extraordinary in some way. The subject could be one of the following:

- a celebrity

- someone who works with celebrities

- an artist or intellectual

- an unsung hero

- an adventurer or explorer

- an eccentric

- a survivor

- someone with a peculiar job

Your list of potential subjects will be broader if you are writing for a school or community publication. For instance, a national newspaper or magazine will not be interested in the new art teacher or exchange student in your school, but the readers of your school's newspaper will be. Similarly, a person closely connected to a story in your local news—a farmer affected by the severe drought in your region or the person who is spearheading the local food drive, for example—will also make an interesting subject for a local publication. Keep your audience in mind as you choose the subject of your profile.

Research

Before you interview the subject, gather all relevant background information. Especially if the person you're profiling is well-known, you should not ask the subject for basic facts, such as his or her birth date, educational background, and so on, during the interview. This information should be readily available from previously published materials. Even if it's the new art teacher you're profiling, find out what you can about him or her—what courses he or she is teaching, what extracurricular activities he or she is running, where he or she has taught previously—before the interview. Although you may need to verify this background information during the interview, having the information will enable you to write more interesting questions, which, in turn, will yield more interesting answers.

You must also do "side interviews"—interviews with people connected to your subject: a friend, family member, colleague, or neighbour. These can happen before your interview with the subject in order to collect background information or they can happen after the main interview in order to fill in gaps and add to the material you got from the subject. Side interviews can add colourful anecdotes to your profile. More importantly, whether the side interviews verify or contradict what the subject says about him- or herself, they help to provide objectivity to the profile.

Some journalists go into the main interview with the angle of their profile already decided. For instance, from a journalist's background research on a singer/songwriter, he knows that he wants to explore how the songwriter draws on her life experience in her songs. He then can write specific questions that will reach for this information. However, since interviewing is an unpredictable process, it is wise not to narrow your focus too soon. Many journalists arrive at the main interview with ideas (and questions) for more than one angle. They also listen carefully during the interview for an angle to present itself that they didn't have in mind before.

Interviewing

Conducting an interview is a complex process. Successful interviewers are known for their keen powers of observation and for their intuition. They know when to let the subject keep talking, when to interrupt with a follow-up question, and when to change the subject. Good preparation will help you tremendously in getting what you need for your story, but experience will help you to grow proficient at the interview process. Following is a list of interviewing guidelines. It may be helpful to do several practice interviews with friends or family members using the following guidelines before you conduct a professional interview.

Before the Interview

Prepare fully for your interview.

- Bring pens and ample paper. If you're tape-recording the interview, you will need to write down your observations and, if the subject doesn't agree to being taped, you'll need to write down information and quotations throughout the interview.

- Bring a working tape recorder with a working microphone. Bring blank tapes. Know how to use the tape recorder. Some journalists prefer to take notes rather than to record and transcribe the interview, but it is difficult to listen attentively to your subject, write down what he or she says accurately, and record your observations all at the same time.

- Memorize the important background information about your subject and his or her accomplishments before the interview.

- Write thoughtful, open-ended questions before the interview. Unless the subject is a celebrity (in which case pretty well all of his or her life will be of interest to the readers), write questions that focus on the parts of your subject's experience that are out of the ordinary or that relate to the angle that your profile will take. Avoid trivial questions about favourite colours or pet peeves, and avoid questions that can be answered in one or two words.

At the Beginning of the Interview

Begin the interview by setting up the parameters: how long the interview will take, where the profile will be published, who else you're interviewing for the story. Ask for permission to tape-record the interview.

Start your interview with easy questions in order to make the subject comfortable and to establish rapport. Leave tough questions, or questions that may make your subject feel uncomfortable, to the middle or end of the interview time. Subjects are more likely to answer difficult questions if you've gained their trust.

During the Interview

Stay in control. Let your subject talk, but gently direct him or her toward subjects you want to hear about. Don't get in the way of the story by commenting unnecessarily, but don't hesitate to redirect your subject if necessary. Knowing when to redirect and when to sit back and listen is tricky—sometimes the tangents your subject takes will be more interesting than the answers to your prepared questions.

Ideally, try to conduct two interviews, the first in the person's home if possible, and the second in a public location such as the person's workplace. This will give you the opportunity to observe the person in different settings.

As the subject speaks, take notes. Don't write down what the subject is saying (unless you're not able to tape-record the interview). Instead, write down everything that you observe—about the environment, about the subject, and about how she reacts with the environment. If you're in the subject's home, look around the room. Describe it with specific details. Observe your subject—not just what she's wearing but what she's eating, drinking, or smoking, what she does with her hands when she speaks, the angle of her chin, her body language and how it changes as she talks about various subjects.

At the End of the Interview

End your interview by asking the subject whether he or she has anything to add. Sometimes you may get an interesting tidbit to include or, more rarely, a whole new angle to use in the profile by opening up the topics for discussion at the end.

Make sure you thank the person you've interviewed and that you have a phone number to reach him or her in case you need to verify any information or clarify a point.

Structure and Content of the Profile

The Lead

A profile, like any other piece of creative nonfiction, begins with a lead whose purpose is to hook the readers. Unless the person you're writing about is widely known, the lead in the profile must show why the reader should be interested in the subject. For example, examine the opening to this profile of first-time novelist Nick McDonell:[22]

There are some things 17-year-old boys should not be able to do. They should not, say, be able to introduce themselves to girls they believe they are in love with without their words coming out all together in a madman's gibber. They shouldn't be able to walk away from an argument sensibly persuaded of the other point of view. They shouldn't be able to avoid cutting themselves shaving before big nights out. And they shouldn't be able to write exceptional satirical novels.

Effortlessly. In their summer holidays. And have them published in nine languages.

Nick McDonell, now 18, is the author of *Twelve*, a smart, sharply written fable of drugs and violence among New York's gilded youth.

Note how this lead immediately highlights what is extraordinary about this new author, making readers want to read on to find out how a 17-year-old manages to write (and publish!) a novel before finishing high school.

APPLICATION

1. Imagine that you were going to interview a new teacher in your school. Write at least 10 open-ended, thoughtful interview questions.

2. Interview a friend about his or her experiences in an extracurricular activity (sports team, club, swimming, dance lessons). As you listen, take notes not on what the friend says, but on his or her body language while answering your questions. For example, your notes might read like this:

   Question #1: She leaned forward, sat up straighter, looked serious—lips pursed.

   Question #2: She smiled broadly, put her hands behind her head.

The Body

The Angle
Your research and interviews usually will yield more material than you can use for your story. Narrow your focus by choosing an *angle*, which in a profile is usually the dominant impression you want the readers to gain about the person you're profiling. This angle will come across in your lead. As you decide what you will focus on, remember that you owe your subject a story that is fair and truthful,

without unnecessary invasion of privacy. However, don't write to please your subject. Your profile should not be like a glamour shot that makes the subject look unbelievably good. Your readers will see through you and dismiss your point of view. Instead, strive to create a distinctive candid snapshot that reveals a slice of the subject's life in a realistic, captivating way. The main focus should be on what makes the person tick, what makes him or her unique and interesting. Don't focus on merely how the person looks or what he or she has done.

The Structure

As you write your profile, go back and forth between paragraphs of description and narration, using quotations frequently so that your subject can speak for him- or herself. You can compare the profile to a hearty stew: to make it as pleasing as possible, you want to put in roughly the same amounts of the different ingredients. Leaving out an ingredient will take away from its appeal. The paragraphs should include the following ingredients:

- background facts and information about the subject: who he or she is and what he or she has done

- anecdotes—stories about the subject's experiences; stories that reveal his or her personality

- quotations by the subject and by others with whom you conducted side interviews

- observations about the subject's appearance, behaviour, reactions, and so on, during the interview(s)

Make sure that each detail helps to create the point of view you've chosen so that your profile will be tight and coherent. Donald Murray[23] advises, "Construct the dominant impression using a sequential body of evidence that does not so much tell the reader how to react but invites the reader to react.... Give the reader a trail to follow through the story, such as narrative, chronology, cause and effect, problem and solution, process, or a walk with the subject."

Revealing Character on the Page

Use the techniques of fiction to describe the subject vividly. Just like short story writers and novelists, the nonfiction writer tries to show rather than tell what his or her subjects are like by describing any or all of the following:

- their physical appearance

- their actions

- how they speak

- what they say about themselves

- what other people say about them

- how they react in certain situations

- their attitudes and opinions

- how they respond to others

- their possessions and surroundings

- how they interact with their environment

Of course, the nonfiction writer, like the novelist, doesn't simply list these details; he or she carefully arranges them so that they tell an interesting story.

Consider your word choice carefully as you compose your story, and use the techniques of description to make your profile vibrant. You can use the following devices:

- vivid word choice: powerful verbs, specific nouns, well-chosen adjectives and adverbs, words with strong connotations

- a simile or metaphor that helps to describe the person

- imagery that uses various senses: the subject's appearance, the sound of his voice, the grip of her handshake, the scent of his cologne

- active voice and present tense to make the story more immediate

- comparison or analogy

- point of view or angle of vision; for instance, you can begin by describing how a passer-by may view the subject and then narrow in to your point of view

- varied sentence patterns

As you read profiles by professional writers, analyze how they reveal character. Examine where and how they use physical description, quotations, their own observations, and anecdotes. Examine how they shift from topic to topic, and how they use the techniques of description to make the subject live and breathe on the page. When you come across an especially powerful profile, imitate its structure and techniques in one or two "practice profiles" of your own.

APPLICATION

1. Examine a profile about an ordinary person (anyone who is not a celebrity).
   - How does the author create interest in the subject and make you feel that he or she is worth reading about?
   - How does the author use both showing and telling to reveal the person on the page?

2. Examine a celebrity profile. Identify which parts of it most likely came from
   - background research;
   - the writer's observations of the subject;
   - side interviews;
   - interview(s) with the subject.

3. Find an interesting person in your school or community. The person could be a retiring teacher, a graduating senior student, a community leader, and so on. (See the section on who makes a good subject for a profile on page 50.) Research this person's background and conduct an interview with him or her. Write a profile that effectively uses the various techniques for revealing the person vividly.

Feature Stories

WHAT IS A FEATURE STORY?

The feature story is a popular form of creative nonfiction, found both in magazines and newspapers. Its purpose is to inform and to entertain. In many magazines, features are the main course—the content that readers "sink their teeth into." The subjects of these stories correspond to the purpose of the magazine: a parenting magazine may offer stories on sibling rivalry or preparing a child for kindergarten; an entertainment magazine will include stories on the new fall line-up of television shows. Feature stories comprise a large part of the content of newspapers as well; here they tie into "hard news" stories or include some kind of hook that makes them seem relevant and timely to the reader. For example, if a company is making front-page news for opening, or closing, a production plant in a region, the local paper may run an accompanying feature story about the history of the company.

The news stories on the front pages of a newspaper focus on facts (who, what, where, when, why, and how) and are deadline oriented. Features, in contrast, can take weeks to write, especially if the topic requires research. They are also different from hard news in that they can reflect the point of view or opinions of the author. Features average 2000 words in length,[24] though some publications prefer very short pieces, and some will run stories of 10 000 words or more.

Here are some of the common types of feature stories. Note that although a particular story may fall neatly into one of these categories, often there may be overlap between two or more categories.

- *List features* are organized into lists, often supplying helpful hints, solutions to specific problems, or pitfalls to avoid when doing an activity or pursuing a goal, for example, ten ways to ace your job interview; useful Internet sites for student writers; steps in creating your own home recording.

- *Roundup features* "round up" people's opinions on a current issue, event, or problem, for example, how students are reacting to having to wear the new school uniforms.

- *Human interest features* explore a contemporary issue, trend, or event, usually with references to individuals' experiences and feelings, for example, the wake-boarding trend—who "wake boards" and why.

- *Personal experience* or *true-life features* record or explore people's unusual experiences, traumas, successes, failures, and so on, for example, how the September 11 rescue workers were coping a year after the disaster.

- *Historical features* provide the history of an institution, place, trend, event, and so on, for example, the history of a local public school, on the occasion of its fiftieth anniversary.

- *In-depth news features* provide depth and meaning to an issue or story in the news, for example, why many of Canada's farmers are struggling to keep their businesses alive.

- *Behind-the-scenes features* take readers beyond the common knowledge of an event or process, for example, the making of *Spiderman*—a behind-the-scenes look at the stunts in the film.

- *Exposé features* are written by investigative or undercover reporters that tell the secrets they've uncovered. For example, immigration officials at an immigration office take bribes in exchange for Canadian citizenship.

- *Satirical/humorous features* make the reader laugh at an issue or at human foibles. Note: often a humorous feature is combined with another kind of feature. An example is a satirical behind-the-scenes feature on a meeting at Parliament Hill.

THE WRITER'S WARM-UPS

Review the types of features listed on pages 58 to 59, and complete the following activities:

- List 10 possible topics for each of the feature types. Choose topics that you would like to read about in the school newspaper. For example, for the list feature, you might list how to survive the first day of school in September, how to take great pictures with the school's new digital camera, and so on.

- For each of the topics you listed, identify what research you will have to do in order to write the feature and explain where you will most likely find the information. For example, for the story on taking great pictures with a digital camera, you might make the following list:

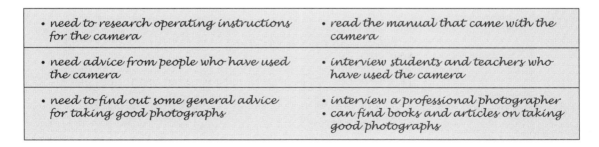

• need to research operating instructions for the camera	• read the manual that came with the camera
• need advice from people who have used the camera	• interview students and teachers who have used the camera
• need to find out some general advice for taking good photographs	• interview a professional photographer • can find books and articles on taking good photographs

- For one of the topics you listed, construct a *source grid* (see the diagram below) and do the research necessary to write the story. (Note: An expert source is someone who would be considered an authority on the issue; a layperson is an average person who may be involved with or affected by the issue but who is not an expert.)

PRIMARY SOURCES	SECONDARY SOURCES
Expert sources:	Background information:
Layperson sources:	Statistics:

 ## THE WRITER'S TOOLKIT

Getting Ideas

Feature stories vary dramatically in their subject, audience and purpose, tone and length. So what do you write about? Anything you want, as long as your topic will interest your audience. Begin with these suggestions:

Who You Are and What You Know

Perhaps you are a second-generation Canadian of Chinese descent, or you have two sets of twins in the family, or you tried out for three sports teams but did not make any of them. Perhaps you had a paper route for three years, you live in a remote part of Canada with few roads, you started a part-time business walking dogs in your neighbourhood, or you have an aunt who collects salt-and-pepper shakers. Perhaps you cope with a disability, you have a unique hobby, or you overcame an addiction to smoking. Each one of these characteristics and experiences could yield several feature stories. For example, with some research your experience of being cut from the team could yield one of the following:

- a "roundup" feature on the question "Are the procedures for choosing teams fair?"

- a personal experience feature on psychological and social effects of not making the team

- a list feature on how to improve one's skills in a particular sport

What You See and Hear

According to journalist and novelist Nora Ephron,[25]

> You can't sit there and wait for ideas to smash into you. It's not a passive process. So much of being a nonfiction writer is forcing your-self to find things to write about. It's an active process of looking at something in the newspaper, or some *thing* that's going around, and thinking: "How do I feel about this?... Can I get anything out of this?... Can I push myself a little further on this topic?"

Every day you will encounter dozens of story possibilities, if you keep your ears and eyes open. For example, consider the following examples:

- A story in the morning paper about a vehicle striking a pedestrian who was jaywalking may prompt you to write an article about jay-walking in your town.

- A conversation with a grandparent about his or her memories of Halloween from his or her childhood may prompt you to write a seasonal article about how Halloween celebrations have changed.

- An announcement at school about reduced bus service may prompt you to write an article about reduced education or city budgets and the impact of the reductions on students.

- The installation of new vending machines in your school may prompt an article on the eating habits of students or on the rela-tionship between schools and commerce.

Professional journalists often keep clipping files of story possibilities—things they read, hear, and witness that can be developed into stories. Consider beginning a similar clipping file. Doing so will encourage you to see the world through a journalist's eyes, always in search of interesting stories. Reading the newspaper daily will also widen your perspective and present you with ideas for feature stories of your own.

What You Want to Know More About

If you are interested in a subject and you are willing to research it, you can probably write a good story—even if you have little or no background knowledge or experience in the subject. Many powerful feature articles are written by authors who become experts on the subject through research. For example, a writer may know nothing about women's shelters, but could visit several shelters, interview workers and residents, and read what others have written about women's shelters in his or her region, gaining enough knowledge to write the article. If you choose this route, you will most likely need to complete a lot of research to gain the knowledge and understanding you will need. You will need to read what others have written on the topic (secondary sources) and to interview both experts on the subject and laypeople who are affected by the subject.

The Content of the Feature

Research

Your story will very likely require research—historical background, facts, and statistics about the topic, as well as interviews with experts and with people involved with or affected by the story. You can use personal experience as well. As you research, look for examples and anecdotes that will make your story come alive. For example, if you are writing a feature exploring the trend of wake boarding, you can find the background information about what wake boarding is and how it started, but you can also interview wake boarders and get stories of their experiences with the sport. For tips on interviewing, see page 51.

1. Make a list of characteristics and experiences that contribute to your identity. Next to each characteristic or experience, write two or more story ideas for feature articles based on that topic.

2. As you go through a typical day, find at least 10 story ideas. Pay attention to what your friends and family members are talking about, what you see as you walk through your school, what you read in a newspaper or on a Web page, and so on.

3. Read the front page and the op-ed (editorial) page of a national or large city newspaper. Brainstorm at least 20 ideas for feature stories based on the issues presented in the pages you read.

The Angle

A feature story presents not just the facts, but your interpretation of the facts. Thus, once you have your story idea or the broad subject you will talk about, you must develop an *angle* on the story—the point of view you are going to take on the topic. For example, if you write a story on pet shelters, there are many angles you could take: that we need pet shelters largely because people buy pets without properly researching how to care for them, that the local pet shelter treats its animals inhumanely, that complex adoption procedures help (or hinder) the animals, and so on. Your angle is a little like a controlling idea in an essay; though you likely won't state your angle directly, it will determine what goes into the article and what you save for a different article. Often your angle will emerge as you do your research, but sometimes you may have to begin writing before you find an angle. As you polish your story, make sure that you can identify for yourself (if not explicitly for your readers) what the angle of the story is. A story without a clear angle is usually cluttered and unfocused.

Structure

The Lead

Begin with a strong lead. In hard news journalism, you begin by summarizing the story, but in features, you can start at any point in the story. Most writers begin with the most compelling part. See page 38 for types of leads to try.

The Body

The body of the feature story usually goes back and forth between narrative paragraphs and expository paragraphs. Frequently, the writer uses *synecdoche*, a literary device in which one person, place, or event represents the broad subject. For example, for an article on how a Canadian city is confronting homelessness, you might begin your article with a description of the typical night in the life of Albert J., a homeless man. As you write the article, you will alternate paragraphs of background information, facts, statistics, and expert opinions with the story of Albert J. In this article, Albert J. will put a face on the issue of homelessness for your readers, and your article will have more interest and impact than a mere recitation of facts.

Feature articles can also use the structural patterns you are already familiar with from your study of essays: chronological order, comparison/contrast, and so on (see pages 43 to 46 earlier in this chapter).

Use transitional words judiciously to guide your readers through the story. Overuse of such devices will bother your reader.

The Closing

Write a memorable closing for your feature story. Turn to page 47 for a list of the kinds of closings you can try.

APPLICATION

1. From a current magazine or newspaper, find a feature story on a contemporary social issue or problem.
   - Identify the angle, and explain how you know what the angle is.
   - Identify what type of lead the article uses and how it hooks you.
   - Identify the pattern of organization used in the article. Explain why it is or isn't the best one for the subject.
   - Identify the transitions used in the article. How do they lead the reader through the article?
   - Identify the type of closing. In your opinion, is it a good ending? Why does or doesn't it leave the reader with "a strong sense of having arrived somewhere"?

2. Read the following excerpt from a feature story on breakdancing.[26]
  - Explain how the article uses synecdoche.
  - Identify where and how the writer moves back and forth between expository and narrative paragraphs.

> If Josh King could shift gears as easily as he shifts from a windmill to a flare, his Celica would be one smooth ride. But this breakdancer, this B-Boy, has only been driving standard for a week—and it shows.
>
> He rides his clutch down Eglinton, grinds his gears along Don Mills. There's no rest for a tranny when a young dancer needs space to move. It's a desire that will drive a young man from the heart of the city to the edge of Pickering, that misunderstood haven of hip-hop.
>
> "Are you kidding me?" he hollers over the loud but tinny sound system. "I wouldn't be driving all this way if I had space to dance at home."
>
> Every Monday and Wednesday, King and his boys converge on Pickering's Petticoat Creek Community Centre to practise breakdancing, breaking, B-Boying.
>
> "I call it B-Boying," shouts King, 22, "because it's the media that calls it breakdancing."
>
> But now that "the media" feels both uncool and unsafe in the passenger seat, it's okay to ask what breakdancing—I mean, B-Boying—is all about. King leans back and rhapsodizes about the culture of this craft that was born in the 1970s, popularized in the '80s, and covert in the '90s.
>
> "What people forget is that this is part of the culture of hip-hop," he says. "We all live the essence of hip-hop—everyone respects each other and looks out for each other. It's about community. We get together and have fun, but we also take it pretty seriously."
>
> By hip-hop culture, King isn't just talking about dancing. He's talking about a love for the music, the style and the sense of fraternity that goes with it. Nicknames are a part of that. King goes by B-boy Tax.
>
> "I'm half native, so I don't pay tax," he shrugs. "That's why they call me that."
>
> Right now, he's lost in Scarborough. He's here to pick up Dyzee, known to his mom as Karl Alba. Weaving through a suburban maze, King talks about Karl, 23, a member of their dance troupe. The Supernaturals.
>
> "He's one of the best in our crew," King says. "When his legs are spinning, he looks like a weed-whacker. His style is off the hook. It's like there's no cartilage in his knees."

Individual style is a big part of B-Boying, King says. Dancers start off with the basic elements of the dance, but eventually take on a distinct flair, inventing moves and techniques.

"Everyone's got a basic style, but that develops into something different," he says.

"Everybody's body moves in a different way. Karl flows well. But I'm known for having good flow in my footwork. Some people are known for having good power moves."

A power move is the showstopper. Like a flare, where the dancer's holding himself up with his hands, kicking his legs up in a giant spinning V. Or a windmill, where a dancer spins with legs in the air with back to the ground, looking like a perpetual motion machine.

They come in handy at competitions. "Battling," as B-Boys call it, is a big part of B-Boying.

"It can start when someone tries to show you up," King explains. "You might take that as an insult and try to show them up, too. It can happen anywhere. It happened to me at a competition. But it usually gets quashed before things get ugly."

After picking up Karl, then fumbling along Hwy. 401, the posse arrives at the community centre. Like much of Pickering, it's a crisp new building parked beside the freeway.

3. Using one of the feature story ideas that you came up with for the activity on page 59, write the story. Make sure that you research and interview as necessary and that you follow the suggestions on page 63 for structuring the article.

Editorials

WHAT IS AN EDITORIAL?

For the purposes of this book, we are defining editorials and editorial writing as writing that takes a position on an issue. In the newspaper, you will find the following types of editorial writing:

- *editorials:* the newspaper's opinions on a current issue

- *opinion/editorials (op-eds):* Written by writers who may or may not represent the paper's view, op-ed columns are position papers or opinion pieces on current issues, "what ifs," and issues that have been around for a long time (for example, gender equality in the workplace), but which may not currently be in the spotlight.

- *letters to the editor:* opinions about articles or editorials that have appeared in the paper

Magazines also have editorials, but they are usually a summary of the major articles covered in the magazine and why or how the stories came about. Magazines almost always have letters to the editor as well as op-ed articles. The latter take a position on one aspect of the broader subject of the magazine (for example, "the trouble with snowboarders," written for a ski magazine; "the yearly hype over new cars," written for a car magazine; "the dangers of labelling children before they enter school," written for a parenting magazine).

Editorial writing puts forward a position, supports it with researched facts, statistics, details, and illustrations, and then discusses what should be done about the situation. The subjects the writers tackle are generally serious, although some writers may choose a sarcastic or humorous tone for their articles. Like all creative nonfiction, you should not pretend to be unbiased. Confirm your biases up front.

THE WRITER'S WARM-UPS

In small groups, brainstorm a list of issues that are current in and relevant to the following:

- your school

- education in general

- your community

- religious institutions in your community

- your province

- your country

- the world

Choose the best ideas from all the lists and use those issues as daily warm-ups. For each warm-up, take a stand on an issue and through your writing, convince your audience to take your point of view.

THE WRITER'S TOOLKIT

Persuasive Writing

Editorial writers must be persuasive. Their job is to present a position and to sway readers' opinion. Therefore it is essential that, as editorial writers, you know your audience. In knowing your audience, you will know how far you can push an argument, which tone is most appropriate, and which appeals will touch the readers' minds (reason) and hearts (emotion). The following sections examine the appeals you can use in your own writing.

Logic

One of the appeals writers use to persuade their audience is *logical reasoning*. There are two types of logical reasoning: deductive and inductive.

If you are using *deductive reasoning*, base your argument on a sound *premise* (an assumption that is considered true because it can be proven). The major form of deductive reasoning follows this order:

Major premise:	All humans need water to survive.
Minor premise:	A teenager is a human.
Conclusion:	Therefore, a teenager needs water to survive.

If one of your premises is inaccurate, then your conclusion will be inaccurate.

Major premise:	All humans need spring water to survive.
Minor premise:	A teenager is a human.
Conclusion:	Therefore, a teenager needs spring water to survive.

The major premise is incorrect because humans don't necessarily need spring water; any source of clean water will do just fine.

If you are using *inductive reasoning*, make sure you have enough facts and reasons to support your generalization. Inductive reasoning works like this:

Generalization:	Brand X is the exceptional product.
Proofs:	Many studies have been conducted that show that the product does what it claims to do.
	I have used the product for 10 years and have been satisfied with its performance.
	I have used other products that claim to do the same thing, but they have not performed as well.
	A survey was conducted of 10 000 people who compared Brand X with Brand Y. Of those people, 9998 thought Brand X was better.

Poor inductive reasoning would look like this:

| Generalization: | Graduates from Confederation Secondary School are exceptional English students. |
| Proof: | Last year I taught two students from that school in my university English class and both achieved As. |

There are too many unknowns in this proof. Were the two young people typical of students from Confederation Secondary School? How did other students from that high school do in university English? Did any other students from Confederation Secondary School take university English? What is the achievement in university English of students graduating in other years from that high school?

Blunders in Logic

While trying to appeal to readers' reason, writers often fall into the trap of *logical fallacies*. The following logical fallacies are used by writers quite frequently and should be avoided. If you make the error of overusing them or using them unwisely, be prepared to have your editorial criticized by observant readers or your ideas discounted. Most respected editors will not accept writing that is riddled with logical fallacies since they have their reputations at stake.

Fallacies of Distraction

Fallacies of distraction use a *logical operator* to distract the reader from the falsity of a certain proposition. In other words, they use the language of logical reasoning, such as cause and effect (if A happens, *then* B will happen) or comparison (*either* this *or* that is responsible). However, despite the logical sound of the statements, one or more of the propositions in the statement are false. Here is an example:

- Either support this cause or the earth will perish. (This argument puts issues or opinions into "black or white" terms, providing only two options when there are more.)

- Since scientists cannot prove that global warming will occur, it probably won't. (This statement assumes that since something has not occurred, then it is false.)

- If we pass laws against fully automatic weapons, then it won't be long before we pass laws on all weapons, and then we will begin to restrict other rights, and finally we will end up living in a communist state. Thus, we should not ban fully automatic weapons. (The sequence of arguments here is an illegitimate use of the "if…then" operator.)

- You should support home education and the right of parents to raise their children according to their own beliefs. (Here, two otherwise unrelated points are conjoined and treated as a single proposition. The reader is expected to accept or reject the entire argument, which is treated as a single proposition. The reader is expected to accept or reject both together, when in reality one may be acceptable while the other may not.)

Fallacies of Definition

The purpose of a definition is to state exactly what a word means. A good definition should enable a reader to "pick out" instances of the word or concept with no outside help. For example, take the word "apple." If its definition clearly explains what it is, then the reader should be able to go out into the world and select every apple that exists—and only apples. If the reader misses some apples, or includes some other items (such as pears), or can't tell whether something is an apple or not, then the definition has failed. However, definitions may have the following fallacies:

- An apple is something that is red and round. (This definition is too broad; the planet Mars is red and round, so it is included in the definition. But obviously it is not an apple.)

- Music is what is played on a piano. (This definition is too narrow: a drum solo cannot be played on a piano, yet it is still considered music.)

- An animal is human if and only if it has human parents. (This definition is circular. The term being defined is "human," but in order to understand "human," we would need to understand the term "human parents." To understand "human parents," we would already need to know what "human" is.)

- An object is beautiful if and only if it is aesthetically successful. (This definition fails to elucidate. The term "aesthetically successful" is harder to understand than the term "beautiful.")

- A society is free if and only if liberty is maximized and people are required to take responsibility for their actions. (This definition is self-contradictory. If a person is required to do something, then that person's liberty is not maximized.)

Numberitis
Though numberitis is not a logical fallacy, it is a type of reasoning to avoid. Numberitis is the inclusion of many numerical statistics to support your point. It is better to use one or two powerful statistics than to overwhelm your readers with numbers they can't understand or won't take the time to understand.

Emotion and Logic
When appealing to the emotions of an audience, you need to determine what might be important to them. Here are some emotional areas to which you could appeal in your writing:

- *basic needs:* air, water, food, sleep

- *belonging:* family, friends, clubs and teams, religious groups, work groups

- *health and safety:* health, protection, security, stability

- *growth:* creativity, novelty, respect, success, economy

- *certainty:* practicality, knowledge, reliability, superiority, comfort

Another grouping is the "emotional food groups," which include love, worth, significance, growth, certainty, and uncertainty. To connect with your readers, you need to appeal to at least one of these emotional triggers.

While you can appeal to your readers' emotions by using emotive language, vivid words, evocative words, and figures of speech, be aware that the following techniques should be used carefully:

- *testimonial*: A celebrity says that a product or an idea is great. What qualifications does that person have to make him or her an expert? Does he or she have a bias? How much money is he or she receiving for endorsement?

- *bandwagon appeal*: Bandwagonning sounds like this: "Everybody is doing it!" You may have used this technique with your parents when you wanted to do something with your friends. But in your writing, a reader may ask who is "everybody"?

- *plain folks*: When a writer says, "Just like you, I ...," an alert reader may view the writer as pretending to be "just like us" to try to convince "us" to go along with his or her ideas.

- *name calling*: Writers may label people who think differently than they do in order to persuade an audience to go against that opposing point of view. Negative labelling, such as "spoiled brat," "whiner," "flaming liberal," and "cheap" all carry negative connotations. What emotion is the writer trying to appeal to? Has the writer any proof that the name is appropriate?

- *glittering generalities*: Abstract words and expressions can be defined in many different ways by many people. Take for instance the slogan "Lemonade is it." An observant reader might ask, what is "it"? People think of "it" in many different ways: the most refreshing, the best tasting, the least expensive, the most popular, the oldest, the greatest. Therefore, try to identify glittering generalities and, if possible, use specific concrete language instead.

Tone

In persuasive writing, *how* you present your reasons is as important as what those reasons are. Your tone can help you to win readers to your way of thinking or it can alienate readers. For a review of how tone is created, see page 35. In the example below, both paragraphs make the points that the soccer team played sloppily and that the players will need to brush up on their skills to improve their game. However, as you read the paragraphs, note how differently you feel about each writer because of the tone that has been employed.

> Last night, our school went down to a humiliating defeat at the hands of a soccer team that, by all accounts, should be a vastly inferior team. Could we have been let down any more completely by our own team? Could the incompetence—no, the lazy betrayal—of our athletes have been any more apparent? What happened to the hard work, the commitment, the spirit, and the will to win that our team used to possess? The fans still had it. The stands were rocking with it last night. But the spoiled louts who dare to wear our school colours on their lazy backs, who dare to pretend they represent us, have obviously forgotten what it takes to deserve to be winners. Maybe with a few kicks in the right places for the right people, last night's humiliation will be a sad but necessary lesson that can put this sorry team back on its tracks.

> Last night, our school gave up a win to its arch rival. We like to characterize Central High as the inferior soccer team, but last night they showed they have what it takes to be winners. Despite a strong showing by our fans—the stands were rocking!—our team couldn't seem to pull it together at many crucial moments. We seemed to be caught off guard. Perhaps, having trounced Central High so many times before, we took our superior strength for granted. But we have always had a team that comes back from defeat, learns from its mistakes, and is stronger for it. With the fans behind the team and last night's lesson in the players' back pockets, this team will soon get back on track.

In general, it is wise to avoid tones that are angry, arrogant, scornful, or lecturing. Keeping your tone positive when you feel strongly about an issue may be difficult, but keep in mind—as the proverb says—that "you'll catch more flies with honey." Also, note how *you* feel when you read a piece with an unpleasant tone—even if you agree with the writer, you may dismiss the arguments because the tone offends you.

Sometimes you will have a great deal of knowledge about a subject, knowledge that you have acquired through study, research, or experience. You may be tempted to talk down to your readers; but again, a positive, respectful tone is more likely to win their ears than a condescending one. As you experiment with writing opinion pieces, work at creating compelling tones.

1. Form a small group and read a week's worth of editorials in a newspaper. (All group members must read the same paper.) Working individually, identify the appeals to logic and to emotion that the writers include in their work. Then, in your group, analyze the appeals you found. Test their logic and their effectiveness.

2. Find examples of politicians' speeches, especially prior to an election or during a candidate's debate. As you read through the speeches, highlight or copy examples of what you consider blunders in reasoning or manipulative persuasion.

3. Discuss current issues that are facing your school. Choose one and write an editorial on that issue. Revise and rewrite. Compare your editorial with those of your classmates. Make a collection of the class's best comments for submission to the school newspaper or magazine or to a local newspaper.

Reviews

WHAT IS A REVIEW?

Reviewers evaluate products. In order to have an audience for their review, they must interest and inform their readers as well as evaluate the product they have been given to review. It is important to remember that reviews are not summaries. Information about the product will be included in the points you are making about it.

Throughout high school you have probably studied and written book reviews, play reviews, movie reviews, and maybe even restaurant reviews. But magazines, newspapers. and Internet sites are filled with reviews of concerts, music, automobiles, athletic equipment, electronics, and games, to name a few. In this next section, we will focus on entertainment (movies, plays, concerts), book, and equipment reviews.

The critical aspect of reviewing is that you have to read the book, see the movie, use the product—that is, you complete the activity that will allow you to write your review. Reviewers develop their own opinions about products, not going by hearsay. Sometimes they go against the tide. For example, a long-awaited new novel by a best-selling author may be panned by the reviewer if he or she didn't like it.

Reviewers research both the specific product being reviewed and the type of product. For instance, if you were going to review the latest science fiction movie, you would not only go to see the movie, but you would learn about the genre and see some other movies in that genre if you hadn't already. If you were reviewing the latest CD by a singer/songwriter, you would not only listen to that CD but listen to the previous work of the singer and know at least a little about the type of music you're reviewing.

Reviews are popular and plentiful. Many people have started their own Web sites devoted to reviews. As you read reviews, note how the writers inspire confidence, or lose your confidence, as they talk about the product.

THE WRITER'S WARM-UPS

Choose one of the following topics for a review:

- a piece of equipment that is commonly found in your classroom or school with which all students in your class have knowledge (computer, overhead projector, videotape player, or portable tape/CD player)

- a book that you have recently read

- a movie that you disliked (you may also write another review of the same movie from a positive point of view)

- a children's "read aloud" book (the audience of your review should be parents, and your review should be written in a way that will make the parents want to buy the book)

- school cafeteria food for a nutrition magazine (remember to consider all that is available, not just what most students like to eat)

- a new music CD or movie comparing it with the artist/director/actor's previous work

- something that has been written for or about a hobby you like (for example, an instructions manual for a camera, a pattern for a knitted sweater, a recipe, or a rule book for a new role-playing product)

- the family car
- a lesson you have recently been given (for example, a school lesson, a swimming lesson, a heritage language lesson, or a driving lesson)

THE WRITER'S TOOLKIT

Structure of a Review

A review is a specialized type of article and, like an article, needs all the elements discussed in other types of creative nonfiction. A review needs a strong lead, a well-developed middle with vivid examples and details, and a powerful end.

The Lead

Reviews need a *lead* that will catch the audience's attention as well as convey something about the content of the article (refer to pages 37 to 43 in this chapter for more information on leads). A reviewer might state his or her opinion in the first sentences. The reader knows what the reviewer thinks and may decide, "That person's opinion is good enough for me," and not read any farther. Other reviewers might start with a description of what they are reviewing, not in a dry way, but in a way that will keep the reader reading. Through the tone of the description, the opinion of the reviewer will probably be evident.

The Body

The *body* of the review contains the information people need to decide whether or not they will spend their money on the product or production. Obviously, the length suggested or required by the publication is going to determine the depth and breadth of the review. What you include in your review will depend on your audience and on your expertise.

Whether you loved or hated the product or production, you need to explain your feelings. "This movie stinks" is not going to make the entertainment section in any newspaper. Give examples. Use quotations if possible and if appropriate.

You may have a bias against a product or production that you are reviewing. For example, you may be reviewing Brand A skis, but you prefer Brand B skis. If Brand A skis are good and you like the way they perform, then you need to say that. Don't let everything you review be coloured by previous experience or bias. Think of a restaurant reviewer who has had a terrible dining experience in a restaurant and five years later revisits that same restaurant—it would be unfair to prejudge the food or service based on past experiences. While the reviewer may mention the previous visit as a point of comparison, he or she must base his or her current review on the current visit.

It's fine to come clean about your bias in a review. If you say nothing, and the readers detect a bias that they think interferes with the review, your opinion will be discounted. Show that you've considered other points of views. Address the opposite point of view and challenge it!

The Conclusion

The *conclusion* can briefly summarize your points (if space allows), should give a recommendation (explicit or implicit), and refer back to the main idea suggested at the beginning of the review.

How Strong Should Your Opinion Be?

While it is probably more fair to a product or production to present a balanced view of it (stating the positives and stating the negatives), it's not as much fun to write or read. Reviewers are known for stating their opinions. As writers, we want our readers to have a reaction to what we've written, not fall asleep as they read.

You can, however, alienate readers with a tone that is know-it-all, lecturing, or superior. When you have finished your review, read it into a tape recorder. Play it back and listen for those words that may push the review into the "distasteful" or "offensive" category. Have a peer editor read it and give you feedback on tone.

Having a strong opinion and expressing it is fine; being insensitive to word choice is not.

Entertainment Reviews

There are many topics or categories you can discuss when reviewing a movie or play. Reviewers need to become fast category experts, knowing each category thoroughly. You can take media courses, read and research, or try to get a job with a production company to learn firsthand! Following are some aspects of a production that you might choose to write about:

- actors
- background/history of production
- camera work
- computer-generated images
- content
- costumes
- dialogue
- editing
- intended audience
- producer(s)
- set
- special effects
- theme
- tone
- animation
- characters
- comparisons with other productions (by same director, with same lead actor, or with similar themes)
- director(s)
- hair/make-up
- music
- script/screenplay
- sound
- structure (flashbacks, framing devices, play within a play)
- type of movie

Naturally you aren't going to write about all of the topics above. You need to decide who you are writing for and the purpose of your review. Every newspaper and magazine has its own audience. What you write about will depend on whether this audience sees a production because of its production values, its story, its actors, its director(s), or a combination of all of these. If your readers know nothing about cinematography, they may not want to read a review that discusses the technical aspects of camera work and editing, but they may want to hear something about cinematography so they can watch for it and become more knowledgeable.

Read the two reviews[27] of *The Lord of the Rings*: *The Fellowship of the Ring*. Look at what each reviewer stresses. How can you discern the audience from reading the reviews? What aspects of the production does each writer discuss? How do the reviews differ from each other? What do the differences tell you about reviews?

The Lord of the Rings—Movie Review
★★★★

The Lord of the Rings is a three-hour-long monster of a film packed with eye candy, awesome acting and some of the coolest monsters ever and now it's finally out on DVD. It's about four hobbits (three-foot-tall people), Frodo, Sam, Merry and Pippin, who have to destroy a magical ring before it's used to kill everyone.

The hobbits hook up with the wizard Gandalf, Aragorn the ranger, Boromir the warrior from Gondor, Legolas the elf and Gimli the dwarf to form the fellowship of the ring and kick some evil butt.

The Lord of the Rings' intro starts off with background info about how the evil super-sorcerer Sauron created the One Ring to "rule them all and in the darkness bind them." Then it delivers a ton of special effects with huge armies going to war, evil wizards blasting stuff, sword fights and more action than the whole NFL season. Once you've recovered, the rest of *The Lord of the Rings* starts and it's time to watch as the fantasy world of Middle-earth is brought to life with awesome acting and incredible special effects.

The Lord of the Rings is loaded with fantasy cities, huge underground labyrinths, massive wizard towers and scary monsters. When the Cave Troll shows up and starts laying the smack down, it's time to hold your date's hand. When the Balrog rips up the screen, it's time to hold your mom's hand! Even the orcs are creepy monsters with freaky eyes and warped faces.

The Lord of the Rings isn't perfect though. It takes serious bladder control to last for three hours watching it straight through but that's no problem now that *The Lord of the Rings* is available on DVD. There are also a few scenes where it's a little rough and where it starts to get boring.

Even with a few flaws *The Lord of the Rings* movie is totally worth watching at least once. Gary went twice to see it in the theaters and he's gonna go rent the DVD!

The Lord of the Rings: The Fellowship of the Ring

Lisa Schwarzbaum

Grade: A

So that's what the fuss is all about. I mean the passion, the devotion, the obsession of people for whom the fate of fictional characters who live in Middle-earth—players named Frodo and Gandalf, Aragorn and Elrond, Gollum and Sauron—means more, at times, than the fate of the real people who live next door. It's not usually necessary, or shouldn't be, to announce one's lack of familiarity with literary source material in order to assess a movie's qualities as a movie. But, remembering the ferocity of high school classmates—boys, mostly—who steeped themselves in Elvish arcana while the girls wallowed in Salinger and Sylvia Plath, I open by saying that I have never read the fantasy series by the tweedy British scholar J.R.R. Tolkien, the modern lit classic known as *The Lord of the Rings* trilogy.

And I follow quickly by saying that *The Lord of the Rings: The Fellowship of the Ring* is thrilling—a great picture, a triumphant picture, a joyfully conceived work of cinema that (based on this first installment, with two more ready for release in the next two years) would appear to embrace Tolkien's classic with love and delight, and rewards both adepts and novices with the highest compliment of all: an intelligence and artistry as a movie independent of blind fidelity to the page. The Middle-earth of this "Fellowship"—as directed by Peter Jackson with all the graceful inventiveness hoped for from the maker of *Heavenly Creatures*—is vibrantly, intricately alive on its own terms. This is what magic the movies can conjure with an inspired fellowship in charge, and unlimited pots of gold.

One of the "Fellowship's" most exemplary attributes is the ease and good instinct with which Jackson regularly shifts perspectives, both structurally and visually, from the epic to the intimate and back again: Thousand-year-old, thousand-creature battles (depicted with of-the-moment computerized assistance) really do look and feel as awesome as such mythological battles ought to but rarely do—and then the focus shifts to the tenderness expressed in the close-up half smile of a gentle wizard. Having laid out the saga's prehistory in a thunderous yet (blessedly) comprehensible prologue—the Great Rings of Power created by the Dark Lord Sauron, the Elven Kings, the Dwarf Lords, the Mortal Men, the one master ring capable of shifting the balance of power in the world, the whole fantastical yada yada— Jackson carries us to the Shire, home of the hobbit Bilbo Baggins (Ian Holm), his young nephew, Frodo (Elijah Wood), and all their pint-size, hairy-footed, pointy-eared fellow hobbits, living in an idyllic village of excellently cozy wee homes such as Real Simple magazine would swoon to photograph.

As Frodo greets the return of Gandalf the Grey (Ian McKellen), the hobbits' wizardly protector who has returned for Bilbo's 111th birthday party, the boy and the graybeard share a wagon ride together into a village detailed enough to delight Munchkins, Breughel, and the kitsch painter Thomas Kinkade alike. Frodo is the hero-as-average-fellow in Tolkien's tale, the very opposite of a strapping action figure, to whom will fall the saga's great heroic assignment—and Wood imbues the role with such a serious, kindly, unmannered goodness that he holds his ground easily even against such attention-getting costars as McKellen, Cate Blanchett as the impossibly dreamy Lady Galadriel (queen of all elves), and Viggo Mortensen (impossibly dreamy himself) as the broody and mysterious Aragorn.

The cast take to their roles with becoming modesty, certainly, but Jackson also makes it easy for them: His "Fellowship" flows, never lingering for the sake of admiring its own beauty. There's no time, anyway. Despite the fact that this first episode runs some two and a half hours—and despite the fact that (scholars tell me) some characters from the book have been excised in the mellifluous screenplay by Fran Walsh, Philippa Boyens, and Jackson—there's a massive amount of story to cover. Every detail of which engrossed me. I may have never turned a page of Tolkien, but I know enchantment when I see it.

APPLICATION

1. With a partner, make a list of words that help create the tone of each of the two reviews. Discuss with the class the tone that is created and how these words underline that tone.

2. Find a negative review of a movie or play you enjoyed. Examine each of the points made by the reviewer and decide whether or not it is valid. Write your own review of this same movie or play.

3. View a movie that is famous for its cinematography (for example, *The English Patient*; *The Moderns*; *Crouching Tiger, Hidden Dragon;* or *Lawrence of Arabia*). Write a review that focuses on cinematography but in language that makes it accessible to a national newspaper audience.

Book Reviews

Probably you are familiar with writing about books in the form of book reports. Book reviews are similar to book reports in that they include some summary of the book, however, reviews focus mainly on analysis and opinion. Like entertainment reviewers, book reviewers can discuss a number of things. Most often, book reviews examine big themes in the work—what the author is saying and how well he or she is saying it. What you discuss will depend on the genre, the purpose of the writing, and the audience for whom you are writing. Following are some aspects of a book that you might choose to write about:

- anecdotes/interviews with author, editor, or publisher
- bibliography/references/glossary/index
- comparison between current book and another by same author
- genre
- language/imagery/symbolism
- objectivity
- plot
- publication details
- readability
- subject
- usefulness
- author
- author's expertise and research
- characters
- comparison between books on a similar theme
- dialogue
- form
- illustrations/tables/graphs/charts
- perceived audience of book
- point of view
- purpose of book
- structure
- theme
- writing style

If you are a book reviewer, it is assumed that you enjoy reading and enjoy thinking about what you read. It is also assumed that you have read extensively and (for literary reviews) that you have studied literature, journalism, or media. When you read in order to review a book, you read with a pencil in hand. Take notes on any or all of the topics listed above. Be aware of the parts in the book that kept you interested and those parts that lost your interest. Don't simply read on at those parts, but examine how the author involved you in the content, characters, facts, or language or why the author lost your interest. When you evaluate a book, you need to support your judgements with examples. With well-documented notes, this job is easier.

When reviewing novels, stay away from simply retelling the story. While you will have to discuss the content, it shouldn't be the focus of the review unless the plot line is the one aspect of the novel that detracts or makes the book.

Reviewing collections of essays, poetry, or short stories by a single author poses a challenge. What you might say about one essay, poem, or story may not hold true for another. You will need to look at broad aspects of the author's writing (for example, the political bent he or she takes in the collected essays, the way he or she uses typography to enhance ideas in the poems, and the types of characters that inhabit the stories). You will probably refer to a few pieces in the collection that exemplify the writer's work in that collection, but not to every single one (unless the collection is very short). For anthologies, you may discuss the editor's choice of pieces for the collection as well as highlight a few pieces.

For nonfiction or for fiction where illustrations and layout are an integral part of the book, be sure to discuss how they add to or detract from the book.

As with entertainment reviews, how much technical information you include in your review will depend on your readers. If you are reviewing for a literary journal, you can afford to be technical since its readership is generally knowledgeable about literature. Likewise, if you are reviewing a book about technology for a highly technical computer magazine, you can assume your reader will understand technical language and terms. If, on the other hand, you are reviewing novels for a local newspaper, you may need to read other articles and editorials in the newspaper to get a feel for the readership. Read the following review with this in mind.[28]

No Great Mischief: A Significant First Novel

Siobhan Moore

Alistair MacLeod's first novel, *No Great Mischief*, is a powerful, intricate work which belies the label "first novel."

MacLeod is not a new author but a quiet literary giant whose other published works include two collections of short stories—*The Lost Salt Gift of Blood* and *As Birds Bring Forth the Sun*. Well-known among Canadian authors, MacLeod's presence has not been felt among the reading public until now with this haunting tale of the MacDonald family.

His mastery of the short story technique is put to good use in *No Great Mischief*, which took the University of Windsor English professor more than 10 years to write.

It was well worth the wait. MacLeod's well-defined structure and clear writing style carefully weave the memories and antidotes of the MacDonald family through the narration of Alexander MacDonald.

A middle-aged Alexander examines the past of his immediate family and ancestry—dating back to 1779 when his great-great-great grandfather Calum moved his large family from the Scottish Highlands to settle in Cape Breton, where he became known, in Gaelic, as the Calum Ruadh, patriarch of Cape Breton clan MacDonald.

The story is set in the mid-'80s as Alexander, an orthodontist whose profession has given him a comfortable Ontario life away from Cape Breton, travels every weekend down the 401 to visit his eldest brother, the Calum Ruadh's namesake, now a suffering alcoholic living in a Toronto rooming house.

MacLeod's description of the highway linking the two men—"It will be true to you if you are true to it and you will never, never, ever become lost,"—underlines the brothers' relationship. The highway is the modern connection between the two, whose lives diverged after their parents and one brother died when Alexander and his twin sister Catriona were three and Calum 16 years old.

The twins are raised by their paternal grandparents, whose delightful, warm hearted personalities and relationship highlight the novel's comedic moments. Grandma decorates a boozy, sleeping Grandpa with Christmas ornaments after he comes home too late to put up the tree. Grandpa is a man "buoyed up by his own good spirits," and Grandma a woman who believes "you should always look after your blood."

But Calum and the two other brothers are forced by the parents' death to set up their own household. Later, as Catriona and Alexander leave for university, Calum and the others leave the island to work in uranium mines, and eventually Elliot Lake where the novel's turning point takes place. Each child goes on into adulthood to "repeat his own small history," as Alexander says.

It is these small histories which MacLeod masterfully weaves against the backdrop of famous ancient battles waged by the Highlanders— Killiecrankie, Culloden and most importantly the Plains of Abraham, where Wolfe used the Highlanders to ensure his victory because, in his words, it was "no great mischief if they fall."

Wolfe's abuse of the MacDonald loyalty, courage and bravery at the Plains of Abraham mirrors the injustices dealt Calum—a man "loyal as hell" and "brave as hell," but a man who, like his ancestors, is felled by those same qualities cherished, respected and expected in his family. It is Calum's struggle which Alexander observes with the despair and fierce love which bring the brothers on a journey back to their birthplace.

The contrasting images are powerful and MacLeod's use of language and dialogue in telling this story are superb. This is not a book you can read only once, for the impact of the pictures left in your mind as painted by MacLeod's words forces you back into the pages of *No Great Mischief* again and again.

It is a tale whose savage, cruel beauty makes you weep at its conclusion.

Copy this chart into your notebook and fill it out using the book review on page 84.

Title of review	Tone of review	Words and phrases that create the tone	Aspects of the book that the author discusses

Product Reviews

Products, from interactive games to telephones, are reviewed every day. To be able to review products, you must have expertise. Without expertise, it is easy to make false statements about the product unknowingly. If you are trying to break into this market, learn as much technical information as you can and get hands-on experience.

Aspects of the product that you could discuss in your review include the following:

- description of the product
- performance
- predecessors (history of product)
- cost
- testing results
- how it has been advertised
- features
- drawbacks
- comparisons with similar products
- what has been said about it

Often reviews are aimed at a specialized audience. For example, examine the following review from Mac*Addict* magazine for an MP3 player.[29] Note the aspects of the product that the writer discusses. The review has a conversational tone, almost colloquial, targeting a young audience. As you read, note the technical terms and jargon that the writer assumes the readers know. The review also provides details on what the product can and cannot do, resulting in a balanced view.

MPIO-DMK MP3 Player

Cathy Lu

If we had a rating called *Freakin' Spiffy* that's exactly what we would give the MPIO-DMK, a near-perfect specimen of an MP3 player. Approximately the size and weight of a spring roll, this futuristic-looking Jetsons-like device ... is the perfect MP3 player for people who want to hit the road without feeling weighed down.

Equipped with 128MB of internal memory (there's also a 64MB version available for $179), the MPIO-DMK is about 3.5 inches long and 1 inch wide, and weighs approximately 29 grams. While Digital Global Network intended users to wear the device around their necks like Bonnie Bell lip gloss circa 1986, you can also wear it on your arm or clip it to your belt via the included accoutrements. The only problem is that you'll need new headphones, since the MPIO-DMK's come attached to the neck strap (and they don't extend vary far). That said, the provided earphones are fairly high quality and produce a rich, full sound.

The player itself is quite slick. We were able to store 30 tunes, equaling almost 2 hours of high-quality music (encoded between 128 and 160 Kbps); a single AAA battery kept the music playing all day long (over 8 hours). You can scroll through tracks via the jog dial on the side of the device, and the display shows information such as track number, song length, bit rate, and song title. An equalizer includes prefab settings like Pop, Rock, and Classical.

Unfortunately, the MPIO-DMK does not include an AM/FM tuner or a digital voice recorder. If those features are not important to you, then we wholeheartedly recommend this player. If they are, well, we don't. Also, the 128MB of memory isn't upgradeable. If you like to run marathons while plugged in or you want to listen to Richard Wagner's Ring Cycle on the go, the MPIO-DMK is probably not for you.

The MPIO-DMK comes with its own Manager software for uploading tunes to the player via USB. The software runs in both Mac OS 9 and the Classic environment in Mac OS X (though it's sometimes flaky), and while the interface isn't pretty, it's simple. Just navigate to your folder of music and click the arrows to upload music. Sadly, if you want to delete music or rearrange tracks, you need to plug your player into your Mac, open the software, and proceed from there—you can't do any of those tasks via the player itself. Also unfortunate is the fact that the MPIO-DMK is not part of the iTunes 2 clique—Apple's digital-music app refuses to recognize the player's presence.

Despite a few minor shortcomings, the MPIO-DMK is one of the lightest, smallest, and coolest MP3 players we've ever had the pleasure of sweating and StairMastering with. It's absolutely worth buying if *little* is a big thing in your life.

APPLICATION

1. Find three examples in three different publications (including electronic publications) of reviews for similar products. Make a list of the topics each covers. From your reading, describe the intended audience for each review.

2. Choose a product that you know about. Decide on an audience. Write a review for the product aimed at that specific audience.

3. Visit a local retailer and find out if you could "try out" a product (in the store, of course) for a review. Gather information from the "tryout," phoning or returning for further information if necessary. Write a review of the product.

Travel Writing

WHAT IS TRAVEL WRITING?

You might think that travel writing is reserved for travel magazines and brochures. On the contrary, articles appear in newspapers and magazines covering a variety of topics relating to travel. Here are a few examples of the topics that appear in a range of magazines and newspapers, all travel-related: motorcycles (how the new touring bike did on a trip to Alaska), health (preventative medicine for travelling to developing nations), weddings (planning the honeymoon trip), food (eating out in Italy), women (keeping safe when travelling alone), sports (the best areas to ski in New Zealand), and business (a comparison of business-class services offered by various airlines).

Photographs are important to travel writing since they help to enhance the words in a piece and put readers in the place that might otherwise be foreign to them. Therefore, as a beginning travel writer, you should also have good photographing skills. (When you are well-known or you work for a specific publication, you will be accompanied by a photographer.) Taking a photography course at your high school or the local college or arts centre is a good idea if you want to write travel articles.

Money is always an issue for the travel writer. Travel is expensive. Not all travel writing, however, is about exotic locations. Start locally. Find subjects of interest in your own neighbourhood. Ask yourself why people would want to visit your city or town. Research your area. Discover its history, interesting geographical features, local heroes, fun campsites, and unique spirit. Find an angle for writing about places within easy reach of your own home.

THE WRITER'S WARM-UPS

1. Describe one of the popular areas of your school (library, cafeteria, or gymnasium, for example) in a way that would encourage others to visit.

2. Write a humorous story about an experience you had with a mode of transportation (excluding cars or motorcycles, unless they were rented).

3. Compare grocery shopping in a variety of locations (outdoor versus indoor markets, markets versus grocery chains, different companies or grocery shopping in different towns, provinces, or countries).

4. Compare summer and winter activities in your region.

5. Write an article on how to pack for a weekend in the country or in the city (wherever you *don't* live).

6. Write a review of a restaurant you've eaten in, or a hotel, bed and breakfast, motel, or lodge you've stayed at.

7. Write a detailed account of an unusual trip you took. It doesn't have to be exotic! Your view of the trip will make it exotic.

THE WRITER'S TOOLKIT

Types of Travel Writing

There are many types of travel writing. For our purposes we will use the following categories suggested by Richard Cropp, Barbara Braidwood, and Susan Boyce in *Writing Travel Books and Articles* and Cynthia Dial in *Travel Writing*:[30]

- *Destination pieces* describe a specific place or attraction. They make readers feel as if they've had a "mini-vacation."

- *First-person travel tales* focus on the writer's thoughts and personal comments, allowing the writer to reflect on the travel experience.

- *Specialty theme stories* focus on one aspect of travel, such as adventure, nightlife, food markets, and public transit.

- In *reviews*, the writer reviews the hotels he or she has stayed at or restaurants he or she has eaten in.

- *Guide books* contain information only: how to get there, places to stay, where to eat, sights to see, and so on.

- *Historic travel stories* are based on travel to an historic place and focus on the history of that place.

- *How-to/travel-tips pieces* cover subjects such as how to pack for a specific type of vacation, how to travel safely in a large city, how to travel cheaply in Japan, and so on.

- *Humour articles* look at the humorous side of travel. Whether it's taking a disastrous day trip or ordering food in a foreign language, there are always humorous things that happen when you travel (some are only funny when you look back on them!).

- *Roundups* compare several places that have a common link (for example, spas, theme parks, sports events, or observation towers).

APPLICATION

Examine a variety of types of publications. Find articles that you would consider travel articles and categorize them using the categories above. Remember there will be many articles that don't fit perfectly into one category but cross over two or more.

Research

All travel writing (whether you're walking to the location, taking a two-seater plane, or riding on a camel) starts with research. Without research you might miss a great deal about your destination. Also, by researching thoroughly you will be able to create a list of possible topics on which to write before you arrive. Research also gives you a focus for what you want to see. It will save you time once you reach your destination. Research includes the following:

- looking up information using print and electronic sources

- talking to people who know about the destination

- visiting the local travel agency

- writing to or e-mailing the local tourist information centre for brochures and pamphlets on local attractions

- reading what others have said about the destination

- visiting a country's embassy if one is local

- studying maps of the location you are visiting (road maps, topographical maps, maps that contain information on industry, agriculture, weather, and so on)

- reading local newspapers (many newspapers are now published on the Internet; if they are in a language you can read, they can provide you with current events in the area)

- reading fiction that takes place in the location to which you are travelling

- learning some common phrases in the language of the country you are visiting (books and tapes are readily available from your library or bookstore, sometimes even from your high school)

Naturally, when you are travelling, you should not restrict yourself to only activities you have researched. Sometimes the most interesting stories come from a spontaneous side trip to a local restaurant or a conversation with a bus driver. You must plan ahead, but be prepared to alter those plans.

APPLICATION

1. Choose a local place of interest and perform research on historical facts or stories you have heard about it. Write a travel article based on your research.

2. Interview someone who has travelled to a location outside your province or territory. From that interview and some additional research, write an article on one aspect of that person's journey.

3. Research a location using some of the approaches listed earlier. Create a brochure for that place of interest for a specific audience (students, senior citizens, gardeners, or athletes, for example). Use a computer program to assist you with the design and layout of the brochure.

THE WRITER'S PROJECTS

Investigating the Writer's Craft

1. Find two feature articles on the same issue. Try to find articles that are of similar length and which are written for a similar audience. Write a comparison of the two articles, looking at angle, lead, organization, use of facts, anecdotes and quotations, and the closing. Which article is more helpful in shedding light on the issue, and why?

2. Examine several editorials written by the same person (the editor of your local newspaper, for instance). What techniques of persuasion does the writer tend to rely on? Explain fully how the writer tries to convince his or her readers. Then, write an editorial that uses the same tools of persuasion. Try to make it sound like the writer you've been analyzing.

3. Find five pieces of travel writing about the same town, city, or region. Look for various kinds of articles: a first-person travel tale, a destination piece, a guide book, a review, a humour piece, a historic travel article, etc. Create a chart to compare the five pieces, using these headings:
   • focus and purpose of the article
   • type of lead

- audience (armchair travellers? budget travellers? adventurers?)
- primary method of development (exposition, description, narration, persuasion)
- facts included about the town, city, or region
- opinions included about the town, city, or region

After you've completed your chart, write a review of the travel articles, explaining which one(s) you would recommend to what kind of audience and why.

Practising the Writer's Craft

1. As a class, collect various types of magazines: fashion, music, car, computer, video game, news, nature, and so on. In small groups, analyze the magazines, identifying both the types of articles each magazine includes and the main style of writing (level of formality, level of difficulty). Then brainstorm a list of new articles that the magazine would be likely to print. Working on your own, write one of the articles that your group thought of. After you revise and edit it (and write a query letter if appropriate—see page 17), submit your article to the magazine.

2. Working in a small group, create a magazine. Decide on your magazine's audience and purpose and choose a title. Then, using a "divide and conquer" approach, write the content of the magazine. Include at least four different types of articles: features, profiles, reviews, editorials, and travel pieces. The topics and the slant of each topic must be appropriate for the magazine as you've created it.

3. Write two feature articles on the same topic, but with different slants or purposes. Choose a topic that would be of interest to secondary school students. For example, you might write two articles on back-to-school shopping, one a "how-to" article aimed at teens, the other a roundup article that compares students' real and perceived needs regarding new clothes and supplies for school. Research as necessary, and share your rough drafts with a partner for peer editing. Polish and, if possible, publish your work in a school newspaper or magazine.

4. Choose a current issue in your school or neighbourhood. Write an editorial on the issue, using techniques of persuasion (see pages 66 to 73). Then write another editorial on the same issue, arguing

the opposite point of view. Try to make the second editorial just as persuasive. Revise your work with your peer editors.

5. Attend a reading by an author and write a review of the reading.

6. Choose a town, city, or region you know well. Write three different types of travel articles about the place you choose. Do all the research necessary to make your articles authentic, useful, and interesting. Make sure you have a specific audience—such as backpackers, armchair travellers, five-star travellers, or young families—in mind for each article. When you have finished your drafts, share them with a group of peer editors and ask them to identify your audience and purpose in each article. Gather suggestions for improving the articles, and revise.

7. Write two reviews for the same movie or play, one positive and one negative.

8. Look inside the back cover of this text and copy the jobs listed for creative nonfiction writers. Choose one and research it. Part of your research should include an interview with someone who has the job you chose. Write an article that informs your readers of the responsibilities, appeals, and drawbacks of the job.

THE WRITER'S READING LIST

The Writer's Craft

Burgett, Gordon. *The Travel Writer's Guide*. California: Prima Publishing, 1991.

Cropp, Richard, Barbara Braidwood, and Susan Boyce. *Writing Travel Books and Articles*. North Vancouver: Self-Counsel Press, 1997.

Daugherty, Greg. *You Can Write for Magazines*. Cincinnati: Writer's Digest Books, 1999.

Fredette, Jean M., ed. *The Handbook of Magazine Article Writing*. Cincinnati: Writer's Digest Books, 1988.

Johnson, Sammye and Patricia Prijatel. *The Magazine From Cover to Cover: Inside a Dynamic Industry*. Illinois: NTC Publishing Group, 1998.

Murray, Donald. *Writing for Your Readers: Notes on the Writer's Craft from* The Boston Globe. Connecticut: The Globe Pequot Press, 1992.

"The Age of Creative Non-fiction: *nidus* Roundtable Discussion." *nidus* (on-line publication supported by the Writing Program at the University of Pittsburgh's English Department, http://www.pitt.edu/~nidus/archives/fall 2001/rt.html.) Copyright 2001, *nidus*.

Zinsser, William. *Speaking of Journalism*. New York: HarperCollins, 1994.

Examples of the Writer's Craft

The Journal of African Travel-Writing. http://www.unc.edu/.

"Lighter Side of Travel." *The Toronto Star*, various issues.

Theroux, Paul, ed. *The Best American Travel Writing, 2001*. Boston: Houghton Mifflin, 2001.

Writers Write: The Internet Writing Journal. http://www.writerswrite.com/journal/.

Endnotes and Credits

CHAPTER 2

1 Toni Cade Bambara, quoted in Caryn Mirriam-Goldberg, *Write Where You Are: How to Use Writing to Make Sense of Your Life: A Guide for Teens*. Minneapolis, MN: Free Spirit Publishing Inc., 1999, 39.

2 John Tierney, "Feature Story," in *Speaking of Journalism*, ed. William Zinsser. New York: HarperCollins, 1994, 10.

3 *Oxford English Dictionary*, compact ed. Oxford: Oxford University Press, 1981. Journal, Journalist.

4 *Oxford English Dictionary*, compact ed. Journalist.

5 Phil Druker, "What Is Creative Non-Fiction?" University of Idaho Web site, www.ets.uidaho.edu/druker/nonfic.html.

6 Donald Murray, *Writing for Your Readers: Notes on the Writer's Craft from* The Boston Globe, 2nd ed. Old Saybrook, CT: The Globe Pequot Press, 1992, 3.

7 Murray, "Interview: David Mehegan," in *Writing for Your Readers*, 22.

8 Adapted from Murray, *Writing for Your Readers*, 194–197.

9 From "Interview with Richard Saltus" in Donald Murray's *Writing for Your Readers: Notes on the Writer's Craft* from The Boston Globe. Connecticut: The Globe Pequot Press, 1983, 29.

10 Murray, *Writing for Your Readers*, 64.

11 Excerpt from "Fans Riot After Guns N' Roses No-Show," November 8, 2002— Reprinted by permission of the Canadian Press.

12 Excerpted from "Flyer Donates Great Escape Journal to Museum" by Rod Mickleburgh. *The Globe and Mail*, August 24, 2002, A3. Reprinted with permission from *The Globe and Mail*.

13 Excerpted from "The Laws of Applause" by William Littler. *The Toronto Star*, August 24, 2002, H1.

14 Excerpted from "Campaign Launched to Stop Auto Idling" by Bob Mitchell. *The Toronto Star*, Saturday, August 24, 2002, G1. Excerpted from "Canadian Open Tourney Will Survive Without Tiger" by Dave Perkins *The Toronto Star*, August 24, 2002, E1.

15 Excerpted from "After the War Is Over" by Renata Salecl. *Index on Censorship*, Vol. 30, No. 4, October 2001, 40. Reprinted by permission of *Index on Censorship*, www.indexoncensorship.org.

16 © Keith Ablow from "The Man Who Loved Trains" in *Discover Magazine*, October 1997. Reprinted by permission of Beth Vesel Literary Agency and the author.

17 Excerpted from "The SUV That's a Car" by Jim Kenzie. *The Toronto Star*, August 24, 2002, G1.

18 Robert L. Baker, "Twelve Ways to End Your Article Gracefully," *Handbook of Magazine Article Writing*, ed. Jean M. Fredette. Cincinnati, OH: Writer's Digest Books, 1988, 110.

19 Max Gunther, quoted in Baker, "Twelve Ways to End Your Article Gracefully," in Fredette, *Handbook of Magazine Article Writing*, 109.

20 From Baker, "Twelve Ways to End Your Article Gracefully," in Fredette, *Handbook for Magazine Article Writing*, 111–116.

21 From L. Perry Wilbur, "Draw Your Readers in with Titles, " in Fredette, *Handbook of Magazine Article Writing*, 88.

22 Excerpted from " 'Twelve' at 17: What Next?" by Tim Adams. *The Observer*, August 10–11, 2002, B1—© The Observer.

23 Murray, *Writing for Your Readers*, 115.

24 Sammye Johnson and Patricia Prijatel, *The Magazine from Cover to Cover*. Chicago: NTC, 1998, 119.

25 Nora Ephron, quoted in Candy Schulman, "The Idea Ideal," in Fredette, *Handbook of Magazine Article Writing*, 24–25.

26 Christopher Hutsul, "No Jiggy, No Bling, Just Dance," *The Toronto Star*, September 3, 2002, D1, D5. Reprinted with permission—Torstar Syndication Services.

27 Reprinted by permission of Kidzworld Media Inc. www.kidzworld.com. Copyright © 2000–2002 Kidzworld Media Inc. All rights reserved; Lisa Schwarzbaum, "Movie Review: *The Lord of the Rings: The Fellowship of the Ring*," Entertainment Weekly's EW.com, December 5, 2001, © 2001 Entertainment Weekly Inc. Reprinted by permission.

28 Siobhan Moore, "No Great Mischief a Significant Novel," *The Toronto Sun*, December 26, 1999. Retrieved from Canoe Web site, www.canoe.ca/JamBooksReviewsN/nogreatmischief_macleod.html. Used by permission of Toronto Sun Syndicated Services.

29 "MPIO-DMK MP3 Player" by Cathy Lu. Mac*Addict*. April 2002, 50.

30 Richard Cropp et al., *Writing Travel Books and Articles*. North Vancouver, B.C: Self-Counsel Press, 1997, 11–12; Cynthia Dial, *Travel Writing*. London: Hodder and Stoughton, 1974, 79–82.

Society of Professional Journalists, Code of Ethics

It always comes back to the same necessity; go deep enough and there is a bedrock of truth, however hard.

MAY SARTON[1]

The following is quoted from the Society of Professional Journalists' Code of Ethics.

SEEK TRUTH AND REPORT IT

Journalists should be honest, fair, and courageous in gathering, reporting, and interpreting information.

Journalists should:

- Test the accuracy of information from all sources and exercise care to avoid inadvertent error. Deliberate distortion is never permissible.

- Diligently seek out subjects of news stories to give them the opportunity to respond to allegations of wrongdoing.

- Identify sources whenever feasible. The public is entitled to as much information as possible on sources' reliability.

- Always question sources' motives before promising anonymity. Clarify conditions attached to any promise made in exchange for information. Keep promises.

- Make certain that headlines, news teases and promotional material, photos, video, audio, graphics, sound bites, and quotations do not misrepresent. They should not oversimplify or highlight incidents out of context.

- Never distort the content of news photos or video. Image enhancement for technical clarity is always permissible. Label montages and photo illustrations.

- Avoid misleading re-enactments or staged news events. If re-enactment is necessary to tell a story, label it.

- Avoid undercover or other surreptitious methods of gathering information except when traditional open methods will not yield information vital to the public. Use of such methods should be explained as part of the story.

- Never plagiarize.

- Tell the story of the diversity and magnitude of the human experience boldly, even when it is unpopular to do so.

- Examine their own cultural values and avoid imposing those values on others.

- Avoid stereotyping by race, gender, age, religion, ethnicity, geography, sexual orientation, disability, physical appearance, or social status.

- Support the open exchange of views, even views they find repugnant.

- Give voice to the voiceless; official and unofficial sources of information can be equally valid.

- Distinguish between advocacy and news reporting. Analysis and commentary should be labelled and not misrepresent fact or context.

- Distinguish news from advertising and shun hybrids that blur the lines between the two.

- Recognize a special obligation to ensure that the public's business is conducted in the open and that government records are open to inspection.

MINIMIZE HARM

Ethical journalists treat sources, subjects, and colleagues as human beings deserving of respect.

Journalists should:

- Show compassion for those who may be affected adversely by news coverage. Use special sensitivity when dealing with children and inexperienced sources or subjects.

- Be sensitive when seeking or using interviews or photographs of those affected by tragedy or grief.

- Recognize that gathering and reporting information may cause harm or discomfort. Pursuit of the news is not a license for arrogance.

- Recognize that private people have a greater right to control information about themselves than do public officials and others who seek power, influence, or attention. Only an overriding public need can justify intrusion into anyone's privacy.

- Show good taste. Avoid pandering to lurid curiosity.

- Be cautious about identifying juvenile suspects or victims of sex crimes.

- Be judicious about naming criminal suspects before the formal filing of charges.

- Balance a criminal suspect's fair trial rights with the public's right to be informed.

ACT INDEPENDENTLY

Journalists should be free of obligation to any interest other than the public's right to know.

Journalists should:

- Avoid conflicts of interest, real or perceived.

- Remain free of associations and activities that may compromise integrity or damage credibility.

- Refuse gifts, favors, fees, free travel, and special treatment, and shun secondary employment, political involvement, public office, and service in community organizations if they compromise journalistic integrity.

- Disclose unavoidable conflicts.

- Be vigilant and courageous about holding those with power accountable.

- Deny favoured treatment to advertisers and special interests and resist their pressure to influence news coverage.

- Be wary of sources offering information for favours or money; avoid bidding for news.

BE ACCOUNTABLE

Journalists are accountable to their readers, listeners, viewers, and each other.

Journalists should:

- Clarify and explain news coverage and invite dialogue with the public over journalistic conduct.

- Encourage the public to voice grievances against the news media.

- Admit mistakes and correct them promptly.

- Expose unethical practices of journalists and the news media.

- Abide by the same high standards to which they hold others.[2]

Endnotes and Credits

Appendix B

1 May Sarton, quoted in Caryn Mirriam-Goldberg, *Write Where You Are: How to Use Writing to Make Sense of Your Life—A Guide for Teens*. Minneapolis, MN: Free Spirit, 30.

2 Code of Ethics from the Society of Professional Journalists Web site http://www.spj.org/ethics_code.asp. Reprinted by permission of Society of Professional Journalists, Indianapolis, Indiana, USA.

Fiction and Poetry

I love writing. I love the swirl and swing of words as they tangle with human emotions.

JAMES MICHENER[1]

Chapter 3: Story Writing

Chapter 4: Scriptwriting

Chapter 5: Poetry Writing

Story Writing

*A wondrous dream, a fantasy incarnate, fiction completes us, muti-
lated beings burdened with the awful dichotomy of having only one
life and the ability to desire a thousand.*

MARIO VARGAS LLOSA[2]

LEARNING GOALS

▸ analyze forms of stories and their elements and conventions
▸ analyze the purpose and audience of a variety of stories
▸ assess authors' choices of techniques, diction, voice, and style
▸ research and analyze selected works by authors from around the world to assess their practices and beliefs about writing
▸ write stories in various forms and for various purposes to practise and develop writing skills
▸ explain and assess—individually and in small groups—the creative choices made in producing one's own writing
▸ revise drafts to produce writing that is effective in content, techniques, diction, voice, and style

WHAT IS A STORY?

A story has a beginning, a middle, and an end. A story might be long (novel or novella length) or shorter (short-story length). For the purpose of this chapter, we will talk about stories in general, not a specific form.

Jack Hodgins in *A Passion for Narrative*[3] says the following about the differences between novels and short stories:

> The successful short story tends to be so finely tuned that every word, every nuance of every word, is contributing to a single final impression. To strike one sentence from a fine short story is to do as much damage as to toss away a line of a good poem. A short story's power lies in its density.

The novel may also build its final effect upon a single impression, but it will be an impression large enough to include within it the strands of more than one plot, perhaps, or several conflicting ways of looking at the single theme, or a complex multiplicity of symbols reaching out to other stories. A novel's power lies in its scope.

Flannery O'Connor says this in her essay "Writing Short Stories":[4]

> A good short story should not have less meaning than a novel, nor
> should its action be less complete. Nothing essential to the main
> experience can be left out of a short story. All the action has to be sat-
> isfactorily accounted for in terms of motivation, and there has to be
> a beginning, a middle, and an end, though not necessarily in that
> order.... A short story should be long in depth and should give us an
> experience of meaning.

Many writers believe that a story has to decide what it wants to be. Oftentimes, a writer will set out to write a short story but the idea is far too big and involves far too many people and subplots. The story struggles to get out of the confines of the structure. In an interview, Raymond Carver[5] said about writing: "I begin the story and it takes a natural course. Most often I'm not aware when I start ... a story, of where it's going until I get there. Not while I'm writing it. The drama enters the story, and the consequences and choices present themselves."

Stories—no matter what length—have several things in common: plot, structure, characters, setting, perspective, imagery, and symbols. Memorable stories have all these ingredients, plus good writing—a variety of types and lengths of sentences, appropriate word choice, and connections between ideas. Like anything else, crafting good stories takes practice. Throughout this chapter you will read about different elements of stories and practise writing them. While we will break down storytelling into various parts, in fact, it is the melding of these parts that makes a story good. At the end of the chapter we will include some suggestions for bringing all the parts together into a whole. As you write, you will start to feel the form that best fits your story.

How to Find Stories

Writers who are just starting out often ask, "Where do ideas for stories come from?" They can come from anywhere: your own life experiences, experiences of people you know, newspaper articles, radio or television news, family history, mythology, textbooks (for example, history, geography, or visual arts), travelling, overheard conversations, or photographs. The possibilities for stories are all around you. As a writer, you have to tune your senses to pick up those possibilities. Listen carefully at your next family reunion or when you next talk to a senior citizen. Look around you. Train your eyes to see things in detail. Take a notebook with you at all times and write your impressions of a street scene, your feelings at a concert, your thoughts about a class discussion, your reactions to a food you've never tasted before. Take notes on even the most mundane things in your life—your part-time job, your daily routines. Become a sensory sponge. Try out new things. Take the bus or a train somewhere. Even if you know nothing about art, go to a gallery. Look at each picture or sculpture as if you are a salesperson trying to sell it, or an artist talking to a potential patron. Attend a concert of music you don't normally listen to. Visit a place you've never been before. Meet with other writers and talk about writing. Go to a reading given by a writer, or set up a series of readings given by you and your fellow writers. Most of all, read. Read writing from different centuries and different countries as well as your own. Read children's literature. Read essays and other types of creative nonfiction. All these things will give you food for writing.

THE WRITER'S WARM-UPS

1. Draw a box in the middle of a page. In the box, write a potential conflict for a story. Above the box, draw some of the events that could lead up to that conflict, and below the box, some ways that the conflict could end.

2. Sketch the opening scene of a story to show the character in his or her setting.

3. As a class, gather your favourite sentences from short stories or novels you've enjoyed. Write each of the sentences on an index card. Be sure to include the specific bibliographic information for each sentence. When you are going to practise writing, randomly pick a card, copy down the line, and use it as a jumping-off point. Compare the different ways your classmates use the same sentence.

4. Write a dialogue where the reader enters in the middle. Make it clear what each speaker wants.

5. Describe a scene that you know very well but that others in the class may not be able to describe with authenticity.

6. Put on a piece of clothing or acquire an accessory (for example, a pipe) that you do not usually wear or use. Become the person that

would wear this clothing or use this article and write from that person's point of view.

7. Describe a person walking through the lunchroom or into a classroom. Try to focus both on character and, more subtly, on location.

8. Write a piece, addressing an unnamed person as "you."

9. Recreate a dream you have had.

10. Start retelling what has happened to you today in as much detail as possible. In the middle, have something impossible happen.

11. Choose three disconnected nouns (for example, garage, dishrag, and bottle of ink). Using these three items, write for 20 minutes.

12. Choose a subject or situation that you find hard to write about. Write about that subject in great detail. Recreate sounds, smells, and feelings.

13. Write about a time you felt like you never wanted to stop what you were doing. Describe it in detail so your reader will feel what you felt.

14. Describe a family meal. Choose a perspective that is not your own.

15. Choose a photograph or a picture from a magazine. Write about the people in that photo and what they are doing.

16. Write about a real event, placing a fictional character you've created at the event.

17. Observe a person for 20 minutes. Make notes on clothing, posture, facial features, actions, and so on. Create a story, using that person as a character.

18. Go to a coffee shop or restaurant. Eavesdrop on a conversation. Use your notes as a jumping-off point for a story.

19. Pick up, hold, and handle an object. Describe that object without naming it or its function. Read your description to a classmate and have him or her identify it.

20. Bring a picture to class. Write a description of that picture.

Plot

Orson Scott Card, a science fiction writer, talks about four factors that are present in every story: milieu, idea, character, and event (MICE).[6] How each story is constructed depends on the importance or weight of each of these factors within the story.

Milieu

The milieu of a story includes all the physical locations (urban, rural, one town, many towns, and the countryside in between) as well as the culture (customs, laws, religions, politics, and so on). A story that emphasizes milieu goes into great detail about the customs and the setting. The characters move through the settings as explorers in these places and cultures, reacting to them as they meet people and deal with societal customs. Jane Austen set her stories in nineteenth-century Britain, where class dictated a person's schooling, friends, and marriage partners. The classist society of Austen's *Pride and Prejudice* becomes as important as the characters, since they must maneuver through its rules and regulations to find happiness. Sinclair Ross's "The Lamp at Noon," Alice Munro's "Mile-High City, Montana," Alistair McLeod's "The Boat," and Gabrielle Roy's "Alicia" are all examples of short stories that focus on milieu.

Writers who focus on milieu do not ignore characters, events, or ideas, but spend time recreating detailed worlds and cultures in which to place their characters and have their events unfold.

Idea

In the idea story, a problem or question is posed and, by the end, it is solved or answered. Murder mysteries and detective fiction fall into this category, along with many other types of writing. The characters rarely change over the course of the story. In Arthur Conan Doyle's Sherlock Holmes stories, the detective is given a case to solve. Over the course of the story, Holmes invariably finds clues that no other person (including, more often than not, his partner Watson) would pick up on, and finds the murderer. Readers who enjoy Sherlock Holmes mysteries know the detective's strengths and his weaknesses, and look forward to seeing how he will outsmart the criminals. Once again, the author of a story that focuses on ideas does not forget milieu, events, and characters, but these are less important than the idea itself.

Character

Card explains, "The character story is about a person trying to change his [or her] role in life ... The character story emerges when some part of a character's role in life becomes unbearable."[7] In Xin Qi Shi's story "Stuck in the Throat," a young woman's boss leads the office staff to believe he is having an affair with the main character. The young woman discovers this, and finds it unbearable. She leaves her job, but not before irreparable damage is done.[8]

Event

In the event story, the main character or characters try to put a world that is out of order back into its natural order. For the narrator's mother in Thomas King's story "Borders," a border guard's not recognizing "Blackfoot" as a citizenship throws the natural order out of line. The character was a member of the Blackfoot nation long before there was a Canada, and she wants recognition of that fact. The story centres on her disagreement with the border guards from both countries. While this story emphasizes an event, it is also a strong character story. It is also possible to have a story that emphasizes both event and milieu or event and idea.[9]

Like every other categorization, MICE is a construct, but a very useful one when thinking about plot. Ask yourself what type of story you think you are going to tell. Or start writing and, as you do, look back on the story to determine the type of story you are telling. From that vantage point, it may be clearer how much emphasis you have placed on plot. You may decide to downplay the importance of the events in your plot and focus more on the characters or the world you are planning to evoke.

APPLICATION

Find at least 10 short stories. Look for stories in a variety of genres (science fiction, murder mystery, and so on) written by authors from around the world. Form a small group and read four to six of the stories. Make notes on the emphasis of each story, based on Orson Scott Card's MICE formula. Be prepared to discuss your findings with the rest of the class.

Structure

Annie Dillard[10] wrote this about structure:

> When you are stuck in a book; when you are well into writing it and know what comes next, and yet cannot go on ... then the trouble is either of two things. Either the structure has forked, so the narrative, or the logic, has developed a hairline fracture that will shortly split it up the middle—or you are approaching a fatal mistake. What you had planned will not do. If you pursue your present course, the book will explode or collapse, and you do not know about it yet, quite.
>
> Acknowledge, first, that you cannot do nothing. Lay out the structure you already have, x-ray it for a hairline fracture, find it, and think about it for a week or a year; solve the insoluble problem. Or subject the next part ... to harsh tests. It harbors an unexamined and wrong premise. Something completely necessary is false or fatal. Once you find it, and if you can accept the finding, of course it will mean starting again.

How you structure your story will in part be dictated by which factor(s) you have emphasized. Telling your story in chronological order from beginning to end might be the best form, especially if you have chosen to focus on an "idea" in your story. Stories emphasizing "milieu" may also be told chronologically as we are introduced to the location(s) and its (their) cultures. This does not mean these types of stories are limited to this method of telling. There are many different ways of telling stories and you need to think about how best to lead your reader through the story you want to tell. How do you want them to see what is happening? Will you start near the end, flash back to what has happened up to that point, and then bring the reader back into the present for the climax? Will you tell the story in chronological order but dip regularly into the past to fill the reader in on some necessary information or event? Jack Hodgins has created a series of visuals that represent various ways to structure your story.[11] The first five diagrams show short-story structures. The last three represent novel structures. Look at them carefully and try to think of short stories or novels you have read that use these structures.

Short Story Structure

When a writer uses the pattern shown below, it is a good idea to start with some information or with an event that will ultimately lead to the big scene and climax. Starting with exposition about something that is not directly related to the conflict and eventual climax is often a waste of the writer's and the reader's time. The reader wonders why the scene is there.

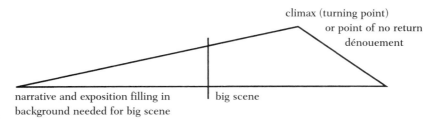

climax (turning point)
or point of no return
dénouement

narrative and exposition filling in
background needed for big scene

big scene

Isabel Allende's story [12] starts with the following sentence:

> She went by the name of Belisa Crepusculario, not because she had been baptized with that name or given it by her mother, but because she herself had searched until she found the poetry of "beauty" and "twilight" and cloaked herself in it. She made her living selling words.

The protagonist is forced to sell speeches to a corrupt Colonel who wants to become president and will stop at nothing to do so. She also gives him two secret words, which haunt him and eventually take all the war out of him. But before the big scene, Allende fills in the reader on how Belisa came to be a word seller and how she used the power of her words. The big scene occurs when she is kidnapped and taken to meet the Colonel. The climax is the Colonel's ultimate "taming," his inability to fight.

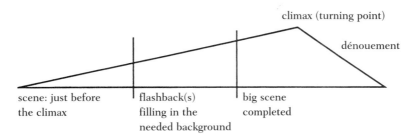

climax (turning point)

dénouement

scene: just before
the climax

flashback(s)
filling in the
needed background

big scene
completed

When using the order shown above, the writer must create a crisis that makes the reader eager to know what led up to this point.

"A West Coast Woman," by Jan Hopaklyissumqwa Gould, begins with an argument between a grandfather and his granddaughter, Sadie, about where Sadie's brother Mark will be buried. The writer starts the story in the middle of the argument with the grandfather's words, "You will not bury him at Saqwiss. He has lost the right."[13] The reader immediately wants to know who the young man is and why he does not deserve to be buried at Saqwiss. We also want to know what is so special about Saqwiss that he can't be buried there. The writer then fills us in on some background that helps us understand the beliefs held by Sadie and her grandfather. After this background, about three-quarters of the way through the story, the grandfather and Sadie finish the argument, which then leads to the climax.

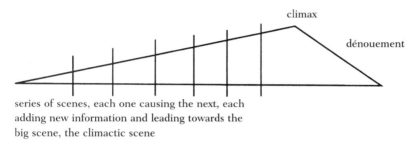

series of scenes, each one causing the next, each adding new information and leading towards the big scene, the climactic scene

Nadine Gordimer's "Once Upon A Time" is an example of the above story shape. The story takes place in South Africa during the apartheid period. A White family—two parents, a little boy, and a dog—live in an all-White neighbourhood, but are increasingly fearful that people of "another colour," who live outside their neighbourhood, want to rob them. In a series of scenes, they fortify their house first with an alarm, then a higher wall, and finally with barbed wire coiled on top of the wall. The story ends with a tragedy, the result of their ever-increasing paranoia and attempts at "protection." Each scene leads inevitably to the next and finally to this tragedy.[14]

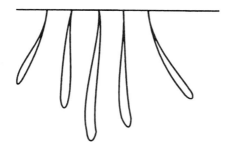

"now," remembering various

"then's" at different parts of the past arranged in an order which is not necessarily chronological

Stephen Vincent Benét's "The Blood of the Martyrs" is the story of a scientist waiting for execution.[15] Throughout the story, he dips into his past and, through this narrative technique, we learn why he is in the prison and facing the firing squad. The diagram above illustrates this structure.

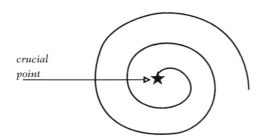

crucial point

circling around the important moment and only eventually showing it directly

On first reading, "No rinsed blue sky, no red flower fences," by Dionne Brand, seems to be developed without structure, but each description, each recollection, each action, adds to the readers' understanding of the despair and hopelessness of the main character—the main idea of the story.[16] Above, this type of structure is illustrated.

Today's short-story writers use a greater variety of narrative shapes than has been used in the past. Alice Monro's "A Wilderness Station" is the story of Annie (McKillop) Herron and Simon Herron, told through a series of letters, newspaper articles, and recollections. Simon Herron is murdered and, through various documents—some contradicting the story of others—the reader pieces together the story of how the murder happened. The structure of your own story may present itself to you from the beginning. You may, however, have to write your story or parts of your story before you know the best way to present it.

1. As a class, choose a short story you have previously read. Individually, rearrange the events of that story in a variety of ways to lead the reader through the action in a different way each time. Discuss your new organizations, focusing on the pros and cons of the various rearrangements you have tried.

2. Sketch or outline a plot you are interested in writing. Think of different ways you could tell the story, keeping in mind Hodgins's various story shapes or others that may not have been discussed in this chapter.

Novel Structure

Hodgins describes three basic novel shapes: horizontal, converging, and vertical.

The horizontal novel (above) follows the characters chronologically. The occasional flashback delves into the past, but basically the plot moves forward. Charlotte Brontë's *Jane Eyre*, Charles Dickens's *Great Expectations*, and Lucy Maude Montgomery's *Anne of Green Gables* are all examples of horizontal novels. This particular shape was popular from the beginnings of the novel to the start of the "modern novel." It is still used widely, especially for "idea" novels, or novels that are plot-based.

In an interview with Eleanor Wachtel, Michael Ondaatje talks about structure in a narrative:[17]

I don't believe stories are told from A to Z anymore, or if they are, they become very ponderous. I'm used to commercial breaks. We discover stories in a different way. I discover something about you after knowing you for X number of years, and then after thirty years I will find out some other changes that occurred five years earlier. That sense of discovery, of memory, and how we reveal ourselves to each other—none of that is chronological.

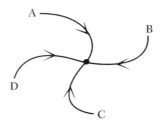

The converging novel (above) has several strands that weave through the story, converging at the end. Jeannette Turner Hospital's *The Tiger in the Tiger Pit* follows the stories of a family, two parents and three grown children, as they prepare to converge for the father's birthday. Each chapter is dedicated to one family member. *The Sweet Hereafter* by Russell Banks is about a tragic school bus accident. We learn about the accident from several different points of view, including the bus driver and the lawyer who is trying to launch a lawsuit on behalf of the parents of the dead children. In *The Jade Peony* by Wayson Choy, we hear the thoughts of each child in an immigrant family living in Canada.

Kent Harris's *Plainsong* explores the relationships between various people in a town. The book is told in third person, but each chapter focuses on a different character.

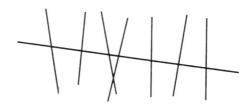

The vertical novel (above) is shaped much like the fourth short-story shape (see top of page 111). The narrator moves into the past from the present, using the past to make sense of the present.

Michael Ondaatje's *The English Patient* combines this technique with the converging technique. We see the lives of four people: Hana, Caravaggio, Kip, and the English patient both in the present and in the past, in a pattern that Ondaatje himself calls "a mosaic."[18] The story is made up of tiny fragments that come together by the end to give the reader a coherent picture. *The Assault* by Harry Mulisch is a story that moves back and forth between a Dutch man's present situation and the events that occurred since he witnessed a brutal Nazi attack on his family when he was a child. Elaine Risley, the protagonist of Margaret Atwood's *Cat's Eye*, returns to Toronto, the place where she grew up. With her return, she is flooded by memories of that mostly unhappy past and tries to make sense of it all now that she is a fifty-year-old, reasonably successful artist.

A_____ | B_____ | A_____

The story-within-a-story is yet another way to shape a novel. The main story (Story B) is bracketed by a shorter story (Story A). The longer story (often a history of some kind) makes sense of the story that frames it. Amy Tan's *The Bonesetter's Daughter* and Timothy Findley's *The Piano Man's Daughter* are two examples of this story shape. In both (simplistically), the main characters learn about their mothers' lives, which helps them make sense of their own.

1. Think back on the novels you have studied through high school. Discuss the different shapes each of these novels took and why the writer might have chosen to tell the story the way he or she did.

2. Look through newspapers to find stories that might make good novels. Think about the shapes those stories could take.

Characters

Character prevails in fiction, just as it does in life.

HILMA WOLITZER[19]

Whether your story focuses on an idea, an event, or a milieu, it will have characters: human, non-human, or animal. Without characters, there is no story. Your characters may take a back seat to the event or the idea, but their actions, thoughts, and words still move through the story and move the story along. As Flannery O'Connor[20] wrote:

> A story is a complete dramatic action—and in good stories, the characters are shown through the action and the action is controlled through the characters, and the result of this is meaning that derives from the whole presented experience.... A story always involves, in a dramatic way, the mystery of personality.

As a writer, your task is to create characters that could exist and characters that people care about. If we didn't care what happened to Bilbo Baggins, the dwarves, and Gandalf, we wouldn't read much of *The Hobbit,* even though Tolkein created that magical place, Middle-earth. If we didn't care whether or not Pip came to terms with his humble beginnings in his classist society, Dickens's *Great Expectations* would never be read. If we didn't care about Kinsey Millhone, Sue Grafton wouldn't be a best-selling detective fiction writer with mystery novels from A to Q and more to come.

I get to know my characters very well indeed before I write a word of the novel. Most of what happens simply proceeds from the interaction of the characters with one another and their environment, their history, their circumstances.

MARGE PIERCY[21]

Building Your Characters

Elizabeth George, the author of many psychological mystery stories, has a detailed process when she is creating her characters. This includes outlining the following:

- a core need

- a psychological profile

- a physical description

- a family history
- "a particular psychological maneuver that he engages in when he's under stress"

She writes all this in a stream-of-consciousness form. Just as with most writers who create detailed character outlines before writing, very little of this information is "told" in her books. The readers see and hear the results of the detailed planning in the actions and voices of her characters.[22]

Not all authors do as much work on characters before their stories are written as do Piercy and George. Some writers think this type of planning stifles the spontaneity of the characters. With or without planning, many authors talk about characters who start to have lives of their own, doing things in the story that their creators had not planned. Whether before or during the writing, it is important for writers to get to know their characters and what their characters want. Be flexible in your writing process. It is fluid, not something that must be followed step by step. You may find that, after having written quite a bit of your draft, you then have to go back to some earlier stages of the process and brainstorm or plan again. You can outline your characters and let them have their say, but things can still go wrong—even for the best and most experienced writers. Here is an example:[23]

> In [Guy Vanderhaeghe's] *Homesick*, the second novel that [he] published, Vera, a character from rural Saskatchewan, goes to Toronto and marries a Jewish intellectual. Vanderhaeghe fell in love with this character—a self-educated autodidact. "He kept getting bigger and bigger in my mind and he began growing larger than his wife in the novel," explains Vanderhaeghe. [Vanderhaeghe] kept writing and then chopping because he knew the relationship between Vera and her husband was "torquing" things out of shape. Finally, he bit the bullet and killed [the husband] off. "I always knew that this guy was going to die and she was going to become a widow," he says. "He just dies sooner and less of their life was described in the book."

There are many ways you can get to know your characters. Following are some suggestions:

Before writing

- Create cue cards (paper or electronic) for your characters with details of their lives, past and present.

- Create a personality profile for each of your characters.

- Write a stream-of-consciousness description (à la Elizabeth George) of your characters.

During writing

- Keep notes on a character and, as new information comes up, jot it down.

- Sketch your characters so you know what they look like as you are writing.

- Create a family tree for your main characters as you write.

- Put your characters in various situations in which they have to react. Note their reactions.

- Write a conversation with a character to find out what he or she wants from a particular scene.

- Write a conversation between two characters on their goals as they see them in the story.

- Stop your story and write about what you like and dislike about your main character(s).

- When faced with a choice the character must make, ask the character about what choice he or she would make (roleplay it or write the character's thoughts).

- Work with two other writers. Have them ask you questions about your character. Sometimes you will find out things you hadn't previously thought about. (Remember to record your answers.)

- Give your character a job. What would it be? How would he or she handle the job? How would the character fill out an application for this job? Whom would he or she use as references?

- Read your work-in-progress to someone else. Ask him or her to comment on the characters.

- Write, write, write. Come back later to questions or problems that arise as you write.

Action and Characters: Show, Don't Tell

In fiction, we learn about characters through these elements:

- their physical appearance
- their actions
- how they speak
- what they say about themselves
- what other characters say about them
- what the narrator says about them
- how they react in certain situations
- their attitudes and opinions
- how they respond to stories and acquaintances
- how they relate to friends and family members
- their memories

To repeat the words of Flannery O'Connor, "Characters are shown through the action and the action is controlled through the characters...."

If you tell your readers about your characters, their pasts and their goals, you will stand a good chance of boring your audience. A combination of showing (scene) and telling (setting) will give your readers the information they need while still engaging them.

Take this excerpt from Shyam Selvadurai's *Cinnamon Gardens*.[24] The novel is set in Ceylon (now called Sri Lanka) in the 1920s. Louisa, mother of Kumudini, Manohari, and Annalukshmi, sees her oldest daughter standing by the bottom step of their front veranda with a bicycle.

> Louisa drew in her breath in astonishment, "What on earth is this?"
>
> "A bicycle," Annalukshmi said, trying to sound as if it were the most normal thing in the world for her to turn up with one.
>
> "I can see it is a bicycle. But what is it doing here?"
>
> "It's Miss Blake's. She gave it to me as a going-away present."
>
> Annalukshmi pushed aside some hairs that had strayed from her plait, which she wore in a knot at the nape of her neck. In her mind, she went over the arguments she had rehearsed with Nancy to combat her family's resistance.

Louisa clicked her tongue against her teeth in annoyance. "Don't talk rubbish, Annalukshmi. You know you can't go around on a bicycle."

"Why not?"

Louisa's face flushed at Annalukshmi's impertinent tone.

Before she could proceed further, her middle daughter, Kumudini, laid a warning hand on Louisa's arm. Arguments between her mother and older sister were often overheated and Kumudini frequently had to step in as peacemaker. "Akka, be reasonable," she said to Annalukshmi. "You can't. People will say all sorts of things."

Though Kumudini was twenty-one, and a year younger than Annalukshmi, she was regarded by everyone as the eldest because she was such a model of propriety.

"And look at the state of your sari." Kumudini continued. "It's ruined." She shook her head. Though only a five-rupee Japanese Georgette sari, it was lovely, with a clover-leaf design on an off-white background. Now there was a grease stain along the bottom of it. Kumudini had, with great care, stitched this sari onto a length of belting because, at the time, a sari was sewn onto belting that hooked around the waist very much like a skirt, the only dressing required being the pleats and the fall draped once about the body and over the shoulder. Her efforts had been in vain. The sari was probably ruined. Further, the white sari blouse had two very unladylike sweat stains under the arms.

APPLICATION

1. From the excerpt, make a list of information we learn through "telling" and information we learn through "showing." Does showing always have to be dialogue? What else can "showing" be?

2. Go back to the list of ways we learn about characters. How do we learn about the characters in this excerpt?

3. This scene takes place near the beginning of the novel. What are some ways you can tell that the reader is meeting many of these characters for the first time? Whom do you think the reader has met previously?

4. Write a scene in which a young person comes into a donut store and meets another person he or she hasn't seen in two years. The relationship between the two was strained when they last met. Show your readers the cause of the strain, how the characters have (or haven't) changed over time, and how they now feel about their history and each other. Use a combination of showing and telling.

Showing State of Mind

Below is a list of ways characters can say things. You could use any of them instead of "he said" or "she said."

WARNING!

Don't overuse these adverbs in your dialogue. Use them only occasionally. *In carefully crafted dialogue, the reader will usually be able to infer the tone of the speaker without descriptions.*

These words can help you describe states of mind your characters find themselves in. Try *showing* your characters in these states of mind. Notice in the excerpt from *Cinnamon Gardens,* the writer does not use any of these adverbs, but *shows* the state of mind the characters are in when they are speaking. Below are some examples of adverbs that can be used to show state of mind.[25]

State of Mind	Examples
angry:	angrily, bitterly, coldly, crossly, darkly, icily, savagely, violently
aggressive:	aggressively, forcefully, nastily, rudely, vehemently
arrogant:	arrogantly, boastfully, immodestly, pompously
bold:	boldly, bravely, courageously, gallantly
flat:	dully, flatly, vapidly
happy:	elatedly, ecstatically, happily, joyously, jubilantly, laughingly
kind:	kind-heartedly, kindly, nicely, warmly
nervous:	edgily, nervously, shiftily
regretful:	badly, regretfully, ruefully
sad:	moodily, mournfully, sadly, woefully
secretive:	discreetly, enigmatically, secretively
spiteful:	malevolently, meanly, spitefully
unfeeling:	nonchalantly, unconcernedly, unfeelingly
zeal:	eagerly, earnestly, effusively, excitedly, zealously

Dialogue

Dialogue is one of the main methods used to "show" your characters. It is also the trickiest part of writing. A writer can't afford to include the "junk words" we so often hear in real speech. The "Hi, how are you?... I'm fine" type of dialogue does not serve a purpose in your writing unless you are making a point about how a character might have changed his or her speech patterns or you are showing leisurely or dull moments. Dialogue has three main purposes in narrative fiction: it furthers the plot, gives information, and develops the characters.

Furthering the Plot

Dialogue can be used to show a change in time and to show a change in location. For example, perhaps in your story the main character has met with his ex-girlfriend. She has asked him to take her back but he only commits to thinking about it. The scene might end with him checking out some books at the library.

> The librarian peers at me over his half glasses. "These books are due in two weeks. Do you have your card?"
>
> I hand him the temporary card I had been issued when Jenna and I started meeting in the library. He runs it reluctantly through the machine.
>
> "Two weeks."

The next scene might take place when the main character is once again meeting with his ex-girlfriend. It could start like this:

> "... a week overdue. That's $1.50."

From the dialogue we know that three weeks have passed and we know that the main character is back in the library. We might guess that he will be meeting his ex again, even though she has not been introduced.

You haven't had to fill in what the main character or the ex-girlfriend has been up to over the three weeks. You may do that later, but for the meantime, you are content to let your audience know that time has passed.

Giving Information

Dialogue can give information about someone else, the main character or narrator, an incident or event, and/or something that happened in the past.

This excerpt from Kazuo Ishiguro's "A Family Supper"[26] illustrates dialogue used for information as well as character development. A young Japanese man has returned from America to Tokyo and to his father's house. The son narrates the story.

"I'm sorry to hear about the firm," I said when neither of us had spoken for some time. He nodded gravely.

"In fact the story didn't end there," he said. "After the firm's collapse, Watanabe killed himself. He didn't wish to live with the disgrace."

"I see."

"We were partners for seventeen years. A man of principle and honour. I respected him very much."

"Will you go into business again?" I asked.

"I am—in retirement. I'm too old to involve myself in new ventures now. Business these days has become so different. Dealing with foreigners. Doing things their way. I don't understand how we've come to this. Neither did Watanabe." He sighed. "A fine man. A man of principle."

The tea-room looked out over the garden. From where I sat I could make out the ancient well which as a child I had believed haunted. It was just visible now through the thick foliage. The sun had sunk low and much of the garden had fallen into shadow.

"I'm glad in any case that you've come back," my father said. "More than just a short visit, I hope."

"I'm not sure what my plans will be."

"I for one am prepared to forget the past. Your mother too was always ready to welcome you back—upset as she was by your behaviour."

"I appreciate your sympathy. As I say, I'm not sure what my plans are."

"I've come to believe now that there were not evil intentions in your mind," my father continued. "You were swayed by certain—influences. Like so many others."

"Perhaps we should forget it, as you suggest."

"As you will. More tea?"

1. Explain what information we learn from this conversation.

2. Look for examples of dialogue in other books that give us important information.

3. Write a dialogue between two family members who have not seen each other in five years. Focus on informing the audience about the past, while still moving the dialogue forward toward the goals of the two speakers.

4. Write a dialogue between two male school friends who have shared some secrets with each other. One of them wants to tell a secret to the girl he thinks he wants to marry.

Developing Character

In dialogue, a character can show emotions and thoughts, and react to a person or situation. This dialogue in "Skipping Stones" by Marvin E. Williams[27] shows the writer using a conversation between a daughter and mother to develop the characters.

> "Who been walking you home from school these last few days?" she asked.
>
> "Just some friends," Zola parried though she knew that would not do.
>
> More loudly now, their mother came back at the slightly trembling Zola, "I say, what boy you have holding your books and darkening my doorway every day?"
>
> Earl and his other siblings crept closer to the hot water. Zola caved in. "His name Daven." A disgusted chupse seemed to raffle the aging galvanize of the roof.
>
> "So who is this Daven? Who he people them be?" Zola hesitated. "I waiting," their mother said, and Earl pictured her arms akimbo, a slap growing to meet her anger.
>
> Earl sneaked a peek over at Sindae and she grinned sweetly, hanging her head to the side in a subtle invitation. He jerked his head upward to singing chincheried whose song was a jazzy hymn to their mating. Birds have it good ... well, pretty good, he thought.
>
> Zola sighed. "He name Daven Granger. His mother is Miss Granger who live just down the road."

Their mother had been fussing nervously with her dresser drawers, but now she slammed one shut. "Listen to me," she tried to calm herself, "you don't bring that damn garrot no where near this house again, you hear me? And I want you to cut off this contact before it go any farther. You hear what I saying?"

Zola sniffled, "Yes, Mammy, I hear what you say."

But their mother wasn't finished. "It have all kinda nice Crucian boys knocking dog on this island. But no. Miss Headache going chatting down to hot up the first island man what smile at she. Since this damn governor open up the school them to cat and dog, every manjack sending down island for they children. Coming here to cause problems for me." She made the sign of the cross, folded her hands as if in prayer and rested them against her breasts, unfolded them to kiss her opened right palm, and flung it to the ceiling. Then she continued: "Girl children is trouble. That's what your granny used to say. And she wasn't wrong. But, by God, I would die first before I see this family drag back to the jungle."

In this dialogue we can see what the daughter wants, what the mother wants, and who wins. We also see, through the short monologue at the end, the mother's beliefs and political views.

APPLICATION

1. Write a dialogue between two people who each want something totally different. Show the struggle and the eventual victory or stalemate.

2. Create a character who holds very strong beliefs. Create a dialogue in which these beliefs come across to the reader but are never mentioned by the person who holds them.

Real Speech Versus Dialogue

Real speech is filled with pauses, repetitions, expressions, filler words, and bad speech habits. Skilled writers learn to capture the feeling of real speech without actually reproducing it. The following is an excerpt from Carol Shields's novel, *Unless*.[28] Four characters are talking over tea about Reta's new editor. Reta calls him smarmy. He has asked to visit Reta's home from New York on January 2, but Reta has suggested January 5. He, in turn, has suggested a later date in January.

"Leave it to a teenager to see through genuine smarm———"

"Especially New York smarm. Or kronk, for that matter. When we were there ———"

"I've talked to him on the phone twice now, and I couldn't help noticing that he always interrupts me just when I'm getting to the point of ———"

"We're always interrupting each other. Have you noticed how we, the four of us ———"

"That's different. It's all right to interrupt each other when there's no power structure to ———"

"Really? Do you believe that ———?"

"It's how the conversation goes, how it gets made, brick by brick, but with these little chipped-in bits of ———"

"But you and Arthur What's-his-name are definitely in a power arrangement, Reta."

"This man's your publisher."

"No, he's her editor, not her publisher."

"But he can decide what is going to be published, what is acceptable to the ———"

"He can definitely influence Reta's novel."

"If you let him."

"At least you'll be on home turf. They always say with football that the home field has a definite ———"

"You know Reta, the very fact that he was 'unable' to come on the fifth as you suggested and changed to the nineteenth ———"

"Definitely signals a power play."

"Absolutely."

"The final say."

"I've done it myself."

"How is it coming, Reta? The novel?"

"Slowly. I've slowed down a bit."

This conversation is a bit of a send-up on the editor, and perhaps on how writers capture "real" speech in dialogue. These characters don't speak like this anywhere else in the book. Reta never gets to the point she wants to make about her editor and, just like her editor, her friends keep interrupting. The excerpt does, however, give you an idea of what we do when we carry on a "normal" conversation—interrupt each other, finish one another's thoughts, change the subject, and/or disagree with one another.

What Shields hasn't included are the "junk" words, the "likes," "ums," "ahs," "you knows," and so on. Neither has she used as much repetition as we do in regular conversation. Notice that, other than

Reta's voice, it's hard (though not impossible) to tell who's speaking. It doesn't seem to be as important for the reader to identify the speaker here as in other parts of the novel.

If Shields always wrote dialogue like this, it might get tiresome. It's almost like she has captured far too much realism with this piece.

To capture some of the naturalness of speech, use contractions, colloquial expressions, accents, and dialects. Include a suggestion of the speaker's speech habits. Look back at the excerpt from "Skipping Stones" by Marvin E. Williams on page 123. The mother definitely has an accent and we hear echoes of her Crucian speech patterns. But the author has made her speech accessible to all readers while maintaining her identity. Had he written the way local people might speak, the dialect could have been much broader and much less effective.

Showing Differences Among Characters

Characters who exist in your writing are all different from one another. We should hear the differences when they speak. Here are some things that make the characters individuals:

- vocabulary

- sentence structures, lengths, patterns, rhythms

- accents or dialects

- favourite expressions

- topics of conversation

- speech habits

- variations in emotion

- how they speak to various audiences

- formality of the situation

- body language and facial expressions that accompany the words

- background

- education

The only way you will learn to write dialogue is to listen. Eavesdrop everywhere you go. Take along your notebook and copy down expressions, topics of conversations, and interesting lines.

Read a variety of types of fiction and a variety of writers from the eighteenth century to today. Buy or borrow literary magazines such as *Room of One's Own, Blood and Aphorisms,* or *The Capilano Review.* They have the newest in short fiction. Read prize-winning novels and try to imitate the way published authors write dialogue.

Read everything you write aloud. Have other people read it aloud to you. Attune your ear. Get rid of what tips the scale to "over the top" and keep what sounds genuine for your character.

APPLICATION

1. Write two short dialogues: one in which you try to capture real speech and another in which you take the first dialogue and edit it to eliminate unnecessary speech habits and junk words while still allowing it to sound real.

2. With another student or students, improvise a scene that you want to include in your story. Tape it and use some of the dialogue (edited) in your work.

3. Write a dialogue using the same character in two different situations, one in which the character is comfortable, and another in which he or she is not. How does your character sound different?

Perspective: Who's Going to Tell the Story?

There are three points of view: first, second, and third person. Because it is the rare writer who can write a narrative effectively in the second person, we will focus on the first and third person.

How do you decide who will tell your story? The following chart summarizes the positive and negative aspects of the different narrative voices you might choose from.

As they do with structures, writers also experiment with narrative voice. Take, for instance, *In the Lake of the Woods* by Tim O'Brien. It is a story of a woman, Kathy, who has gone missing. The story is told by an unnamed investigator. Following is an excerpt from an interview[29] with Tim O'Brien about his narrator:

> Interviewer: Why did you choose to make the narrator a character in the novel? Who is he intended to be? Is the reader meant to trust his interpretations? Is he any more reliable than John himself?

PERSPECTIVE	FLEXIBILITY	RELIABILITY
First person in which the main character is the narrator	The main character is limited by what he or she has experienced, heard, and read. The reader feels intimate with this narrator.	The main character may not be the most reliable narrator unless he or she has distanced him- or herself from the events, or the character presents the event as it happens and lets the reader pass judgement. The character only tells us what he or she wants us to see.
First-person observer	The observer can observe from a variety of places where the main character may not be present, thus observing incidents that might affect what happens to the main character but that even the main character doesn't know about. The observer is probably not with the main character 24 hours a day. The reader knows the narrator but may not feel intimate with the narrator.	The observer cannot get inside the main character's head; thus the reader is told only what the observer sees. The observer may hear things that the main character won't, so the reader might get a more rounded view of the main character and the events. The observer may hold a less biased opinion of the main character than the character holds about him- or herself. On the other hand, depending on the relationship between the main character and the narrator, the viewpoint may be more biased.
Third-person omniscient	This god-like narrator knows all and sees all; thus, he or she is the most flexible of all narrators. The reader feels distanced from the narrator.	This narrator is the most reliable, since he or she knows and sees everything. Reliability could be affected by what the narrator chooses to show the reader and how that biases the way the reader interprets the action.
Third-person limited omniscient	This narrator is most like the first-person narrator. The reader sees the action over the shoulder of a limited number of characters. The narrator's flexibility is less than the omniscient narrator's because the narrator sees the action from a more limited viewpoint. The reader feels very involved with the character on whom the narrator focuses, but does not feel involved with the narrator.	This narrator is fairly reliable, although, because the narrator chooses the viewpoint from which we see the story, the view could be biased.
Third-person reporter	There is little flexibility in this narrative voice. The narrator tells what he or she sees or hears without comment or bias. The narrator is very distanced from the characters and the readers.	This narrator is as reliable as his or her ability to observe. If the reporter misses some important event, so does the reader.

Tim O'Brien: He's more trustworthy. Imperfect, though—limited by all that he does not and cannot know. Like all of us. I saw the narrator as a biographer, a medium, a storyteller like [Joseph] Conrad's Marlow [in *Heart of Darkness*]. He's trying to present an accurate flow of events, periodically stepping back to make sense of what he's relating. Marlow is fallible just as my own narrator is fallible. There's always the problem of ignorance. There's always so much we can never know about.... There's so much we can never know about what happened at that cottage on Lake of the Woods. There's always the wall of ignorance, beyond which the narrator can only speculate. And that's the heart of the novel. On the plot level, we will never know what happened to Kathy. On the psychological level, we can't read the hearts of other human beings. We can't penetrate the minds of our own husbands and wives. We can't read their motives or secret thoughts. We can only guess. We can only hypothesize. Certain things in life will always remain pure mystery, and this both frustrates and fascinates us. In a footnote I use the example of the way Lizzie Borden endures in American mythology. Custer's Last Stand, the Kennedy assassination, the disappearance of Amelia Earheart—we don't know what happened; we can't know. If these mysteries were to be solved, we'd stop caring. We don't go to movies about Herbert Hoover dying of old age. We go to movies like *JFK*. Human beings are entranced by mystery. Whole religions are built around the condition of profound human ignorance. What happens to us after we die? How did we all get here? What caused the universe to exist?

To enhance the mystery of Kathy's disappearance, O'Brien inserts a series of third-person accounts called "Evidence." The juxtaposition of these with the investigator's narration keeps the readers asking, "What happened?"

Chuck Palahniuk's *Fight Club* is narrated in the first person by one of the main characters. The reader has no reason to question the reliability of this narrator. It is only at the end, when we discover the identity of Tyler Durden, that we feel as duped as the main character and want to reexamine his entire narration.

In *A Catcher in the Rye*, the reader is warned from the beginning that something is not "right" with the narrator, so we always take Holden Caulfield's observations, recollections, and opinions with a grain of salt. He is not a reliable narrator.

Time and the First-Person Narrator

It is important to ask yourself some questions when you have decided to write in the first person.

- How long ago did the event or series of events occur?

- How old was the narrator at the time?

- How old is the narrator now?

- How has the narrator changed since the event(s)?

The answers to these questions will affect the way your story is told. Generally, if the events have happened in the near past, or are happening as the narrator is speaking, the narrator's perspective on the events will be limited.

If the events happened in the distant past, some of the details might have been lost or the narrator may have chosen to remember only certain things. However, the narrator will have more of a perspective on the events.

The age of the narrator will affect the *voice* of the story. The vocabulary, the sentence structures, and the perspectives of a child will be very different from those of an adult.

Sandra Birdsell's narrator Lureen in "Stones"[30] is still a child when she tells the story about her mother and their neighbour, the doctor's wife. There is an innocence in the way she talks about sabotaging her mother. The tone of her narration is childlike: "I tiptoed around the house feeling nervous because she hadn't noticed that it was past my bedtime," which, when juxtaposed with her actions, makes the story that much more savage.

The distance between the events and the telling about those events in Patricia Grace's "It Used to Be Green Once"[31] is slightly greater than in "Stones," but the narrator is still young. The narrator is embarrassed by her mother's driving habits and her car.

> Off she'd go on a Wednesday morning, and once out on the road she'd start tooting the horn. This didn't sound like a horn at all but more like a flock of ducks coming in for a feed. The reason for the horn was to let all her mates and relations along the way know she was coming. And as she passed each one's house, if they wanted anything they'd have to run out and call it out loud. Mum couldn't stop because of not having any brakes.

The voice is young. She uses colloquial English and grammar that is casual and conversational.

In both stories, the narrators are still fairly close to the event and aren't able to reflect on the event with much insight. Instead, the writers allow their narrators to tell their stories and give the job of reflection to the readers.

In the following excerpt from Alistair MacLeod's "To Every Thing There Is a Season,"[32] the narrator tells the story as it happens, yet Alistair MacLeod has chosen not to tell it in the voice of a child. The narrator is younger than 13 and is at the stage where he knows there is no Santa Claus but wants to believe in him anyway.

> My mother has been fairly tolerant of my attempted perpetuation. Perhaps because she has encountered it before. Once I overheard her speaking about my sister Anne to one of her neighbours. "I thought Anne would *believe* forever," she said. "I practically had to tell her." I have somehow always wished I had not heard her say that as I seek sanctuary and reinforcement even in an ignorance I know I dare not trust.

The voice of this child rings with adult sentence structures, vocabulary, and reflection. We know this is an adult writing about a passage out of childhood with a wisdom that comes with age, even though MacLeod has written it as if the event is happening to the narrator as we read it. Contrast the voice of the narrator in "It Used to Be Green Once" with the voice of the narrator in "To Every Thing There Is a Season." They are both first-person narrators, both children, both slightly different, and both effective for the story they are telling.

Although the first-person narrator seems like an easy type of narrator to use (many novice writers use the first person), it is difficult. It is easy to fall into the trap of telling the story instead of showing the story when writing in the first person. Looking back at the excerpts, you can see the subtleties necessary to make the narration effective.

1. Take part of a story you have written and change the perspective. Examine the differences in the story as a result of the new perspective.

2. Choose a story from a newspaper or magazine. Start to tell that story using one perspective and then change to another. What difference does it make?

3. Study several stories written in the first person. For each story, look at the distance between the event and the telling of that event. Examine the voice of the narrator. How old is the narrator? How has the writer captured the voice of the narrator—or has the writer chosen to give the narrator a voice that does not reflect the narrator's age?

4. Write a story from the point of view of a person you know little about (for example, a prisoner, a priest, a person from a different cultural background, or a person of the opposite sex). You may want to do some research into the culture or environment of the person before taking on his or her voice.

5. Write a description of an event that has happened to you recently. Rewrite that event three times, using a third-person omniscient, a third-person limited omniscient, and a third-person reporter perspective.

6. Research the controversy in the literary world about appropriation of voice.

7. Read Robert Browning's dramatic monologue "My Last Duchess." Write the story from the point of view of one of the servants in the family household.

Setting

There is a kind of spectrum for the importance of setting to your story.

Not very
important ———————————————————————————— Essential (or setting
at all   as character)

Essential Settings

If you are writing a story that depends heavily on "milieu," then the details about time and place will be essential to the plot and the characters. "Journey" or "quest" stories, such as Stephen Vincent Benét's "By the Waters of Babylon,"[33] depend heavily on description. In the following excerpt, the young protagonist goes to "The Place of the Gods," a land that is forbidden by his culture. One morning on his journey, he wakes to find a dog sitting and watching him.

> I looked about me—not far away there was a great, broken god-road, leading North. The towers were high enough but not so high, and while many of the Dead Houses were wrecked, there were some that stood. I went toward this god-road, keeping to the heights of the ruins, while the dog followed. When I had reached the god-road, I saw that there were others behind him. If I had slept later, they would have come upon me asleep and torn out my throat. As it was, they were sure enough of me; they did not hurry. When I went into the dead-house, they kept watch at the entrance—doubtless they thought they would have a fine hunt. But a dog cannot open a door and I knew, from the books, that the gods did not like to live on the ground but on high.

This story takes place in a post-nuclear age, and although the main character's discoveries are important thematically, the description of this world and the beliefs that have grown up around it are just as important.

Setting as Character

Whenever the protagonist battles with the elements or against society, setting becomes a character in the story. In Jack London's novel *Call of the Wild*, Buck, the dog from whose point of view the story is told, and John Thornton, his master, battle the elements to stay alive. Two young men are lost in the wilderness in Farley Mowat's *Lost in the Barrens* and have to survive the winter.

Society is a major character in Vikram Seth's *A Suitable Boy*. The story gives the readers an insight into the rules and traditions that face a young woman whose family is trying to find her a husband. It also, however, provides readers with a history lesson about India after its independence from Britain.

Setting as Symbol

Settings can be used as symbols. In Stephen King's novella *Rita Hayworth and the Shawshank Redemption*, Shawshank prison is the setting. The story is about Andy Dufresne, an accountant who is sent to this notorious prison because he has been convicted of killing his wife and her lover. Within the prison, the library and his own cell become symbols for freedom. The author does not talk about them in that way. It is only when the readers have heard the whole story that we understand what each of these locations has become.

"Milieu" stories will often contain several elements related to setting that have become well-known symbols. The following chart contains some typical symbols that may be used as part of a setting:

SYMBOL	MEANING OF SYMBOL
under ground, caves, dark basements, prisons	descent into the underworld: hell
mountain tops, high places with great light, rising above the clouds	apotheosis, heaven
seasons: spring summer fall winter	 birth, rebirth height of maturity aging death
weather: snow sun rain	 danger, death, isolation health cleansing, sorrow

These are just a few elements that have taken on symbolic meanings in Western literature. They can be used to foreshadow events or can be reversed to surprise the reader.

Setting as Atmosphere

How the setting is described can contribute to the atmosphere of the scene. The following is an excerpt from Margaret Atwood's *The Handmaid's Tale*.[34]

> We turn in at a more modern building, a huge banner draped above its door—WOMEN'S PRAYVAGANZA TODAY. The banner covers the building's former name, some dead President they shot. Below the red writing there's a line of smaller print, in black, with the outline of a winged eye on either side of it: GOD IS A NATIONAL RESOURCE. On either side of the doorway stand the inevitable Guardians, two pairs,

four in all, arms at their sides, eyes front. They're like store mannequins almost, with their neat hair and pressed uniforms and plaster-hard young faces. No pimply ones today. Each has a submachine gun slung ready, for whatever dangerous or subversive acts they think we might commit inside.

The Prayvaganza is to be held in the covered courtyard, where there's an oblong space, a skylight roof. It isn't a city-wide Prayvaganza, that would be on the football field; it's only for this district....

A number of the Wives are already seated, in their best embroidered blue. We can feel their eyes on us as we walk in our red dresses two by two across to the side opposite them. We are being looked at, assessed, whispered about; we can feel it, like tiny ants running on our bare skins.

Here there are no chairs. Our area is cordoned off with a silky twisted scarlet rope, like the kind they used to have in movie theatres to restrain the customers. This rope segregates us, marks us off, keeps the others from contamination by us, makes for us a corral or pen, so into it we go, arranging ourselves in rows, which we know very well how to do, kneeling then on the cement floor.

Feel the tension created by the description of the "Prayvaganza"—the young men with machine guns, the approving and disapproving looks of the Wives, the herding like cattle into a pen, and the kneeling on bare cement.

Generic Settings

On the other end of the spectrum are the stories in which setting (time or place) are of little importance. The locations are generic and the stories could happen any time.

"Games at Twilight" by Anita Desai is set in India.[35] For a non-South-Asian audience, aspects of this setting will be unfamiliar (for example, the heat of the day, the sari the mother wears, the description of the garden). However, this story is not about setting at all but about games children play and how hurt and isolated a child can feel growing up. The story starts with a game of hide-and-seek:

The children, too, felt released. They too began tumbling, shoving, pushing against each other, frantic to start. Start what? Start their business. The business of the children's day which is—play.

"Let's play hide-and-seek."

"Who'll be It?"

"You be It."

"Why should I? You be ———"

"You're the eldest ———"

"That doesn't mean ———"

The shoves became harder. Some kicked out.

This scene could take place anywhere. In real life, it probably does. Desai's story is about a common experience of childhood. Take away the "band of parrots suddenly [falling] out of the eucalyptus tree" and make them a flock of sparrows flying from their nests in an old cedar tree, and the story could take place in Canada. The descriptions in the story add verisimilitude and beauty, but Desai is more interested in how her main character feels than where he lives.

APPLICATION

1. a) Choose a location with which you are very familiar. Describe that location using as many of the senses as you can to re-create it for your reader.

   b) Write about how that location could take on symbolic significance.

2. Write a scene from a story in which setting becomes a character.

3. Create a new world. Describe the customs, religion, and politics in this new world.

4. Read Thomas More's *Utopia*. Show how the society becomes the main character in the book.

5. Find several short stories in which setting (both time and place) are incidental to the story.

6. Go somewhere you've never been before. Start taking notes from the moment you arrive until you leave. Make this place a backdrop to a story you create.

7. Research a specific time in history. Create a fictional character in that time period or fictionalize a story about a real character from that time.

Language

When you analyzed and discussed great literature in your English classes, you learned how successful writers use imagery, symbolism, and figures of speech to bring their writing alive. You examined an author's use of specific sentence structures, types, orders, and lengths to emphasize ideas. You understood that English grammar could be manipulated for effect and that not every sentence in a novel or a short story is grammatically correct. Finally, you investigated the writer's word choices in both narration and dialogue and considered the effect it had on the audience. Through this study, you learned valuable lessons about writing.

The most common question students ask about rhetoric and language is "Did the writer mean to do it?" The answer is always the same: maybe yes, maybe no. Sometimes imagery and symbols that extend through a narrative are accidental—that is, maybe the writer didn't start his or her story by saying "I'm going to include a red boat in my book that is going to be a symbol of my voyage into evil." Some images and symbols live in our subconscious or in our backgrounds and, because they exist in us, they come out in our writing.

Sometimes a writer notices an object or setting start to take on symbolic meaning as he or she is writing and decides to build on that meaning. At other times, writers deliberately choose names or colours, settings, or even plot lines that are symbolic.

The same is true for sentence constructions and word choice. Some will be deliberate, some happy accidents, and others the result of careful revising and editing.

The only way to know whether or not a writer "meant" to do what he or she did is to ask. And often we don't have that luxury. Instead of asking "Did the writer mean to …?" ask "How did the writer do that?" Focusing on a writer's craft rather than on his or her intentions is both more productive and more useful to you as a writer.

You can learn a great deal from visual artists. They often learn and practise technique by copying the great masters (never, of course, passing them off as their own). As writers, you need to learn from other writers. If you didn't pay attention to all those analyses in English class, pay attention now. Look at the work of your favourite authors. Scrutinize their language choices. Try to imitate their style. Study with the best, whether they are writing now or wrote 200 years ago. Copy the styles of the great masters of literature. Try different styles, from Ernest Hemingway to Barbara Gowdy; from Jane Austen to Rohinton Mistry. As has already been suggested in every other chapter, *read*. Read everything you can. When you are reading, you are learning to write.

WRITER'S PROJECTS

Investigating the Writer's Craft

1. Choose four writers from around the world and research what they have said about creating characters. Draw some conclusions or inspiration for your own writing from this research.

2. Read a novel and write a personal essay on what you learned from the novel about developing characters in your own writing.

3. Examine several short stories written by the same author. Present an oral report that compares the structures of these stories.

Practising the Writer's Craft

1. Write a story emphasizing one of the milieus suggested by Orson Scott Card (see page 106).

2. Use a line from your favourite novel or short story as a jumping-off point for a story. Include the line as an epigraph.

3. Write a story that has as its subject "broken promises."

4. Write a short story and then structure the various plot elements in two or three different ways. Reflect on the effect that the different orders have on the story.

5. Create a detailed character chart for a character in a draft you have written. Explain how this chart will help you revise the story you have written.

6. Write a story for readers your own age. Explain how your characters are designed for this specific age group.

7. Choose a writer whose stories focus on character (for example, Mordecai Richler or Alice Munro). Write your own story emulating the style of this writer.

8. Write a story in which a character from your age group is immersed in an alien culture.

THE WRITER'S READING LIST

The Writer's Craft

Bell, Julia and Paul Magrs. *The Creative Writing Handbook*. London: Macmillan, 2001.

Bell, Madison Smartt. *Narrative Design*. New York: WW. Norton, 1997.

Bernays, Anne and Pamela Painter. *What If?: Writing Exercises for Fiction Writers*. New York: Harper Perennial, 1990.

Brown, Rita Mae. *Starting From Scratch: A Different Kind of Writer's Manual*. New York: Bantam Books, 1989.

Card, Orson Scott. *Characters and Viewpoints*. Cincinnati, OH: Writers Digest Books , 1988.

Dillard, Annie. *The Writing Life*. New York: Harper and Row, 1989.

Fryxell, David A. "The Core Need of Elizabeth George." *Writer's Digest*, Vol. 82, No. 2, February 2002, pages 32–33.

Hodgins, Jack. *A Passion for Narrative*. Toronto: A Douglas Gibson Book, McClelland and Stewart, 1993.

O'Connor, Flannery. "Writing Short Stories." *Writing Prose*; ed. Tom Bailey. Toronto: Oxford University Press, 1987.

Piercy, Marge. "Life of Prose and Poetry: An Inspiring Combination." *Writers on Writing: Collected Essays from the New York Times*. New York: Times Books, Henry Holt, 2001, pages 178–184.

Rubie, Peter. *The Elements of Storytelling: How to Write Compelling Fiction*. New York: John Wiley & Sons, 1996.

Saunders, Jean. *How to Write Realistic Dialogue*. London: Allison and Busby, 1994.

Schumacher, Michael. "Raymond Carver." *On Being a Writer*; ed. Bill Strickland. Cincinnati, OH: Writer's Digest Books, pages 11–20.

Wachtel, Eleanor. *Writers and Company*. Toronto: Alfred A Knopf Canada, 1993.

Wolitzer Hilma. "Embarking Together on Solitary Journeys." *Writers on Writing: Collected Essays from the New York Times*. New York: Times Books, Henry Holt, 2001, pages 263–268.

Examples of the Writer's Craft

Beresford-Howe, Constance. *A Serious Widow*. Toronto: McClelland and Stewart, 1993.

Brand, Dionne. *Sans Souci and Other Stories*. Stratford: Williams-Wallace, 1988.

Clark, Eliza. *What You Need*. Toronto: Somerville House, 1994.

Gibson, William. *Neuromancer*. New York: Ace Books, The Berkley Publishing Group, 1984.

Hospital, Jeannette Turner. *The Tiger in the Tiger Pit*. Toronto: McClelland and Stewart, 1983.

Irving, John. *A Prayer for Owen Meaney*. Toronto: Vintage Canada, a Division of Random House of Canada, 1989.

King, Thomas. *One Good Story, That One*. Toronto: HarperCollins, 1993.

Lamb, Wally. *She's Come Undone*. New York: Pocket Books, Washington Square Press, 1992.

MacLeod, Allistair. *Island: The Collected Stories of Allistair MacLeod*. Toronto: McClelland and Stewart, 2000.

MacLeod, Allistair. *No Great Mischief*. Toronto: McClelland and Stewart, 1999.

McLean, Stuart. *Vinyl Café Unplugged*. Toronto, Penguin Books Canada, 2000.

Mills, Ian W. and Judith H. Mills, eds. *The Arch of Experience*. Toronto: Holt, Rinehart and Winston of Canada, 1987.

Morrison, Toni. *Beloved*. New York: Penguin Books, 1988.

Morrissey, Michael, ed. *The Flamingo Anthology of New Zealand Short Stories*. Auckland, NZ. Flamingo, HarperCollins Publishers, 2000.

Palahniuk, Chuck. *Fight Club*. New York: Henry Holt and Company, 1996.

Selvadurai, Shyam. *Cinnamon Gardens*. Toronto: McClelland and Stewart, 1998.

Stephenson, Craig, ed. *Countries of Invention*. Toronto: Addison Wesleyand Rubicon, 1993.

Urquhart, Jane. *The Underpainter*. Toronto: McClelland and Stewart, 1997.

Waters, Erika, J. *The Caribbean Writer*. 15th Anniversary Issue, Vol. 15, 2001.

Endnotes and Credits

CHAPTER 3

1 James Michener, quoted in Caryn Mirriam-Goldberg, *Write Where You Are: How to Use Writing to Make Sense of Your Life—A Guide for Teens*. Minneapolis, MN: Free Spirit Publishing Inc., 1999, 114.

2 Mario Vargas Llosa, quoted in *Writers on Writing: Collected Essays from the New York Times*. New York: Times Books, Henry Holt, 1990, 124.

3 Jack Hodgins, *A Passion for Narrative: A Guide for Writing Fiction*, A Douglas Gibson Book, McClelland and Stewart, Toronto, 1993, pp. 161–164.

4 Flannery O'Connor, "Writing Short Stories," in *Writing Prose*, ed. Tom Bailey. Toronto: Oxford University Press, 1987, 601.

5 Michael Schumacher, "Raymond Carver," in *On Being a Writer*, ed. Bill Strickland. Cincinnati, OH: Writer's Digest Books, 1989, 17.

6 Orson Scott Card, *Characters and Viewpoints*. Cincinnati, OH: Writer's Digest Books, 1988, 48.

7 Card, *Characters and Viewpoints*, 52–53.

8 This story has also been reprinted in Sue Harper and Douglas Hilker, *Foundations of English 12*. Toronto: Harcourt Canada, 2002, 127–140.

9 This story has also been reprinted in Douglas Hilker and Sue Harper, *Elements of English 9*. Toronto: Harcourt Canada, 1999, 127–140.

10 Annie Dillard, *The Writing Life*. New York: Harper and Row, 1989, 9, 10.

11 From *A Passion for Narrative* by Jack Hodgins. Used by permission, McClelland & Stewart Ltd. *The Canadian Publishers*.

12 Isabel Allende, *The Stories of Eva Luna*. Lester & Orpen Dennys. Copyright © 1990. Reprinted by permission of Key Porter Books.

13 This story appeared in Ian W. Mills and Judith H. Mills, *The Arch of Experience*. Toronto: Holt, Rinehart & Winston Canada Ltd., 1987, 77–82.

14 This story has also been reprinted in Hilker and Harper, *Elements of English 9*, 54–58.

15 Stephen Vincent Benét, *Thirteen O'Clock: Stories of Several Worlds*, Freeport, NY: Books for Libraries Press, 1971.

16 Dionne Brand, *Sans Sonci and Other Stories*, Stratford, ON: Williams-Wallace Canada, 1988.

17 Eleanor Wachtel, *Writers and Company*. Toronto: Alfred A. Knopf Canada, 1993, 59.

18 Wachtel, *Writers and Company*, 59.

19 Hilma Wolitzer, "Embarking Together on Solitary Journeys," *Writers on Writing*, 2001, 267.

20 O'Connor, "Writing Short Stories," in *Writing Prose*, 599.

21 Marge Piercy, "Life of Prose and Poetry: An Inspiring Combination," *Writers on Writing*, 1990, 181.

22 David A. Fryxell, "The Core Need of Elizabeth George," *Writer's Digest*, Vol. 82, No. 2, February 2002, 33.

23 Excerpted from "Fear and Loathing at the Laptop" by Sandra Martin. *The Globe and Mail*, June 29, 2002, R1, R9. Reprinted with permission from *The Globe and Mail*.

24 From *Cinnamon Gardens* by Shyam Selvadurai. Used by permission, McClelland & Stewart Ltd. *The Canadian Publishers*.

25 This list is based on Jean Saunders, *How to Write Realistic Dialogue*. London: Allison and Busby/Wilson & Day, 76–77.

26 Kazuo Ishiguro, "A Family Supper" Copyright © 1982 by Kazuo Ishiguro. Reproduced by permission of the author c/o Rogers, Coleridge & White Ltd., 20 Powis Mews, London W11 1JN. This story has also been reprinted in Sue Harper, Douglas Hilker, and Peter J. Smith, *Elements of English 11*. Toronto: Harcourt Canada, 2001, 244–250.

27 Reprinted by permission of the author, Marvin E. Williams, from *The Caribbean Writer*, Volume 15 (2001), pgs 121–22.

28 "Unless" by Carol Shields. Copyright © 2002 Carol Shields. Reprinted by permission of Random House Canada.

29 "Reading Guides: *In the Lake of the Woods* by Tim O'Brien." From Penguin Putnam Web site, December 3, 2002. http://www.penguinputnam.com/static/rguides/us/lake_of_the_woods.html#interview.

30 See Douglas Hilker and Sue Harper, *Elements of English 9*. Toronto: Harcourt Canada, 1999, 69–71.

31 Patricia Grace, "It Used to Be Green Once," in *Skins: Contemporary Indigenous Writing*. From *The Dream Sleepers and Other Stories*. Reprinted by permission of Pearson Education, New Zealand. A copy of this story appears in Harper and Hilker, *Elements of English 12*, 2–6.

32 Excerpted from "To Every Thing There Is a Season" by Alistair MacLeod. From *Island* by Alistair MacLeod. Used by permission, McClelland & Stewart Ltd., *The Canadian Publishers*. A copy of this story appears in Sue Harper, Douglas Hilker, and Peter J. Smith, *Elements of English 11*. Toronto: Harcourt Canada, 2001, 32–36.

33 Excerpted from "By the Waters of Babylon" by Stephen Vincent Benét. *Thirteen O'Clock: Stories of Several Worlds*, Freeport, NY: Books for Libraries Press, 1971.

34 From *The Handmaid's Tale* by Margaret Atwood. Used by permission, McClelland & Stewart Ltd. *The Canadian Publishers*.

35 Anita Desai, "Games at Twilight," in *Games at Twilight*, copyright © 1978, Anita Desai. Reproduced by permission of the author. This story has also been reprinted in Harper and Hilker, *Elements of English 10*. Toronto: Harcourt Canada, 2000, 122–128.

Scriptwriting

Affecting the audience is why one writes a play to begin with. You don't write it for yourself, the actors, or the director. You're there to do something to the audience.

LEE BLESSING[1]

LEARNING GOALS

▸ analyze forms of scripts and their elements and conventions

▸ analyze the purpose and audience of a variety of scripts

▸ assess authors' choices of techniques, diction, voice, and style

▸ research and analyze selected works by authors from around the world to assess their practices and beliefs about writing

▸ write scripts in various forms and for various purposes to practise and develop writing skills

▸ explain and assess—individually and in small groups—the creative choices made in producing one's own scripts

▸ revise drafts to produce scripts that are effective in content, techniques, diction, voice, and style

WHAT IS SCRIPTWRITING?

Scriptwriting can take many forms. We will focus on screenplays, stage plays, and radio plays in this chapter. Each of these forms depends on dialogue to create characters—the dialogue conveys their emotions, establishes relationships between them, and shows the inner workings of their minds. Dialogue also conveys the script's tone, provides necessary background, creates tension, and moves the action forward.

Not all scripts work in exactly the same way. Screenplays, television plays, and stage plays can depend on actors' facial expressions and body language to support and even substitute for dialogue. In television and cinema, camera work (shots, angles, movement), music, and special effects can also do some of the work of the dialogue. While stage-play writers can work with music, some special effects, and some set changes, they may need to lean more heavily on both the dramatic and narrative functions of dialogue, depending on the budget of the production. Radio dramatists rely solely on dialogue, with sound effects and music supporting, rather than adding to, the dialogue.

All scripts have some things in common.

- They are meant to be heard.

- Speakers are identified by name, title, job, or some other "label."

- Stage directions, indicating the actions, emotions, or thoughts of the characters, are included in the script.

- Scripts must hold the audience's attention: the audience must be engaged by characters and get caught up in the momentum of the action; they should feel that the ending is meaningful, no matter how predictable or shocking.

The following chart provides a summary of the differences and similarities between the types of scripts you might write:

Film	Television	Stage	Radio
Acts and Scenes			
A film script is rarely delineated into obvious acts and scenes, although change of setting, cuts, and changes in the central character in a scene are clues. The most common shape for screenplays is three acts (simply put: the beginning, middle, and end). Storyboards are often used to suggest the types of camera shots, angles, and movement for each scene.	Television scripts are similar to film scripts but scenes may correspond to commercial breaks. For an episodic show, the most common plot shape is two acts in which the beginning, middle, and end must fit. Serial shows may not use the traditional act structure, but may move as each character's story moves.	Stage scripts may be delineated into acts and scenes indicated by a scene change, movement of characters on and off the stage, or intermission. The number of acts varies with the play; a play may have as little as one act or may have many more.	Radio scripts may be delineated into acts and scenes indicated by sound effects, musical interlude, or commercial breaks.

Action			
Generally, actions of characters speak for themselves.	Generally, actions of characters speak for themselves.	They may have a chorus or narrator (who might be a character) to tell about the action in addition to the actors.	They may have a chorus or narrator (who might be a character) to tell about the action; actors take on more responsibility for telling the audience what is happening since the audience cannot see the action.

Actors			
Actors can range from "real" to animated or digitized ("synthesbians"). Actors get multiple opportunities to perfect their performances with multiple takes.	Actors can range from "real" to animated or digitized. Except when they are performing on live television, actors get multiple opportunities to perfect their performances with multiple takes.	Actors may be real or "created" (e.g., puppets, marionettes, or projections on a screen). Live performers get one opportunity to make each performance the best it can be.	Actors must be real. Actors have multiple opportunities to perfect their performances if the play is prerecorded.

Special Effects			
Special effects are limited only by budget and technology.	Special effects are limited only by budget and technology.	Special effects are limited by budget, technology, and venue; many productions now include multimedia where effects are created with film and slides as well as music, sound, lighting, and props.	Special effects are limited to music, sound, and dialogue.

Dialogue			
Dialogue is enhanced by actions, facial expressions, use of voice, camera work, sound, location, and special effects.	Dialogue is enhanced by action, facial expressions, use of voice, camera work, sound, location, and special effects.	Dialogue is enhanced by movement of characters, facial expressions, use of voice, sound, and interaction with props and set.	Dialogue is enhanced by music and sound.

Setting (Time and Place)			
Setting is flexible. Time and space can be easily manipulated through camera shots and editing.	Setting is flexible. Time and space can be easily manipulated through camera shots and editing.	There is some flexibility in the set, but less than on film or television; some plays have only one setting. Time and space are less easily manipulated, although movement through time can be suggested by set, lighting, and sound.	There is flexibility in setting; the change in setting must be indicated through sound or dialogue. Time and space are easily manipulated, as both are limited only by the imagination of the listener.
Imagination			
Viewer imagination is triggered through scripts, acting, camera work (establishing mood, creating visual motifs), music (repeating themes, mirroring emotion), and lighting (creating mood).	On some shows, the thinking is done for the viewer through picture and sound elements (especially laugh and applause tracks), but imagination can also be triggered through scripts, acting, camera work (establishing mood, creating visual motifs), music (repeating themes, mirroring emotion), and lighting (creating mood).	Viewer imagination is essential because of limited special effects (except with multimedia performances) and the limitations of the stage; less concrete detail is provided than on film; there is more suggestion and less confinement to what's real.	Most need for imagination; listeners must imagine appearance of characters and setting.

 ## THE WRITER'S WARM-UPS

These warm-ups focus on writing dialogue, the mainstay of any script. Any time you write dialogue, remember that every person speaking has his or her own agenda—a reason for speaking. The dialogue must move the characters and thus the action forward. Try to eliminate "junk words," words that don't have any purpose.

Try some of the following exercises:

1. Transcribe or tape a conversation between two people. Make notes on how the two voices differ from each other. Try to imitate the speaking style of one of the characters in a monologue or both characters in a dialogue.

2. Study two characters from a published script. Make notes on the differences between the two voices. Write a short dialogue between two characters and make notes on the differences between your own characters.

3. Copy four interchanges between two characters from a published script. Write a continuation of the conversation, imitating the particular style of each of the characters.

4. Script a conversation between two characters in which one character wants to talk about something that the other character is trying to avoid discussing.

5. Script a conversation in which one person is trying to "one up" the other.

6. Script a conversation between two characters in which each has his or her own agenda. Show the agenda of each of the characters without having him or her tell about it directly.

7. Script a conversation between two characters who are experts on a certain subject (e.g., snowboarding, computers, fly fishing). Have them sound like experts, but make the dialogue comprehensible to the average person.

8. Imagine you come face to face with a talking animal. Script the conversation that ensues.

9. Script a dialogue between you and the person you would most want to bring back from the dead.

10. Script a conversation that might take place around the family dinner table. Shape your dialogue with a clear beginning, middle, and end.

11. Script a conversation between two detectives as they arrive at a murder scene.

12. Script a conversation between two people who meet on the street after having not seen each other for five years. Through the dialogue, show the audience the type of relationship they had in the past without being too obvious about it.

13. Choose a well-publicized event from the news (for example, a local plane crash, an international tragedy, or the conviction of a famous criminal). Place two strangers in the vicinity of the event and script their conversation. Try to convey the differences in what is important to each of these characters.

14. Tape a conversation. Take notes on the changes that would have to be made in order for this conversation to be part of a screenplay or radio drama. Rewrite the conversation for one of these genres.

15. Have a partner read aloud some scripted dialogue you have written. As you hear it, take note of the places that don't sound right. Revise your work.

16. As a group, come up with a line that could be said by anyone. Use a character you've created in one of these exercises or for a script you have previously written, and have that character respond to the line your group has created.

THE WRITER'S TOOLKIT

Dialogue and Its Functions

When Canadian writer Timothy Findley died, many articles written about him talked about his ability to capture the human voice in his dialogue, whether in scripts, short stories, or novels. He attributed this gift to his early work as an actor.

Because scripts are written to be spoken and performed, it is important for you to read aloud the excerpts provided in this chapter. You need to hear the words, feel the words and the emotions they carry. When you write, you should read your work aloud or hear your own words read by others.

The script is the most important element of any production, and the dialogue is its main tool. Dialogues perform many functions, both narrative and dramatic as outlined here.

Narrative Functions

Dialogue can serve to do the following:

- reveal the conflict

- move the play forward (ending a scene, projecting what will happen in the next scene)

- add new information

- help the audience understand events that happened before

- explain previous relationships between characters

- introduce or reinforce a recurring symbol

- convey the play's tone

The following scene from the screenplay *Smoke Signals* by Sherman Alexie, serves a strong narrative function.[2] It is a flashback to a conversation between the two main characters, Thomas and Victor, who have grown up together on the Coeur D'Alene reservation. As an infant, Thomas was saved from a house fire by Victor's father. Thomas's parents were killed in the fire. The two boys are standing, one on either side of a burning barrel.

YOUNG THOMAS: Hey, Victor, what do you know about fire?

YOUNG VICTOR: Thomas, I don't know what you're talking about.

YOUNG THOMAS: No, really, Victor. I mean, did you know that things burn in color? I mean, sodium burns yellow and carbon burns orange. Just like that. You can tell what's in a fire by the color of the flames.

(beat)

Hey, Victor, I heard your dad is living in Phoenix, Arizona, now.

YOUNG VICTOR: Yeah, Thomas, what about it?

YOUNG THOMAS: Man, he's lived everywhere since he left you, huh?

Victor ignores Thomas.

YOUNG THOMAS:

(con't)

I mean, he lived in Neah Bay, and then in Eureka, and then in Riverside, and then in Tijuana, and now in Phoenix, Arizona.

(beat)

Man, Phoenix is like a million miles away from here, enit?

YOUNG VICTOR: Is that so Thomas?

(beat)

You know I was wondering. What color do you think your mom and dad were when they burned up?

Young Thomas is hurt by this. He is silent for a moment.

YOUNG THOMAS: You know, your dad ain't coming back.

YOUNG VICTOR: Yes, he is.

YOUNG THOMAS: No, he's gone. When Indians go away, they don't come back. Last of the Mohicans, last of the Sioux, last of the Navajo, last of the Winnebago, last of the Coeur d'Alene people...

YOUNG VICTOR

(interrupting Thomas)

Shut up, Thomas. Or I'll beat you up again.

Long beat.

YOUNG THOMAS: What does it mean?

YOUNG VICTOR: What does what mean?

YOUNG THOMAS: What does Phoenix, Arizona, mean?

This scene serves the following narrative functions:

1. Helps the audience understand events that happened before

   - Victor's father has left the family.

   - The father has lived in many different places.

   - Thomas's parents died in a fire.

2. Adds new information

   - The father is now living in Phoenix, Arizona.

3. Reveals conflict

   - Victor doesn't want to believe that his father will not be coming back.

4. Explains previous relationships between characters

   - The boys are not really friends; their speech contains an undertone of rivalry.

   - This dialogue sets up the relationship between the two boys.

5. Introduces or reinforces a recurring symbol

   - The symbol of fire recurs throughout the play.

   - The absent parent is also a recurrent symbol.

6. Conveys the play's tone

   - An edginess that permeates this play is introduced from this early scene.

A playwright can also write a scene with a narrative function by using a character or a narrator to narrate the scene. The opening scene of the radio drama *One Ocean* by Betty Quan[3] is narrated by the daughter in the play.

Scene 1: Narration, inside memory
MUSIC Establish theme, fade under:

DAUGHTER (*older*): A long time ago. It was my favourite. A story. No, our story. Just a Chinese folktale. Yes. About the Jingwei bird and why she is always dropping sticks and stones in the ocean. When I was small, I used to pretend I was that little bird. I would soar through our communal courtyard with arms for wings. That was when you were still allowed to enjoy our stories, (*becomes overwhelmed*) to tell our stories, before, before ... (*controls herself*) Bah-bah. Father. Do you remember like I do? Father. Tell me about the Jingwei. Yes, like you used to when I was small. You told me that story when I left Hong Kong for Canada. Do you remember? I was sad. We were both sad. Like a bird in your hand I was until you set me free across the sky, across the ocean. Such a long time ago, yet so close I can still see it unfolding before me. Father? Tell me a story. Like you used to do. (*as if repeating what she hears, in memory*) "A long time ago." It seems like yesterday. A long time ago. But that is how we begin our stories, isn't it? We begin with "a long time ago."

This short monologue serves several narrative functions.

1. Reveals the conflict

   • There is a suggestion that the father betrayed the daughter when he "set her free" across the sky and the ocean.

   • The political conflict in China (from where the protagonist and her family escaped and moved to Hong Kong) is suggested by the line, "when you were still allowed to enjoy our stories."

2. Helps the audience understand events that happened before

   • The audience recognizes the special relationship the daughter had with her father.

   • The audience also understands that she has left Hong Kong for Canada.

   • The audience assumes she has left alone, since she uses the singular pronoun "I" in "when I left Hong Kong for Canada."

3. Introduces or reinforces a recurring symbol

   • The bird becomes a recurring symbol in the story.

4. Conveys the play's tone

   • The opening monologue has a nostalgic tone—the daughter wants to be taken back to the past by a story her father used to tell her.

Dramatic Functions

Dialogue can serve to do the following:

• convey characters' emotions, needs, and beliefs

- involve the audience in the lives of the characters

- show how others react to the main character's words, decisions, and actions

In James W. Nichol's adaptation of Margaret Laurence's *The Stone Angel*,[4] the dialogue shows us the emotions, needs, and beliefs of three characters: Hagar, Marvin, and Doris. In this scene, Marvin approaches his mother, Hagar, with the idea of selling her family home and moving to a smaller house. His wife, Doris, also believes this is the best idea. Hagar does not.

MARVIN: Big, Mother ... this house is too big ... now that the kids have moved away.

HAGAR: What?

DORIS: Too big ... too big ... with neither of the kids here now ... except at holidays and that.

HAGAR: What kids?

DORIS: Why, Tina and Steven, of course. Who else? Who do you think we were talking about?

MARVIN: Tina and Steven, Mother.

DORIS: Tina and Steven!

HAGAR: (*Offended*) That's right ... Tina and Steven. Tina moved away a month ago or more. Well, didn't she? (*A challenge*) Didn't she?

DORIS: (*Reluctantly*) Yes.

HAGAR: Well, that's what I said. (*Sitting in her chair*) What did you think I said?

DORIS: (*Handing out the lemon slice*) Anyway ... getting back to the subject at hand ... this house is too big.

HAGAR: Nonsense!

MARVIN: It might be a good idea to sell this house, Mother. Get an apartment, smaller, easier to keep, no stairs ...

HAGAR: You'll never sell this house! It's my house! It's my house, Doris ... mine!

MARVIN: (*Painful for him*) No. You made it out to me when I took over your business matters, don't you remember?

HAGAR: (*Not remembering*) Yes ... yes, of course. But that was just for convenience, wasn't it? It's still my house. Marvin, are you listening to me? It's mine. Isn't that so?

MARVIN: Yeah, alright ... it's yours.

DORIS: Now just wait a minute! Just you hold on one minute!

MARVIN: The way she talks ... you'd think I was trying to do her out of her blamed house! Well, I'm not. Understand?

HAGAR: No!

MARVIN: Well, if you don't know that by now, Mother ... what's the use of talkin'?

DORIS: Maybe you're forgetting ... I'm the one who has to look after this place. It's me that trots up and down these stairs a hundred times a day ...

MARVIN: I know.

DORIS: ... and lugs the vacuum cleaner up twice a week. I ought to have some say!

MARVIN: I know ... I know that.

HAGAR: But it's still my house!

MARVIN: Yes, I know that too.

DORIS: And who am I? Some stranger?

MARVIN: No, no ... of course not.

HAGAR: Oh, I always swore I'd never be a burden!

MARVIN: Oh, we don't think that ... we never said that. Did we, Doris? Did we?

DORIS: (*Reluctantly*) No.

HAGAR: (*Teary-eyed*) I wouldn't want the house sold, Marvin ... I wouldn't want that.

MARVIN: Then let's forget it.

DORIS: Forget it?

MARVIN: Please! I can't stand all this racket! (*Retreating upstage*) We'll see. We'll leave it for now. Right now ... I'm going to see what's on TV.

Marvin exits.

Doris and Hagar stare at each other ... stalemate. Doris takes back Hagar's plate.

DORIS: I'm going to evening service, Mother. Care to come along? You haven't been for some time now.

HAGAR: Not tonight thanks. Next week perhaps.

Doris exits.

HAGAR: Sell my house? I bought it with my own money.

1. As a class, discuss the dramatic elements of the dialogue in this scene.

2. With a partner, improvise a scene in which a young person tries to convince his or her parents to allow him or her to attend a university in another province. Consider all the reasons why a parent would want to discourage the move (financial reasons, family obligations, lack of trust, the young person's home-sickness, parents missing their child, and religious or cultural reasons), and all the reasons the young person may want to go (courses offered, friends who are also going, cheap housing, desire for independence or a scholarship). Create several improvisations of the same situation, working towards a scene strong in both narrative and dramatic elements. Be prepared to perform your scene and discuss it with the class.

Listening for Differences in Dialogues

Not everyone speaks alike. Differences in your characters' voices are a result of many different influences, some of which are listed here:

- the area in which they were raised

- their parents' backgrounds

- their education level

- their experiences

- their interests

- their friends

- their values and beliefs

- what they watch on television

- the music they listen to

- what they read

As a class, add to the list of influences on the way a character might speak. Then, as a class, write a few lines of dialogue that you might hear in a coffee shop. Improvise how these lines would change depending on the background of the speakers.

Characters will also speak differently

- in various situations (formal, informal);

- in various moods;

- for different audiences;

- when they want something;

- when they disagree with something that has been said;

- when they are trying to hide something.

Read the following three excerpts from *LOUIS and DAVE* by Norm Foster.[5]

Characters
> LOUIS and DAVE are in their early twenties

Setting
> DAVE's car. Two chairs, side-by-side, make up the set.
> (LOUIS and DAVE are cruising a downtown city street. DAVE is driving. When they are yelling at women, their speeches may overlap.)

LOUIS: Hey sweetheart! Hey! You in the pants!

DAVE: Hey! Hey gorgeous!

LOUIS: You wanna go for a ride? Huh? Whadya say? Go for a little ride?

DAVE: Hey! We're goin' to a party. You wanna come? Come on, climb in!

LOUIS: Come on! Hey! I think I love you! I'm in love! Marry me! Whadya say?

DAVE: How about your friend there? She wanna go to a party? Whadya say, baby? Huh? *Party!!*

LOUIS: I love you!

DAVE: *Party!*

LOUIS: I mean that!

DAVE: *Party!*

LOUIS: I want you!!

Pause.

DAVE: Are they lookin'?

LOUIS: No.

DAVE: Snobs.

LOUIS: Stuck up is what they are.

DAVE: Icebergs.

LOUIS: A couple of glaciers.

. . .

LOUIS: (*Pause.*) So, what do you think, Dave, the Flames gonna do it this year or what?

DAVE: Definitely.

LOUIS: You think so?

DAVE: No question. They've got it together this year. They've got the coaching, the scoring punch, they're okay in the nets. They'll be there.

LOUIS: I think you're right, man. I really do. The only ones who can give 'em a run are the Bruins. Maybe the Rangers. (*Pause.*) The Kings too maybe.

DAVE: Hey, don't count them out.

LOUIS: They're tough. They're tough.

DAVE: (*Pause.*) And you got the Habs too.

LOUIS: Yeah, they're always there at the end. Could be, could be. Oh, here come three more. Slow down, slow down. Hey, sweetheart! Hey! Hey, honey! You wanna go for a ride?

In the first part of the play we see two young men who appear sexist and chauvinistic, interested in typical male activities like hockey. They seem crude, maybe even uneducated by the way they drop the ends of words and the way they use slang. As we read on, we are surprised by one of the characters who breaks the stereotype the playwright has created.

LOUIS: God, I love Saturday nights.

DAVE: They're the best.

LOUIS: How long we been doin' this now, Dave?

DAVE: Gee, don't know. Three, four years.

LOUIS: Like clockwork, right?

DAVE: Every Saturday.

LOUIS: Damn right. And one of these nights we're gonna score.

DAVE: No doubt about it.

LOUIS: Damn right.

DAVE: Gotta happen.

LOUIS: We're due.

DAVE: Absolutely.

LOUIS: You got it.

DAVE: Absolutely.

LOUIS: (*Pause.*) Hey, the Jeff Healy Band's in town next Thursday. You wanna go?

DAVE: Jeff Healy?

LOUIS: Yeah.

DAVE: They're gonna be in town?

LOUIS: Next Thursday.

DAVE: All right! You're not kiddin' me, are you?

LOUIS: No way.

DAVE: All right! Dig it.

LOUIS: So you wanna go?

DAVE: Definitely.

LOUIS: All right!

DAVE: Oh, wait a minute. I can't next Thursday.

LOUIS: Why not?

DAVE: My reading club meets every Thursday.

LOUIS: Your what?

DAVE: My reading club. Damn. Talk about bad luck.

LOUIS: What reading club? What the hell is that?

DAVE: It's a reading club. We meet every Thursday and read books.

LOUIS: Books?

DAVE: Yeah.

LOUIS: You read books?

DAVE: Yeah.

LOUIS: What kind of books?

DAVE: All kinds. Everything from Hemingway to Plato to Camus.

LOUIS: To what?

DAVE: Camus.

LOUIS: What, you mean that killer whale thing?

DAVE: No, that's Shamu. Camus was a French writer. An existentialist.

LOUIS: Oh.

. . .

LOUIS:...Wanna get together and watch some football tomorrow?

DAVE: Uh...No, I can't. Geez, the Niners are playin' tomorrow too, aren't they?

LOUIS: Niners and the Bears. A classic.

DAVE: Oh, man. What a day for the symphony to be in town.

LOUIS: The what?

DAVE: The symphony. They're giving a concert tomorrow afternoon and I've got tickets.

LOUIS: The symphony?

DAVE: Yeah. I mean, I'd skip it, but it's Mahler.

LOUIS: Smaller than what?

DAVE: No, not smaller. Mahler. The composer. And done the way Mahler should be done, well, it can be very moving.

He spots some more women.

Oh, here we go. Look at this. Four of them! And dressed to kill. Hey, honey!! Hey! You girls wanna go for a spin?? Whadya say?

It turns out that Dave is an intellectual who belongs to a reading club, goes to symphonies and political rallies, and dances in the ballet. He has known Louis since eighth grade but has always been afraid to talk about his interests for fear of losing Louis's friendship.

APPLICATION

How has the author changed the way Dave speaks from the first excerpts to the second? Write five additional lines for Dave in which he discloses one of the other activities he does. Try to capture his reluctance to expose his hidden life.

The following excerpt is from Anton Chekov's *A Marriage Proposal.*[6] This humorous opening depends on the dialogue to suggest the conflict, to establish the relationship between the suitor and his potential father-in-law, and to help the audience understand the suitor's views on marriage. By his own words, Lomov also gives us a detailed description of himself.

Characters

CHUBUKOV: *A wealthy, middle-aged gentleman who owns an estate in nineteenth-century Russia*

NATALIA: *His daughter, an unmarried woman ready to take a husband*

LOMOV: *A neighbour gentleman, a neurotic bachelor of thirty-five (Chubucov's mansion—the living room. Lomov enters, formally dressed in evening jacket, white gloves, top hat. He is nervous from the start.)*

CHUBUKOV: (*Rising*) Well, look who's here! Ivan Vassilevitch! (*Shakes his hand warmly*) What a surprise, old man! How are you?

LOMOV: Oh, not too bad. And you?

CHUBUKOV: Oh, we manage, we manage. Do sit down, please. You know, you've been neglecting you neighbours, my dear fellow. It's been ages. Say, why the formal dress? Tails, gloves, and so forth. Where's the funeral, my boy? Where are you headed?

LOMOV: Oh, nowhere. I mean, here; just to see you, my dear Stepan Stepanovitch.

CHUBUKOV: Then why the full dress, old boy? It's not New Year's, and so forth.

LOMOV: Well, you see, it's like this. I have come here, my dear Stepan Stepanovitch, to bother you with a request. More than once, or twice, or more than that, it has been my privilege to apply to you for assistance in things, and you've always, well, responded. I mean, well, you have. Yes. Excuse me, I'm getting all mixed up. May I have a glass of water, my dear Stepan Stepanovitch? (*Drinks*)

CHUBUKOV: (*Aside*) Wants to borrow some money. Not a chance! (*Aloud*) What can I do for you, my dear friend?

LOMOV: Well, you see, my dear Stepanitch ... Excuse me, I mean Stepan my Dearovitch ... No, I mean, I get all confused, as you can see. To make a long story short, you're the only one who can help me. Of course, I don't deserve it, and there's no reason why I should expect you to, and all that.

CHUBUKOV: Stop beating around the bush! Out with it!

LOMOV: In just a minute. I mean, now, right now. The truth is, I have come to ask the hand ... I mean, your daughter, Natalia Stepanovna, I, I want to marry her!

CHUBUKOV: (*Overjoyed*) Great heavens! Ivan Vassilevitch! Say it again!

LOMOV: I have come humbly to ask for the hand ...

CHUBUKOV: (*Interrupting*) You're a prince! I'm overwhelmed, delighted, and so forth. Yes, indeed, and all that!

(*Hugs and kisses Lomov*)

This is just what I've been hoping for. It's my fondest dream come true. (*Sheds a tear*) And, you know, I've always looked upon you, my boy, as if you were my own son. May God grant to both of you His Mercy and His Love, and so forth. Oh, I have been wishing for this ... But why am I being so idiotic? It's just that I'm off my rocker with joy, my boy! Completely off my rocker! Oh, with all my soul I'm ... I'll go get Natalia, and so forth.

LOMOV: (*Deeply moved*) Dear Stepan Stepanovitch, do you think she'll agree?

CHUBUKOV: Why, of course, old friend. Great heavens! As if she wouldn't! Why she's crazy for you! Good God! Like a lovesick cat, and so forth. Be right back.

(*Leaves*)

LOMOV: God, it's cold. I'm goose flesh all over, as if I had to take a test. But the main thing is, to make up my mind, and keep it that way. I mean, if I take time out to think, or if I hesitate, or talk about it, or have ideals, or wait for real love, well, I'll just never get married. Brrrr, it's cold! Natalia Stepanovna is an excellent house-keeper. She's not too bad looking. She's had a good education. What more could I ask? Nothing. I'm so nervous, my ears are buzzing. (*Drinks*) Besides, I've just got to get married. I'm thirty-five already. It's sort of a critical age. I've got to settle down and lead a regular life. I mean, I'm always getting palpitations, and I'm nervous, and I get upset so easy. Look, my lips are quivering, and my eyebrow's twitching. The worst thing is the night. Sleeping. I get into bed, doze off, and, suddenly, something inside me jumps. First my head snaps, and then my shoulder blade, and I roll out of bed like a lunatic and try to walk it off. Then I try to go back to sleep, but, as soon as I do, something jumps again! Twenty times a night, sometimes ...

1. As a class, create a chart that compares the speech of Chubukov to that of Lomov. Use as many points of comparison as possible.

2. Study Lomov's speech in this excerpt. Show how it changes depending on the situation and on his emotions. Write an additional speech in which Lomov reflects on the advantages of being single. In your writing take the character through at least two different emotional states during his reflection.

3. With a partner, write a continuation of the script in which Lomov meets with his future bride. Maintain the voice of Lomov and create a new voice for Natalia based on what you know about her family and what you have learned about her from the script so far.

Crafting from the "Mess" of Natural Speech

Conversational language ... is a mess, though a mess that we are entirely used to dealing with.

RIB DAVIS[7]

It is essential that dialogue sound like it *could* take place with the characters you have created and under the circumstances they find themselves in.

When we speak, we don't speak in standard Canadian English. We don't think about what we are going to say and craft our thoughts into the best possible sentences. The following are some of the messes we have learned to deal with:

- interrupting in order to have our own say

- talking over another person's voice

- leaving out parts of a sentence

- starting to speak, rethinking, and then revising what we are going to say

- interrupting someone's sentence in order to agree, disagree, or confirm that what they have said has been heard

- completing other people's sentences

- changing the subject without warning

While it is important to have your script sound authentic, it is inadvisable to copy, unedited, real speech into your script. On top of the list of messes listed above, we often pause during a thought, sometimes even losing that thought because we are distracted. We repeat ideas. Think about the number of junk words like "um," "ah," and "like" that we put into our speech. If you included all of our poor speech habits in your script, your dialogue would sound sluggish and your audience would lose interest in it.

You need to give your audience the *idea* that your characters' dialogue is natural, but you must carefully craft this naturalism by including some of our messy speech habits, while not overdoing it. As an example, read the following transcript of a real conversation.[8] Notice that even though this is a real conversation, it sounds contrived. If you were to hear this in a script it would not capture your interest.

Scene 6

Setting: Ms. Brown's class. Camera on group two.

A: Right, yo. This is stupid, man. It really is stupid. Okay, you look at this picture right here. Everyone has advantages.

K: They all have advantages, but the school—

A: You can't have everybody's way ...

K: Yeah, but they're saying that you should be conscientious to everybody's needs.

A: The moral of the story is you can't have everybody's way.

K: Okay. Everybody has different needs .... S, do you know what the moral is?

S: It's basically what you're saying. Nobody's good at everything; everybody's good at something.

(W is writing, while A is singing)

K: Okay. B, discuss how the story relates to schools and students today. Everybody has different interests and strengths in school .... And you can't be good at everything. You can't do good in all your subjects.

A: Everybody has their strengths and weaknesses.

W: How do you spell subjects? How do you spell weaknesses?

A: S, my boy, how come you're not saying anything?

K: You guys agree with the moral?

A: Nah. I don't agree with this.

S: Well, the story's right. Everybody has strengths and weaknesses.

A: For example, the duck can't run and swim. It can fly. Therefore, everyone has strengths and weaknesses.

K: Does that make sense to you? Do you agree with the moral? I have to go to work after school.

A: Students don't like schools like that.

.   .   .

K: Okay, what are you guys good at?

A: I'm good at playing basketball.

K: Sports. Just write a list.

A: We're all good at sports. Just like K here is good at hockey.

K: S, what are you good at?

S: I don't know. I play video games.

A: I'm good at arguing a lot swearing ...

Teacher: Please focus on the positives ...

K: I got beginner French. That's why I got ninety percent.

A: Well, I'd change the curriculum by taking the subjects I'm good at the first semester and the next semester I wouldn't have to worry about it. I'd take the bad subjects.

K: I'd take out history because I hate history.

W: I suck at science.

K: I'd take out art. I'd have more choices.

A: I would take out English. Ha, ha! We would take out the subjects that we are not good at like—

K: History, science, art, and more extra-curricular activities like sports.

K: I'd add driving.

A: Dating!

K: And social subjects.

W: A period for talking. Socializing.

K: What else?

A: That's it. That's it. We're done. We're done!

The following short excerpt from Norm Foster's stage play, *The Visit*,[9] gives the impression of natural language but does not overdo it:

Characters

> *RICHARD: Richard Penny, a lawyer.*
> *RHONDA: His mother.*
> *LLOYD: His father.*

Setting

> *Richard's law office. The present.*
>
> *(As the scene opens, RICHARD is sitting at his desk, talking on the phone.)*

RICHARD: Well, hopefully my meeting won't last too long. I should be at your place by five-thirty. Mmmm I can't wait. Have the wine chilling ... Oh, listen, can I get one of your fabulous back-rubs tonight? I've got some tension knots like you wouldn't believe ... Well, you do mine, and I'll do yours.

> *(The office door opens and RHONDA and LLOYD enter. RHONDA carries a picnic basket.)*

RHONDA: Hello, Counsellor. Mind if we come in?

> *(They enter and close the door.)*

RICHARD: (*To the phone.*) I gotta go ... Yeah, see you then. (*He hangs up the phone.*) Mom, Dad, what are you doing here?

RHONDA: We brought lunch. Ooh, look at this office, Lloyd. Is this the office of a big wheel lawyer or am I Joan of Arc?

LLOYD: Very nice, Ricky.

RICHARD: Mom, it's three-thirty. I've already had lunch.

RHONDA: Well, so you'll have some more. You're too thin anyway.

LLOYD: It's lobster.

RICHARD: Lobster? You brought lobster?

RHONDA: McLobster. Your father insisted.

LLOYD: I happen to like McLobster.

RHONDA: (*to RICHARD.*) I brought some vegetables and a cold plate for us, Richard.

> *(She sets the basket on his desk.)*

RICHARD: Mom, really, I don't have time. I have a meeting. And how did you get by my secretary?

RHONDA: I told her I was your mother. She sent us right in. It's a woman thing. She's rather trampy-looking, isn't she?

> *(She sits.)*

RICHARD: Who, Tammy?

RHONDA: Tammy? Well, say no more. Lloyd, are you going to sit?

LLOYD: I'm looking at the office. Very nice, Ricky.

RICHARD: Thank you. Mom, listen to me ...

RHONDA: Listen nothing. You've been in this office for almost a year now and you haven't invited us to see it once. So we're smashing.

RICHARD: Crashing.

RHONDA: Whatever. Now, sit down and have some food. Your meeting can wait twenty minutes.

RICHARD: Mom ...

RHONDA: Sit.

The occasional use of everyday expressions and interruptions gives the impression of an ordinary conversation between parents and child. This conversation, in real life, would probably sound much different.

APPLICATION

1. With a partner, write the dialogue above the way it might sound if it were real speech. Read it aloud to the class. Explain why it wouldn't work as well as the "cleaned up" speech of the characters in Foster's script.

2. Script a dialogue between two teenagers suggesting the messiness of natural speech while moving the needs and desires of the characters forward.

3. Work with two classmates. Each of you should adopt the characteristics, attitudes, and viewpoints of someone you know well. Don't tell your classmates whom you have chosen to be. Decide on a situation in which the three of you find yourselves and start a conversation staying true to the character you have chosen to be. When you have improvised for about five minutes, start to script the dialogue for a radio or stage play.

4. Write two monologues on the same subject from the perspectives of two people from different backgrounds. Craft their speech to capture their point of view and their emotions while maintaining momentum and interest.

As stated at the beginning of this chapter, quality dialogue is essential for successful drama (unless you are staging a mime show). A writer must understand the limitations or advantages of each medium in order to write effective dialogue for each. Radio is the most dependent on dialogue. The radio dramatist has only four things he or she can work with to create characters: dialogue, music, sound effects, and silence. Drama written for the stage can rely less on dialogue and more on facial expressions, body language, and blocking (actors' movements on stage) to develop characters and their relationships with others. On the screen, camera angles, movements, and shots combined with an actor's facial expressions, body language, and movement can speak volumes about the character without a word being uttered.

Before writing your script, decide on the medium and tailor your dialogue to that medium.

Structuring Your Script

Because scripts are crafted differently depending on the medium, this section on structure focuses on scripts for screenplays, for radio, and for the stage. Whatever medium you are writing for, you will have to discover your own writing process. Some writers plan out the structure of their scripts from beginning to end, knowing exactly the way the story will be told. Others start to write and let the story dictate the structure. There is no "correct" way to write your script. You need to experiment to find your own method. Even when you think you've found it, you can just as easily change it from script to script.

Screenplays

While there are many elements in screenplays, such as picture and sound elements, costumes and editing, this section will focus on the structure of a screenplay.

Screenplays are more like poetry than like fiction. Screenplays ... have form. Like sonnets, actually. Just as there are expectations of form, meter, and rhyme in a sonnet, there are the same kinds of expectations for screenplays.

SHERMAN ALEXIE[10]

A page of script is approximately a minute of movie. Thus, a two-hour movie takes about 120 pages. Screenplays traditionally fall into three acts. Within each of these acts are scenes indicated by changes in locations and/or characters.

Act I

In Act I, the writer introduces the characters, their goals, and the overall tone of the film. The writer also sets up the audience for the complications that will happen in Act II.[11] The first act must interest the viewers enough to keep them in their seats.

Syd Field, in *The Screenwriter's Workbook*,[12] designed this paradigm to represent the screenplay:

The Story:

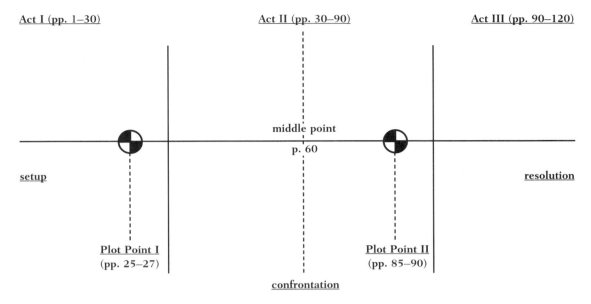

middle point

p. 60

<u>setup</u>

<u>resolution</u>

<u>Plot Point I</u>
(pp. 25–27)

<u>Plot Point II</u>
(pp. 85–90)

<u>confrontation</u>

Act I generally ends with a "reversal" or plot twist (plot point I) that propels the viewer into the second act. This reversal (so named because the direction of the story is reversed, as are the expectations of the viewers) must be logical within the overall story, yet still be a surprise to the audience. The plot twist must carry the second act of the movie.[13]

Act II

Act II is made up of a series of obstacles that threaten to prevent the characters from achieving their goals but also keep the story moving forward. The obstacles should grow logically out of the reversal at the first plot point and increase in size, thus building suspense as the story spins towards its end. At the end of the act, a second plot point or reversal will again propel the action forward into the final act. Remember that your second reversal or plot point, like the obstacles that you have designed, must grow logically out of the characters, their goals, and their actions. Surprises are good, but not if the audience can't believe they could happen.

Act III

The final act is the place in which the characters either attain or fail to attain their goals. It grows naturally out of the reversal or plot point in Act II as well as through the characters as they have been developed in the story. Most screenplays do not have long denouements, since audiences don't want to sit through them.

The three-act structure is a handy tool to use when you are writing your screenplay. It is not, however, the only way to structure a screenplay. An extreme example of breaking away from the traditional structure is Christopher Nolan's screenplay *Memento*. The audience sees the climax first and then works backwards through time to learn how and why the main character ended up where he did. Some viewers find the structure confusing; others enjoy the writer's innovation.

APPLICATION

Write a four-page treatment for a screenplay using the steps below, adapted from Syd Field's exercise in *The Screenwriter's Workbook*. The purpose of this exercise is to dramatize and define your story line in four pages, double spaced, using broad strokes without being specific or precise. This exercise helps you tell a story before you write the screenplay.

The Paradigm

- Draw the *paradigm*. It should look like the paradigm structure on page 167.

- Lay out the subject of your story—the action and character—according to the dramatic structure of the paradigm; choose your ending first, then your beginning, then plot point I and plot point II and record them on the paradigm structure.

- Based on your story line, what should your opening be? Where does it take place? What is the character doing? Sketch it out in broad terms. You don't have to know *everything* yet—and you can always change it later.

Act I (one page)

- Write the narrative action that opens the story, about half a page. This will be the setup for your opening; you haven't hit the opening yet. Here is an example:

Night. A car slowly weaves through the streets. It turns a corner, the lights go out, and it coasts to a stop in front of a large office building. Silence. In the distance, a dog barks. JOE sits silently behind the wheel, a radio transmitter on the seat next to him. He slips on a pair of earphones, slowly turns the dial to pick up police calls. Then he sits. And waits.

- Write the opening sequence in broad, general terms. Use a few lines of dialogue if you need to.

- On the remainder of page 1, write a couple of paragraphs describing the action that takes you to the plot point at the end of Act I. This dramatizes the action in Act I.

Act II (two pages)

- On the first half of the page, write the plot point at the end of Act I. Where does it take place? What does the character do? Without being specific or precise, write it out, focusing on plot point I.

- Now you're ready to move into Act II, a unit of dramatic action. Before you begin writing, think about the following: What dramatic context or *confrontation* will hold this act? What obstacles will you create that your character has to overcome to achieve what he or she wants to win or gain—his or her *dramatic need*? Your story becomes how your character overcomes (or does not overcome) all the obstacles in the way of his or her dramatic need. Think about the two or three major obstacles that will generate conflict within the progression of your story and that will move your story *forward* to the end of Act II.

- Write the action of Act II in about a page, focusing on your character confronting these obstacles. Once again, be general.

- Now write the plot point at the end of Act II, about half a page. How does the plot point at the end of Act II "spin" the action around in Act III? Use dialogue if needed. Remain general.

Act III (one page)

- What happens to your character? What is the resolution? How does it end? Describe the resolution simply on the last page (you may not need the full page).[14]

Radio Plays

Radio drama ... begins with nothing at all, with absolute silence.... To this utter emptiness the playwright, bit by bit, using only sound, adds setting, period, characters and everything else needed to tell a dramatic story.

WILLIAM ASH[15]

Radio dramas, like stories, have a beginning (introduction and inciting incident), middle (rising action which includes a series of growing crisis), and end (the climax and resolution). The opening scene of a radio drama must catch the listener's attention immediately. Remember, there aren't any visuals to help with the words of the script. Once your listeners have tuned out or changed the station, it will be impossible to get them back.

Unlike stage plays or screenplays, on the radio there is no scenery to look at or costumes to interest the audience. This listener can't see the reactions of actors or other audience members. As a radio playwright, you need to engage your audience's imagination. Through your words and your listeners' imaginations, visual words are created. To keep the imaginations of the audience engaged, you must include action.

Drama and Action

Tim Crook[16] says, "Don't give [your listeners] a warm bed with comfortable pillows and a hot water bottle ... parachute [them] into a top dramatic moment." This means you need to choose a dramatic point to start your play, a point where your listeners' attention will be immediately captured, propelling your audience into the middle of the action. Because radio is an aural medium, many novice playwrights think they should *tell* the story. Giving them the history of the play and all the characters before any action begins is almost guaranteed to turn them off. Like both stage and screenplays, radio plays must "show," not "tell."

The beginning scene is not the only place that should have a strong drama. Radio plays are often 50 minutes long, start to finish, if they are not presented episodically. Your play must take the shortest route between two points. This means doing the following:

- telescoping some events

- making some events happen "off-stage" and having characters refer to those events

- bringing the audience into a scene in progress, close to its climactic point

What you decide to include, exclude, shorten, or lengthen will depend on how these events affect the flow of the play—the way the play moves towards the climax. Re-creating some scenes may make the play slow down too much, whereas leaving a scene out may make the play leap forward too quickly. Sometimes you may wish to draw out a scene to create suspense. No matter how slow or how quick, each scene has the same general shape as the overall drama: a rising action, a climax, and a resolution. It also has to lead the listener into the scene that follows. Every plot twist must carry the "dramatic promise," that is, that it will lead to a logical yet not blatantly obvious conclusion.

Plot Line and Characters

Like stage and screenplays, radio plays can have more than one plot line. It is important not to complicate the plot too much, however, since oftentimes audience members are doing other things as they listen and need to be able to pick up on the action if their attention has temporarily lapsed. For the same reason, it is important not to have too many characters. Listeners have to be able to tell the difference between characters by voice and can only remember so many voices before they start confusing them.

Sound Effects

Whatever your plot line, as a radio playwright, you must think in terms of sound. It is difficult to think of what a plot line might look like and then try to adapt it to a sound medium. Think "sound" from the beginning. William Ash[17] makes the following suggestions for helping writers think in "sound pictures":

- Create incidents in the story that could take place around sound (concerts, car races, auctions, parties).

- Design characters that could be involved with sound (musicians, singers, public speakers).

- Use sound devices like telephone calls, taped conversations, and voicemail.

- Let the audience hear how a person struggles to open a window, is winded after a long run, "surfs" radio stations, and honks the horn while sitting in a traffic jam.

Setting

The joy of writing for radio is that you are not restricted by place or time. To keep up the aural interest, you can move from an outdoor to an indoor scene, from a battlefield to an underground war room where generals are plotting strategy. You can be in a crowded bar one minute and at the top of the CN Tower the next. Of course, a boring plot is not going to be "fixed" by a variety of sounds in a variety of locations, but variety can add to an already interesting plot.

APPLICATION

In a small group, decide on a subject you would like to write about. Write a simple plot line that develops that subject (it doesn't have to be original). With this basic plot line in mind, create an opening scene for a radio drama, keeping in mind William Ash's tips for thinking in "sound pictures" and his suggestion to start in the middle of the action.

Stage Plays

A typical stage play that takes 90 minutes will generally have two acts. A long stage play (approximately 120 minutes) will often have three acts. Ends of acts are most often signified by intermissions.

Act I

Following is Richard Toscan's diagram of a typical plot structure for a two-act play (page 173).[18] The "point of attack" is the first thing the audience is introduced to in the act. All stories have a history. The playwright must decide in which point of the history to begin telling the play's story. That will be his or her point of attack. The point of attack is followed very closely by the inciting incident, the point at which the conflict begins.

Because history has taken place before the point of attack, you may have to bring some of that into your script. Give the audience only what they need to know when they need to know it.

The high point of act one is the peak of a crisis, but it is not the climax. It is suspense-filled and tense, but it does not resolve the conflict. This point is followed by the "curtain line," which may twist the plot and should leave the audience wanting to know what will happen next. It should move the action into the second act, and if it is given before the intermission, should make the audience want to return. The curtain line can be any of the following:

- a line of dialogue

- a physical action by a performer

For me the opening moments of a play are most important, in terms of form. I might begin a play a hundred times until I get it absolutely right. Because if I don't get you in those first few minutes, I've lost you. I want to get you caught up as fast as possible. You hear something, you see something, there's enough to drag your butt into that play .... Once I'm dead certain of the opening moments, the rest is a lot simpler.

CHARLES FULLER[19]

- a visual image

- a sound effect

Act II
Act II is shaped much like Act I. It starts at a lower point than the end of Act I, but then moves up to the climax and, finally, to the resolution of the conflict (lower than the climax).

Scenes
Many plays contain scenes within the acts. The endings of these scenes act as "mini-intermissions" and allow a change of setting or time. When writing scenes, you need to shape each scene much like you shaped Act I, starting with a point of attack, moving toward a crisis, and ending with a "curtain line."

Throughout your script, and through the twists and turns of the plot, the audience will take an emotional ride, hitting highs and lows as they follow the characters over each of their obstacles. The climax should leave the audience feeling satisfied—not necessarily happy, but satisfied that the ending you have written flows logically from the conflict, the crisis, and the characters. It must be believable.

Structural Diagram of a Two-Act Play

In Three-Act plays, Act II repeats Act I

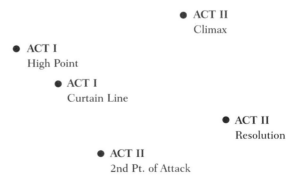

● **ACT II**
Climax

● **ACT I**
High Point

● **ACT I**
Curtain Line

● **ACT II**
Resolution

● **ACT II**
2nd Pt. of Attack

● **ACT I**
Pt. of Attack | Inciting Incident

Read a short story from an anthology you use in school or that you borrow from the library. Describe the order in which the story is told. Now look at it from a dramatist's point of view. Where in the story would an adaptation for the stage begin? What events would be kept for the stage production? Which ones dropped? In what other ways would the stage play adaptation differ from the short story? How would it differ if you were to write it for radio?

Layout and Design of Scripts

Radio and stage plays generally start in the same manner, with a list of characters, perhaps who they are, and a description of the setting. Following is an example from *The Illegal Playwriting Class* by John Lazarus.[20]

Characters

DOCTOR

MADAME

RECEPTIONIST (a voice on the intercom)

CAPTAIN

Setting

DOCTOR's office. Desk, chairs, sofa, bookshelves. Leather and wood, of quality but now old and a bit shabby. Set and costumes seem of another time, suggestive of the '30s or '40s, though a desktop computer sits beside the old-fashioned black phone. They are also foreign: the books bear titles in an unknown language, and there is a large wall map of a nonexistent country, with place-names in the same mysterious language, as are the books and framed diplomas. This exercise was inspired by Glenn Gould's fugue "So You Want to Write a Fugue." For the record, the novelist quoted by the DOCTOR is Voltaire; the actor is William Hutt; the director is Keith Johnstone; and the Greek philosopher is probably Aristotle.

> *(Tableau: DOCTOR stands at the window, peering out through the blinds, while MADAME, hatted and veiled, peers at him from beneath the veil. She drops the veil as he drops the Venetian blinds and turns to her.)*

The same goal is accomplished in screenplays and television scripts through a description of the shot, for example, inside (INT.) or outside (EXT.); the location of the shot; whether it is day or night. Following this is the description of the action and the characters, if they have not been previously introduced. Some screenplays go into more detail than others. Here is an example from the opening of the screenplay *The Straight Story* by Mary Sweeney and John Roach.[21]

> 1. *EXT.—NIGHT SKY*
> *Autumn evening FULL of STARS. Music plays over as credits roll.*
> *DISSOLVE TO:*
>
> 2. *DAY—LAURENS, IOWA*
> *It is a hot day in early September in Laurens, a small rural community in north central Iowa. The main drag, all of four blocks, is bookended by a giant grain elevator and a John Deere dealership. No cars on the road.*
> *CUT TO:*
>
> 3. *EXT.—DAY SMALL HOUSE & NEIGHBORING HOUSE*
> *At the neighboring house, DOROTHY, a rather large woman, 50ish, with bleached blond, cropped hair is sunbathing in a chaise lounge. She is wearing bermuda shorts, a tank top and eye protectors over her eyes. Next to her is a small table with a plate on it. Out of the other house, which has chipped siding and faded, peeling window frames, comes ROSE (late 30s, brown hair in a pixie cut, stocky, in jeans and a cotton shirt). The door slams and Rose heads down the walk. Dorothy doesn't move a muscle or remove her eye protectors.*

Stage and radio scripts are formatted similarly. The name of the speaker is written justified left in capital letters followed by a colon. If there are directions for a specific way to perform the line, they follow the character's name, are enclosed in parentheses and written in italics. Stage directions, music, or sound effects are also italicized and enclosed in parentheses. They are indented beneath the last speaker's line (see the scene from Norm Foster's play on page 164).

Storyboards

Storyboards are visual representations of how a script is going to be shot. If you are making a movie or video, a storyboard will help you see what each of your shots will look like. Storyboards may be composed of thumbnail sketches or highly detailed drawings.

Each frame is drawn as if you were looking through the lens of a camera. A person looking at each frame of the storyboard should be able to tell the camera distance and camera angle, as well as the shot content. Beside or underneath each frame, you should describe each of the following:

- shot content

- camera distance

- camera angle

- camera movement

- audio

- shot duration in seconds

THE WRITER'S PROJECTS

Investigating the Writer's Craft

1. Using print and electronic resources, research a variety of playwrights through interviews they have given. Make a list of pieces of advice they have given about writing scripts. Revise a scene you have already written, using one piece of advice they have suggested. Write a journal entry on how it helped or hindered your writing.

2. Research a playwright from another country. Read at least three plays he or she has written. Write an analysis of the writer's work based on one aspect of scriptwriting you have studied in this unit.

3. Read a book on scriptwriting. Write a critique of one of your scripts, based on at least three points the scriptwriting author has said are essential to good scripts.

Practising the Writer's Craft

1. Form a group of three. Explore a variety of authors from around the world and find several short stories that would adapt well to radio drama. Choose one story and write a radio adaptation. Below are some things you should consider as you are writing:
   - how to limit the number of characters in the script
   - how to best manipulate the structure of the story for radio listeners
   - how the voices of the characters differ in the original and how you will distinguish them further for your script
   - what sound effects would enhance the action and meaning
   - what music would enhance action and meaning
   - how a central image or motif, if there is one, could be worked into the script

   Record your play and listen for strengths and weaknesses in your writing. Revise your work, re-record it, and have another group provide you with revision suggestions. Record a final version with sound and music.

2. Choose a screenplay or television movie script and create a storyboard for at least 10 sequential shots. If the writer has not suggested audio or music, write in your own suggestions.

3. Go back to your warm-up activities at the beginning of this chapter (page 146) and use one of them as a basis for developing a script.

4. Write a script for radio, stage, or screen.

THE WRITER'S READING LIST

The Writer's Craft

Ash, William. *The Way to Write Radio Drama*. London: Elm Tree Books, 1985.

Catron, Louis E. *The Elements of Playwriting*. New York: Macmillan, 1993.

Cox, Kerry and Jurgen Wolff. *Successful Scriptwriting*. Cincinnati, OH: Writer's Digest Books, 1988.

Davis, Rib. *Writing Dialogue for Scripts*. London: A&C Black, 1998.

Field, Syd. *The Screenwriter's Problem Solver.* New York: Dell/Bantam Doubleday Dell, 1998.

Field, Syd. *The Screenwriter's Workbook.* New York: Dell/Bantam Doubleday Dell, 1984.

Frank, Anne, ed. *Telling It: Writing for Film and Television in Canada.* Toronto: Doubleday Canada, 1996.

Paice Eric. *The Way to Write for Television.* London: Elm Tree Books, 1987.

Sautter, Carl. *How to Sell Your Screenplay.* New York: New Chapter Press, 1988.

Toscan, Richard. *The Playwriting Seminars,* http:// www.vcu.edu/artweb/ playwriting.

Examples of the Writer's Craft

Stage Drama

Chekov, Anton. *A Marriage Proposal* in *The Brute and Other Faces*; compiled by Eric Bentley. (This play has also been reprinted in Douglas Hilker and Sue Harper, *Elements of English 9.* Toronto: Harcourt Brace Canada, 1999, 111–120.)

Cooper, Beverley. *Out of Body* in *Instant Applause: Twenty-six Very Short Complete Plays* Vol. 1. Winnipeg: Blizzard, 1997, 52–57.

Lazarus, John. *The Illegal Playwriting Class* in *Instant Applause: Thirty Very Short Complete Plays* Vol. 2. Winnipeg: Blizzard, 1999, 23–37.

Nichol, James W. *The Stone Angel.* (An excerpt of this play appears in Sue Harper, et al., *Elements of English 12,* Toronto: Harcourt Canada, 2002, 134–181.)

Taylor, Drew Hayden. *Girl Who Loved Her Horses.* Toronto: Talonbooks, 2000. (This play has also been reprinted in Sue Harper, Douglas Hilker, and Peter J. Smith, *Elements of English 12,* Toronto: Harcourt Canada, 2002, 99–118.)

Radio Drama

Carley, Dave, ed. *Airplay: An Anthology of CBC Radio Drama*. Winnipeg: Scirocco Drama/J. Gordon Shillingford, 1996.

Chislett, Anne. *Venus Sucked In* in *Airborne: Radio Plays by Women*, ed. Ann Jansen. Winnipeg: Blizzard, 1991, 51–68.

Jansen, Ann, ed. *Adventures for (Big) Girls: Seven Radio Plays*. Winnipeg: Blizzard, 1993.

Schmalz, Wayne, ed. *Studio One: Stories Made for Radio*. Regina: Coteau Books, 1990.

Sher, Emil. *Making Waves: Three Radio Plays*. Toronto: Simon & Pierre, 1998.

Screenplays

Coen, Ethan and Joel Coen. *O Brother, Where Art Thou?* London: Faber and Faber, 2000.

Darabont, Frank. *The Green Mile: The Screenplay*. New York: Scribner Paperback Fiction, Schuster and Schuster, 1999.

Figgis, Mike. *Collected Screenplays 1*. London: Faber and Faber, 2001.

Sweeney, Mary and John Roach. *The Straight Story*. New York: Hyperion Books, 1999. (Excerpts of this screenplay appear in Sue Harper and Douglas Hilker, *Foundations of English 12*, Toronto: Harcourt Canada, 2002, 303–331.)

Endnotes and Credits

Chapter 4

1 Lee Blessing, quoted in "Beginnings: The Point of Attack," Virginia Commonwealth University Web site, www.vcu.edu/artweb/playwriting/pointattack.html.

2 From SMOKE SIGNALS by Sherman Alexie. Copyright © 1998 Sherman Alexie. Reprinted by permission of Hyperion.

3 *One Ocean* by Betty Quan. Originally broadcast on radio by CBC—*Morningside*. Copyright © 1994 by Betty Quan.

4 James W. Nichol, *The Stone Angel*. Reprinted by permission of James W. Nichol.

5 Norm Foster, *LOUIS and DAVE*. Reprinted by permission of Norm Foster and Playwrights Guild of Canada.

6 *A Marriage Proposal* by Anton Chekov. Edited by Eric Bentley. Copyright © 1958 by Eric Bentley. All Rights Reserved. Reprinted by permission of Applause Theater & Cinema Books, LLC.

7 Rib Davis, *Writing Dialogue for Scripts*. London: A&C Black, 1998, 3.

8 Excerpted from an actual class transcript. Courtesy of Patricia Westerhof.

9 Norm Foster, *The Visit* in *Instant Applause: Thirty Very Short Complete Plays*, Vol. 2. Winnipeg: Blizzard, 1996, 76–77. Reprinted by permission of Playwrights Canada Press.

10 Sherman Alexie, "Introduction," in *Smoke Signals*, x.

11 Kerry Cox and Jurgen Wolff, *Successful Scriptwriting*. Cincinnati, OH: Writer's Digest Books, 1988, 23.

12 From THE SCREENWRITER'S WORKBOOK by Syd Field, copyright © 1984 by Syd Field. Used by permission of Dell Publishing, a division of Random House, Inc.

13 Carl Sautter, *How to Sell Your Screenplay*. New York: New Chapter Press, 1988, 18.

14 From THE SCREENWRITER'S WORKBOOK by Syd Field, copyright © 1984 by Syd Field. Used by permission of Dell Publishing, a division of Random House, Inc.

15 William Ash, *The Way to Write Radio Drama*. London: Elm Tree Books, 1985, 11.

16 Tim Crook, "Principles of Writing Radio Drama," www.irdp.co.uk/scripts.htm.

17 Ash, *The Way to Write Radio Drama*, 19–20.

18 "Structure of a Two-Act Play." Reprinted by permission from The Playwriting Seminars Web site by Richard Toscan.

19 Charles Fuller, quoted in "Inciting Incident," Virginia Commonwealth University Web site, www.vcu.edu/artweb/playwriting/inciting.html.

20 John Lazarus, *The Illegal Playwriting Class*, in *Instant Applause*, Vol. 2., 23. Reprinted by permission of Playwrights Canada Press.

21 From THE STRAIGHT STORY by Mary Sweeney and John Roach. Copyright © 1999 Mary Sweeney and John Roach. Reprinted by permission of Hyperion.

Poetry Writing

The crown of literature is poetry. It is its end and aim. It is the sublimest activity of the human mind. It is the achievement of beauty and delicacy. The writer of prose can only step aside when the poet passes.

W. SOMERSET MAUGHAM[1]

LEARNING GOALS

▸ analyze forms of poetry and their elements and conventions

▸ analyze the purpose and audience of a variety of poems

▸ assess poets' choices of techniques, diction, voice, and style

▸ research and analyze selected works by poets from around the world to assess different poets' practices and beliefs about writing

▸ write a variety of forms of poetry for various purposes and to practise and develop writing skills

▸ explain and assess—individually and in small groups—the creative choices made in producing one's own poems

▸ revise drafts to produce poems that are effective in content, techniques, diction, voice, and style

WHAT IS POETRY?

You can find almost as many famous definitions of poetry as there are well-known poems. Some definitions focus on poetry's power; others on its beauty. Emily Dickinson,[2] for example, wrote, "If I feel physically as if the tip of my head were taken off, I know that is poetry." Most definitions are poetic themselves: E.E. Cummings called poetry "the algebra of the heart"; William Carlos Williams described a poem as "a small machine made out of words"; while Canadian author Susan Musgrave described poetry as "a kind of wild justice." Elizabeth Drew[3] aptly comments, "Has any poet or critic successfully defined poetry? They talk about it in such very different terms that it is difficult to believe that they are describing the same activity."

Part of the difficulty in defining poetry comes from the many forms it takes. Early ballads—like many song lyrics today—use rhyme, repetition, and a regular rhythmic pattern to tell a story. Another common poetic form, which you'll recognize from your study of Shakespeare, consists of unrhymed lines with a regular rhythm and number of syllables per line. In the twentieth century, free verse became popular: poetry that uses neither rhyme nor regular rhythm, but instead focuses on compressed language, powerful imagery, aural devices and careful, creative arrangement of words on the page. Although some contemporary poets, especially songwriters, prefer more traditional forms, most poets today write in free verse.

Not only does poetry come in many forms, but the subject matter ranges widely, from human emotions to ideas, insights, and experiences. What the poet sees, thinks, or feels is the starting point for poetry. However, poems are more than self-expression; the raw material of the poet's experience is communicated *aesthetically*, using not only the words' meaning, but their sound and the way they look on the page. Because poetry speaks to readers in such a rich, compressed way, it is intuitive and emotional. Bronwen Wallace explains this in "Shyly Slipping a Poem from the Purse":[4]

> What I like about poetry is the economy of its communication, the way it uses the surprises of an image to say what it takes most of us paragraphs to say. In a poem called "When You Go Away," for example, W.S. Merwin says everything about the pain of being left and how hard it is to talk about it in two lines:
>
> My words are the garment of what I shall never be
> Like the tucked sleeve of a one-armed boy.

Good poetry moves the reader; it enchants, shocks, amuses, delights, surprises, angers, and relieves. It can make us look at a tired subject in a fresh way. It can name our experiences and deepest feelings. It can make us laugh. It can broaden our understanding of ourselves or the world around us. Because poetry is so intricate and versatile, it can capture the astonishing range and complexity of human experience.

In this chapter you will examine and experiment with various techniques of poetry and poetic forms. We will look at how to make decisions about your approach to the subject, your word choice, and poetic form. Many of the activities will focus on wordplay to help you develop your creativity and craftsmanship.

1. Reread the quotations about poetry from the "What Is Poetry" section at the opening of this chapter. Write your own poetic definition of poetry.

2. Cut 30 words at random out of an old magazine. Make sure you include some basic words such as *of, or, is,* and *and,* as well as endings such as *-ed* and *-ing.* Using as many or as few of the 30 words as you want, create as many different poems as you can.

3. In a journal entry, record a powerful memory in as much detail as you can. Then change your prose into a free-verse poem, focusing on using powerful verbs and adjectives.

4. Take the first line from a poem in an anthology or collection, and write your own poem using that line in the beginning, in the middle, or at the ending of your poem. Be sure to indicate the source of the line you borrowed.

5. Choose a page at random from a science or math textbook, or from a business manual. Using only words and phrases from that page, write a poem.

6. Find an ode (Pablo Neruda's "Ode to my Socks" is a good one). Write an outline of the poem, noting shifts in tone, content, and approach to the subject. Then, using the outline, write an ode of your own on a subject of your choice.[5]

7. Write a poem describing a favourite or feared place. Use all the five senses in your description. Try to show how you feel about the place through your description of it.

8. Generate a list of your favourite words. Write a short poem that uses at least three of those words.

9. Generate lists on several topics. Examples of lists are *things that come in handy, lies I've been told, what won't happen today, things I remember about* _____. From one of your lists, develop a poem.

10. Begin a poem with the punchline of a joke.

11. Find a poem more than 200 years old (a Shakespearean sonnet works well). Rewrite the poem using contemporary language and free verse.

12. Write a poem about a dream. Write the dream details as if they were real. Use as many senses as possible in your description.

THE WRITER'S TOOLKIT

Subject and Tone

So what should you write poems about? Many people see poetry as
an outlet for deepest feelings. A powerful emotion is a good starting
point. E.E. Cummings, in the famous essay "A Poet's Advice to
Students," says:[7]

> A poet is somebody who feels, and who expresses his feeling through
> words.
>
> This may sound easy. It isn't.
>
> A lot of people think or believe or know they feel—but that's think-
> ing or believing or knowing; not feeling. And poetry is feeling—not
> knowing or believing or thinking.
>
> Almost anybody can learn to think or believe or know, but not a
> single human being can be taught to feel. Why? Because whenever
> you think or you believe or you know, you're a lot of other people; but
> the moment you feel, you're nobody-but-yourself.

The danger of making a feeling the starting point of your poem is
that the writing can become more a diary entry than a work of art. If
your purpose in writing is to identify your emotions or to work something out for yourself, then you will be writing self-expression—which
is an important sort of writing, but it is not poetry. In writing poetry
you must consider two things. First, your purpose is to communicate
with your reader. "The writer is both an eye-witness and an I-witness,
the one to whom personal experience happens and the one who
makes experience personal for others," explains Margaret Atwood.[8]
Second, your poem needs an aesthetic dimension; that is, it must
communicate by including elements such as sound, form, imagery,
or wordplay to convey emotion or purpose to the reader and to make
the poem work on several different levels. Consider, for example,
Margaret Atwood's poem, "you fit into me":[9]

> you fit into me
> like a hook into an eye
>
> a fish hook
> an open eye

Atwood could merely have said, "Our relationship is painful to
me," but that would not be a poem. Moreover, it would not evoke the
savagery that the imagery does. It is more work to communicate
ideas and feelings in this way—one wonders how many images

Atwood rejected before finding this one. Yet the end result is far more powerful than a literal expression would be.

Good poems don't need to be difficult. In fact, you may wish to strive to use everyday language and accessible imagery in your poetry. However, rather than telling the readers how you feel or how they should feel, show the emotion in a way that leaves room for the reader to enter the poem, to see or even to experience the feelings with the speaker. Consider this poem by Eve Merriam:[10]

New Love

I am telling my hands
not to blossom into roses

I am telling my feet
not to turn into birds
and fly over the rooftops

and I am putting a hat on my head
so the flaming meteors
in my hair
will hardly show.

This poem is playful and accessible. It uses everyday language to present its ideas and emotions. But it doesn't name the emotions, relying instead on aesthetic elements such as imagery and wordplay.

APPLICATION

Write a short poem about falling in love or ending a relationship. Don't name your feelings; rather, reveal them through imagery or wordplay.

The Sympathetic Contract

According to John Ciardi, every poet takes a particular attitude and tone towards his or her subject in a poem. If the reader is not willing or able to sympathize with the poet's position, then that poem fails for that reader. When a poem fails, Ciardi holds, it is not for technical reasons: not because of forced rhyme or use of clichés, though technical flaws can add to the problem. However, poems that are technically flawless can certainly be bad poetry. The failure comes from the reader's inability to believe the speaker or take him or her seriously.[11] Consider the following poem (author unknown).[12]

Friendly Obstacles

For every hill I've tried to climb,
For every stone that bruised my feet,
For all the blood and sweat and grime,
For blinding storms and burning heat,
My heart sings but a grateful song
These are the things that made me strong!

For all the heartache and the tears,
For all the anguish and the pain,
For gloomy days and fruitless years,
And for the hopes that lived in vain,
I do give thanks, for now I know
These were the things that helped me grow!

'Tis not the softer things in life
Which stimulate man's will to strive;
But bleak adversity and strife
Do most to keep man's will alive.
O'er rose-strewn paths the weaklings creep,
But brave hearts dare to climb the steep.

Although no doubt the writer means to be sincere in this poem, many students are unable to take this poet seriously. The speaker's response to the many hardships described seems unrealistic: "My heart sings but a grateful song." The last two lines strike many readers as judgmental rather than inspirational. Ciardi explains the problem with a poem like this one:[13]

Every poem ... by its choice of tone and attitude is a mask the poet assumes. In one mask he may present himself as heroic. In another as flightily gay. In another as philosophically detached, or as wistful, or as torn two ways.

But whatever the mask, the poet must make the role resound winningly within the reader. Poetry is not an ornamental exercise. It is man's best means of perceiving most profoundly the action and the consequence of his own emotions. Every poem addresses in some way, however slight, the question: "What is a man?" The reader tries on the mask through which the poet addresses that question and wills himself vicariously into the role the poet is playing; but he must then feel that the role is well and meaningfully played, and he must resist any effort by the poet to win him to shoddy emotions. Such identification is the essence of the sympathetic contract. The poem asks the reader to "be someone," but it must be someone the reader can reach to by an ideal extension of his own sympathies. "Yes," he must conclude, "on these premises I can accept this way of taking the subject and myself as meaningful."

When, on the other hand, the poet becomes untrustworthy within his mask (and let "mask" be taken to mean "the total complex of tone and attitude"), then the reader has no choice but to look down on the poet.

APPLICATION

1. Put the quotation from "The Sympathetic Contract" into your own words. Think of a poem that breaks the sympathetic contract for you. If you can't think of a poem, use song lyrics. Share your choice and explanation with a partner.

2. Write a poem with a subject similar to the one on page 186 (enduring hardship or growing stronger from difficult experiences). Have your speaker talk about his or her experience in a way that will enable your audience to feel a connection with the speaker. This will likely be harder than it appears! You may wish to work with a partner, or use peer editors to "test" your lines on.

Sentimentality Versus Authentic Feeling

One common way that writers break the sympathetic contract is through sentimentality. *Sound and Sense: An Introduction to Poetry*[14] explains that sentimental literature

> aims primarily at stimulating the emotions directly rather than at communicating experience truly and freshly; it depends on trite and well-tried formulas for exciting emotion.... It oversimplifies; it is unfaithful to the full complexity of human experience.

Examine the following poem (author unknown).[15] What parts of it feel authentic to you? Where does it oversimplify or rely on "well-tried formulas"?

Keep Believing in Yourself

There may be days
when you get up in the morning
and things aren't the way
you had hoped they would be.

That's when you have to
tell yourself that things will get better.
There are times when people
disappoint you and let you down,

but those are the times
when you must remind yourself
to trust your own judgments and opinions,
to keep your life focused on believing in yourself

and all that you are capable of.
There will be challenges to face
and changes to make in your life,
and it is up to you to accept them.

Constantly keep yourself headed
in the right direction for you.
It may not be easy at times,
but in those times of struggle

you will find a stronger sense of who you are,
So when the days come that are filled
with frustration and unexpected responsibilities,
remember to believe in yourself

and all you want your life to be,
because the challenges and changes
will only help you to find the goals
that you know are meant to come true for you.

In contrast, examine the following poem by Langston Hughes on a similar subject.[16] Does it avoid sentimentality? If so, how?

Mother to Son

Well, son, I'll tell you:
Life for me ain't been no crystal stair.
It's had tacks in it,
And splinters,
And boards torn up,
And places with no carpet on the floor—
Bare.
But all the time
I'se been a-climbin' on,
And reachin' landin's,
And turnin' corners,
And sometimes goin' in the dark
Where there ain't been no light.
So, boy, don't you turn back.
Don't you set down on the steps
'Cause you finds it kinder hard.
Don't you fall now—
For I'se still goin', honey,
I'se still climbin',
And life for me ain't been no crystal stair.

Perhaps you do not feel bothered by sentimentality. If so, you are not alone. The commercial success of "easy listening" pop songs, greeting cards, and collections of inspirational poems and stories demonstrates the wide audience for material that, though predictable, is quickly accessible and makes its audience feel good. And if you are skilled at writing sentimental verse, you will likely have a more financially secure future than your high-brow, purist cohorts! However, you may find pleasure and accomplishment in getting the feeling on paper just right, describing it in a way that resonates, and which is unique. You will all have different examples of poems or song lyrics that resonate for you. Think of one and take a few minutes to identify why it speaks to you and *how* it speaks to you. Does it use powerful words or phrases? Does it use imagery? repetition? pleasing sounds? Naming what you like about other poets' works will help you to find ways to present authentic emotion and experience in your own poems.

Sometimes sentimentality occurs when a writer uses poetic conventions, tones, rhythms, and rhyme schemes that seem old-fashioned to the contemporary reader. For example, read the following poem (author unknown).[17]

Out in the Fields with God

The little cares that fretted me,
I lost them yesterday
Among the fields above the sea,
Among the winds at play,
Among the lowing of the herds,
The rustling of the trees,
Among the singing of the birds,
The humming of the bees.

The foolish fears of what might pass
I cast them all away
Among tile clover-scented grass,
Among the new-mown hay,
Among the hushing of the corn,
Where drowsy poppies nod,
Where ill thoughts die and good are born—
Out in the fields of God.

Though the poem has a timeless subject—the beauty of nature and its effect on the speaker—if you addressed the subject in this way today, your poem would certainly sound dated and simplistic. The sing-song rhythm, the outdated use of words such as *fretted* and *ill*, and even the sentence structure in the first two lines of each verse would strike today's readers as old-fashioned. Thus, though the poem has both insight and charm, mimicking the style in this poem would make your work sound old-fashioned and sentimental.

Again, if you rely on imagery and detail to present emotion rather than describing how you feel or how the reader should feel, you are more likely to avoid sentimentality. You saw some examples of this technique in Merriam's "New Love" (page 185) and Atwood's "you fit into me" (page 184).

Examine how the following poem by Bobbi Katz reveals the speaker's feelings about fall and nostalgia for summer:[18]

October Saturday

All the leaves have turned to cornflakes.
It looks as if some giant's baby brother
has tipped the box
and scattered them upon our lawn—
millions and millions of cornflakes—
crunching, crunching under our feet.
When the wind blows,
they rattle against each other,
nervously chattering.
We rake them into piles—

Dad and I.
Piles and piles of cornflakes!
A breakfast for a whole family of giants!
We do not talk much as we rake—
a word here—
a word there.
The leaves are never silent.

Inside the house my mother is packing
short sleeved shirts and faded bathing suits—
rubber clogs and flippers
in a box marked SUMMER.

We are raking,
Dad and I.
Raking, raking.
The sky is blue, then orange, then gray.
My arms are tired.
I am dreaming of the box marked summer.

Note again that poems needn't be complex in order to present authentic feeling. Rather, they need to describe experiences in a vivid, not clichéd way, and let the imagery speak for itself. Instead of writing, "My baby's left me and I feel so all alone," Jean Hillabold[19] wrote this poem:

Disappointment

I waited for you
Until the avocados on my table
Turned to dust;
Until my curtains faded
From the heat of my stare;
And my feet wore down the carpet
And the wood under it;
Until my plants all died
And the cat ran away
To find a normal life;
Until my alarm clock exploded
And my fingernails became long knives;
Until the snow piled up to my third-floor windows.

I wanted you to know
That I moved to a better location
Where time trots faster.
I have a new Persian rug
And some healthy philodendrons
That complement my colour scheme.
The members of my Tuesday-night group
Are so witty
That I'm collecting their *bon mots*
With some of my sketches and photographs
For a book to be published in time for Christmas.
Do look for it.
My phone number is unlisted.
I don't give out my address
To just anyone,
And I'm rarely home.

If you tried to contact me, I wouldn't know it.
If you pounded on my door,
Sobbing my name,
The neighbours wouldn't recognize you
And would call the police.
You could have sent a letter to my old address,
Saying "sorry," and "please," and "let me know,"
But it never reached me.

If I still cry sometimes;
If I still wear the necklace you gave me
In the hope of absorbing your strength,
The better to fight you
And to break hearts,
You never ask.
Your silence coats my walls
Like ice on rock.

The image in the final two lines suggests the depth of pain and loneliness of the speaker despite the efforts she's made to change her life. Finally, examine the following haiku by Kaneko Tota:[20]

After a heated argument
I go out into the street
And become a motorcycle

In just fourteen words, the poet conveys both the event and his physical and emotional reaction to it. The poet's choice of the word *become* rather than *ride* is the key to expressing the speaker's rage and frustration so powerfully and compactly.

APPLICATION

1. Examine a collection or anthology of poetry, paying particular attention to poems about specific emotions or with first-person speakers. How does (or doesn't) the poet avoid sentimentality?

2. Choose a specific feeling. (There are many charts of "feeling words" on the Internet if you need help.) For the feeling you choose, do the following:
   • describe it using three or four adjectives
   • show it through a metaphor or an extended metaphor
   • show it through imagery
   You can develop one image in 8 to 10 lines (or more), or you can present a series of images that suggest the emotion.

3. Find an example of a sentimental verse (greeting cards are a good resource here). Identify the dominant emotion and the message of the verse; then rewrite the verse to communicate the intention in a more poetic way.

4. What is the place of sentimentality in our lives? Should we shun sentimental verse altogether or does it have its uses? Discuss these questions in your class.

Freshness

Another simple way to get closer to expressing yourself in your own way is by avoiding clichés. Clichés are worn-out expressions such as "apple of my eye" or "burning your bridges." A cliché may once have been a powerful expression, but it has lost its effect from overuse. Using "burning your bridges" in a poem, for example, is unlikely to cause the reader to pause and picture those bridges on fire (unless, perhaps, you extended the metaphor). (See pages 28 to 30 for more information on clichés.) Pay attention to your reading process as you read the following poem (author unknown) from an inspirational poetry Web site.[21] What do you picture as you read the words?

Wisdom for the Road

Cherish things while you still have them,
before they're gone,
and you realize how precious they really are.

Life can only be understood backwards,
but it must be lived forwards.

Everything in life is temporary.
So if things are going good,
enjoy it because it won't last forever.
And if things are going bad,
don't worry because it won't last forever either.

Destiny is not a matter of chance,
it is a matter of choice;
it is not a thing to be waited for,
it is a thing to be achieved.

A journey of a thousand miles
begins with a single step.

Never cross a bridge
without knowing how to swim the tides.

If you can't add years to your life
Add life to your years.

Though this poem gives good advice, you have probably heard a lot of it before, stated in similar words. When phrases sound so familiar, it's hard to gain insight, or to experience surprise or delight while reading them. Consider instead, the following song lyrics, which could also be called "wisdom for the road." This poem by Michael Bennett uses an old Irish blessing as its refrain.[22]

The Rocky Road

May the rocky road you're travelling
Be a stone's throw from your dreams
May the Lord above be gracious
Should you stumble in between

Toss a coin in every fountain
Make a wish on every star
But if it's not on love you're counting
That won't get you very far

> *May you find the One who loves you*
> *May you always keep your head*
> *'May you be in heaven half an hour*
> *Before the devil knows you're dead'*

With no worries for tomorrow
And no cares for yesterday
May you find your courage laughing
As your troubles kneel to pray

Ain't it tragic, ain't it lovely
How this life will spin you 'round
May you always find the strength
To get your feet back on the ground

Interestingly, this song, too, uses clichés. However, Bennett connects and extends the clichés in ways that cause the listener to picture the image: "May the rocky road you're travelling / Be a stone's throw from your dreams." The playfulness here makes the imagery come alive, unlike the overused phrases in "Wisdom for the Road." Though pop music listeners tend to be more forgiving of trite language, clichés, and sentimentality than are readers and writers of other kinds of poetry, successful songwriters, like today's free verse poets, also strive to use imagery in surprising ways. Thus, as you express yourself in poetry, strive for authenticity in what you say and innovation in how you say it.

1. Sometimes setting limits or rules for your poetry will help you to see a subject in a new light. For example, writing poems by cutting out words from old magazines or books limits you to the words you can find in them, but it can produce fresh and intriguing images and phrases. Your cut-out words can become rough drafts that you alter to craft a finished poem.

   Similarly, choosing to write a sonnet on your subject, sticking carefully to the required regular rhythm, structure, and rhyme scheme can help you to think about your subject in new ways as you seek for words that fit the needs of the form.

2. Have a peer editor go through an earlier piece of your writing (free writing or poetry). He or she should underline phrases that are trite or clichéd. Find better replacements.

Words

Whenever W.H. Auden met a young person who said "I have important things to say," he offered no encouragement, but if the budding writer said "I like hanging around words, listening to what they say," he knew this might be a poet.

JOEL CONARROE[23]

Words are, of course, the building blocks of any piece of writing. In poetry, they are perhaps more important than in other forms of writing because there are fewer of them. Poetry is a compressed way of speaking, and every word must contribute to the overall impact of the poem. Consider Coleridge's advice:[24] "I wish our clever young poets would remember my homely definitions of prose and poetry; that is, prose—words in their best order; poetry—the best words in their best order."

Finding the best words requires some specialized knowledge of language and how it works. An understanding of English grammar, for instance, will certainly help you to craft your work effectively. We don't have room here to give you a refresher course in grammar, but as a writer, you will need to consult a good English handbook regularly. Simple grammatical concepts such as keeping verb tense consistent and using passive voice sparingly will strengthen your writing. In this section we will look at a number of concepts to apply specifically to the poetry you write in this unit and more generally to all of the writing you do.

Vocabulary

Poets need substantial vocabularies, not because they need to use impressive or flowery diction, but because they need to find the *best* word for their purpose, that is, the most exact word for their meaning and the word that looks and sounds the best in its context. When we speak to one another, we have many nonverbal ways to lend clarity to our messages: facial expressions, gestures, intonation, pauses, and so on. Furthermore, speaking is usually interactive, so the listener can ask questions, probe further, or clarify. In writing, however, the communication is one way. The words do all the work. Thus, you must choose your words with care. It is, of course, easier to be specific and exact if you have many words from which to choose. Just as textile dyers can distinguish between dozens of shades of red because they have names for all of them, so will you want names for the emotions, experiences, and ideas that you want to write about. Poet Eve Merriam says,[25] "I've sometimes spent weeks looking for precisely the right word. [The right word] is like having a tiny marble in your pocket; you can feel it."

Reading widely will help expand your vocabulary quite effortlessly (assuming you, like most writers, enjoy reading). However, you can be quite intentional about expanding vocabulary by looking up unfamiliar words as you come across them, by deliberately using new words in your writing, and by studying synonyms, antonyms, common prefixes, and suffixes. Your local bookstore will carry books with vocabulary-building exercises. You can also subscribe to an on-line vocabulary-building course. At the time of this printing, A.Word.A.Day, http://www.wordsmith.org/awad/, offers its subscribers a free word-of-the-day service with definitions and etymologies (histories) of the words it features.

Using words well will make your writing both more evocative and more authentic. For example, examine the following excerpt from Earl Birney's "David."[26] The poem, set in the mountains of British Columbia, describes the experiences of two young mountain climbers. (The "Finger" in the first line refers to a challenging mountain peak the young men plan to climb.)

> But always we talked of the Finger on Sawback, unknown
> And hooked, till the first afternoon in September we slogged
> Through the musky woods, past a swamp that quivered with
>   frog-song,
> And camped by a bottle-green lake. But under the cold
>
> Breath of the glacier sleep would not come, the moon-light
> Etching the Finger. We rose and trod past the feathery
> Larch, while the stars went out, and the quiet heather
> Flushed, and the skyline pulsed with the surging bloom

Of incredible dawn in the Rockies. David spotted
Bighorns across the moraine and sent them leaping
With yodels the ramparts redoubled and rolled to the peaks
And the peaks to the sun. The ice in the morning thaw

Was a gurgling world of crystal and cold blue chasms,
And seracs that shone like frozen saltgreen waves.

Note how the words in this excerpt are specific and appropriate for the territory Birney is describing: *the feathery larch, the heather, the moraine, ramparts, peaks, chasms, seracs.* But more than being accurate, the words evoke the landscape in the reader's mind. Powerful word choice will fire the imagination of your reader.

Denotation and Connotation

Denotation refers to the dictionary definition of a word. *Connotation* refers to the emotional associations a word has for its users. For example, *house* and *home* both mean "the place one lives." However, for most people, the word *home* has connotations of safety, security, and comfort. Consider the words *plump* and *obese.* Both mean "overweight," but to most people, *plump* sounds more attractive.

As you write, you need to be aware of the nuances of meaning in the words you use. While you can't control the associations your readers will bring to your words, you can choose the word that conveys most precisely what you intend. For example, examine the following sets of words with similar denotations. What are the shades of meaning or connotations of each synonym? Compare your feelings about each word with a partner. Do you bring the same associations?

- poor, broke, needy, impoverished, insolvent

- thin, skinny, lithe

- aggressive, pushy, self-assured, domineering

- dad, father, papa, daddy, my old man

Beware of importing words from a thesaurus to "improve" your writing unless you know the precise meaning of the word. Building your vocabulary is a better strategy than always consulting a thesaurus.

Examine "The Lonely Land" by A.J.M. Smith,[27] and identify the words with strong connotations. Note how the words are *consistent* in their connotation, working together to create a mood of isolation and strange beauty.

The Lonely Land

Cedar and jagged fir
uplift sharp barbs
against the gray
and cloud-piled sky;
and in the bay
blown spume and windrift
and thin, bitter spray
snap
at the whirling sky;
and the pine trees
lean one way.

A wild duck calls
to her mate,
and the ragged
and passionate tones
stagger and fall,
and recover,
and stagger and fall,
on these stones—
are lost
in the lapping of water
on smooth, flat stones.

This is a beauty
of dissonance,
this resonance
of stony strand,
this smoky cry
curled over a black pine
like a broken
and wind-battered branch
when the wind
bends the tops of the pines
and curdles the sky
from the north.

This is the beauty
of strength
broken by strength
and still strong.

When words have or acquire many negative connotations, we tend to invent *euphemisms* to use in the place of the unpleasant word. For instance, instead of stating that someone died, we say she "passed away," "passed on," "went to live with God." Some euphemisms are flippant, making light of the painful or unpleasant. For example, we say someone "kicked the bucket," "bit the bullet," or "is pushing up daisies." Avoid euphemisms in your writing unless you are using them to reveal the character of your speaker or for another specific reason.

APPLICATION

1. Write a free verse poem in which you describe a place. You may use A.J.M. Smith's "The Lonely Land" on page 199 as a model. Use specific details and powerful adjectives. When you finish, choose approximately one word per line and look up synonyms for that word. Rewrite the poem, including at least two synonyms for each word you chose. For example, if you used the first four lines of Smith's poem, the revised poem might look like this:

   Cedar and [jagged, ragged, prickly] fir
   uplift [sharp, pointy, razor-sharp] barbs
   against the [gray, bleak, dreary]
   and cloud-piled sky;

   Now share your poem with a small group or the full class and ask them to choose the best word for each line, justifying their choices. Your discussion will help you become more attuned to the connotations and nuances of different words. After the discussion, write a final version of your poem, choosing the words that you feel are most exact and appealing.

2. Create a poem that is a monologue by a speaker from a specific subculture (teenagers, computer hackers, a cultural group that you know well, and so on). Use the specialized vocabulary and expressions of that speaker. For example, examine "united colours of benneton" by amuna baraka-clarke (page 202).

Sound

I've always striven for a rhythm in the poem that is an exact echo of the content it seeks to explore or expose ... I've always counted syllables in my poems in order to achieve a rhythmic effect that the speaker of the poem can rely on. A poem is a musical score for voice.

PATRICK LANE[28]

Perhaps you already have a well-tuned ear, that is, an ear that listens to the sounds of the words as you write. For you, a word or phrase is right because it just *sounds* right. However, if the starting point of your poems is usually an idea or image, perhaps you need to work at the aural elements of poetry. Sound is not something the average person is good at describing. In our visual culture, we are surrounded by sounds, but we have a hard time describing what it is we like or don't like about a noise. For example, try describing the sound of someone's fingernails on the chalkboard. Likely, you described it by describing its effect on you ("It makes my teeth clench"). As you become a more sophisticated writer, you will craft your poems with the sounds of the words in mind. Following are some concepts with which to experiment.

Rhythm

Rhythm in poetry refers to the measured flow of words, a wave-like recurrence of beat or accent. When the rhythm in a poem is regular—that is, if the accented syllables occur at regular intervals—then we talk of *meter*. If you are a fluent speaker of English, and you tap along to the following nursery rhymes, you will naturally tap on the accents. Try tapping as you read these examples:

> Hey Diddle, Diddle
> The cat and the fiddle

(Did you tap on the "Hey," the second "Did-," "cat," and "fid-"?)

> If all the world were apple pie
> And all the sea were ink
> And all the trees were bread and cheese...

(Did you tap on every second syllable—"all," "world," "ap-," and "pie" in the first line; "all," "sea," and "ink" in the second; and "all," "trees," "bread," and "cheese" in the third?)

You can have a lot of fun writing and reading poems that rely heavily on rhythm for their effects. Perhaps you've read Dennis Lee's poems for children in *Alligator Pie*. Look at this poem by Meguido Zola.[29] It is made up entirely of Canadian place names (better yet, read it aloud).

Canadian Indian place names

Bella Bella, Bella Coola,
Athabaska, Iroquois;
Mesilinka, Osilinka,
Mississauga, Missisquois.
Chippewa, Chippawa,
Nottawasaga;
Malagash, Matchedash,
Shubenacadie;
Couchiching, Nipissing
Scubenacadie.
Shickshock
Yahk
Quaw!

Several vibrant movements in poetry, both in the last century and in the present, depend on rhythm as a primary device. A current example is dub poetry, a genre that originated in Jamaica. Dub poetry, often written in Jamaican Creole, is strongly influenced by African Caribbean oral tradition and by reggae music. Dub poetry is made to be performed, and some well-known dub poets like Canada's Lillian Allen have produced recordings of their poems. Following is an example of a dub poem written by amuna baraka-clarke.[30] Read it aloud to hear the rhythm.

united colours of benneton

what a gwan benneton
what a gwan wid benneton

when i taking dih train
i see dem ads at every stop & i cry out in pain
becuz the images
of i & i
perpetuate all dem
white lies

dem seh blk is bad & white is right
all whitey look like gold
all we is blk as nite
but dat nuh right
dis sight of oppression
so stop all of dis exploitation

cuz it nuh right dese signs if downpression
mih nah 'low dem fih dis fih we blk nation

what a gwan wid benneton ...

everywhere i turn
& everywhere i look
i see dem clothing ads wid jah people
scattered all aroun babylon neighbourhood

i see white goldilocks
& a blk child fox
for dat picture dem need a good box

i see blk ooman
ah nurse white baby
& dem ave dih nerve fih seh dem end slavery

& dere's a white wolf
ready fih nyam blk sheep
lawd how dem love depict we as enemy

& mih nuh understand
how dem so presumptuous
fih show a white man ah grab mih fih mek mih im love

what a gwan wid benneton ... boycott haffi go on!

Along with dub poetry, many contemporary forms of music such as hip hop and rap use rhythm and other sound devices in playful, innovative ways.

APPLICATION

Write a poem of at least ten lines that is made to be spoken. Your poem can be serious, comical, or even nonsensical, as long as it uses rhythm in a pleasing way. Perform it for your classmates or have the class perform it together.

Rhythmic Patterns

Rhythmic patterns have names based on the number of accented syllables in comparison with the unaccented syllables, as well as on the number of accented syllables per line. This is less complicated than it sounds. There are five basic kinds of meter or rhythmic patterns.

1. **Iambic**: This pattern consists of an unaccented syllable followed by an accented syllable. Iambic meter most closely resembles the rhythm of everyday speech in English.

ˇ / ˇ / ˇ / ˇ / ˇ /
If all / the world / were ap / ple / pie

ˇ / ˇ / ˇ /
And all / the sea / were ink

2. **Trochaic:** This pattern consists of an accented syllable followed by an unaccented syllable. Trochaic meter sounds forceful and powerful. Read the following lines from Dionne Brand:[31]

/ ˇ / ˇ
Branch es / fall ing

/ ˇ / ˇ
Rain drops / fly ing

/ ˇ / ˇ
Tree tops/ sway ing

/ ˇ / ˇ
Peo ple / run ning

/ ˇ / ˇ
Big wind / blow ing

3. **Anapestic:** This pattern consists of two unaccented syllables followed by an accented syllable, as seen in these lines from Edgar Allan Poe's "Annabel Lee."

ˇ ˇ / ˇ ˇ / ˇ ˇ / ˇ ˇ /
For the moon / ne ver beams / with out bring / ing me dreams

ˇ ˇ / ˇ ˇ / ˇ ˇ /
Of the beau / ti ful An / na bel Lee

4. **Dactylic:** This pattern consists of one accented syllable followed by two unaccented syllables, exemplified in these lines in "Charge of the Light Brigade" by Alfred, Lord Tennyson.

/ ˇ ˇ / ˇ ˇ
"For ward, the / light Bri gade!"

/ ˇ ˇ / ˇ ˇ
Was there a / man dis may'd?

5. **Spondaic:** This pattern consists of two accented syllables. Spondees are usually used for variation within another pattern. Compound words are examples of spondees.

/ / / / / /
heart break   child hood   base ball

The following line from Milton's *Paradise Lost*, which is written in iambic meter, begins with three spondees.

Rocks, caves / lakes, fens / bogs dens / and shades / of death

Along with identifying the rhythmic pattern, we can also talk about the number of metrical feet per line. A foot is a unit of meter. For the first four types of meter listed (iambic, trochaic, anapestic, and dactylic), a foot consists of one stressed syllable and the unstressed syllables that go with it. So, for example, the line "If all / the world / were ap/ple pie" contains four metric feet. So does, "For the moon / never beams / without bring/ing me dreams." The names for metrical lines are as follows:

monometer	one-foot line
dimeter	two-foot line
trimeter	three-foot line
tetrameter	four-foot line
pentameter	five-foot line
hexameter	six-foot line
heptameter	seven-foot line
octometer	eight-foot line

Traditionally, most poetry was written in regular verse forms that used a consistent rhythmic pattern. You are probably familiar with some of these verse forms, such as the ballad, the couplet, or the sonnet, from your study of poetry in other English courses.

APPLICATION

Write a four-line verse in each of the following patterns:
- iambic pentameter
- trochaic tetrameter
- anapestic dimeter
- dactylic trimeter

Which meter do you prefer and why? Do the different meters seem to lend themselves to certain styles or tones of writing? Which was easiest to write in? Which was the hardest? Are you pleased with your drafts? Why or why not?

Rhythm in Free Verse Poetry

Today, many poets prefer to write in free verse, meaning they do not use a regular rhythmic pattern or a regular rhyme scheme (see page 207 for a discussion of rhyme scheme). However, free verse poets do not ignore rhythm. When you write free verse, you can use rhythm to emphasize certain words or phrases, and to make the words flow, even with no consistent rhythmic pattern. William Stafford, a contemporary American poet who uses free verse, says this about using sound in his poems:[32] "I want all the syllables to be in there like a school of fish, flashing, relating to other syllables in other words … fluently carrying the reader by subliminal felicities all the way to the limber last line." Stafford's free verse poems generally use the language of everyday speech and mostly regular stanza lengths and line lengths. Read the following example aloud and listen to the flow of the words.[33] How does Stafford use rhythm to please the ear?

One Time

When evening had flowed between houses
and paused on the schoolground, I met
Hilary's blind little sister following
the gray smooth railing still warm from the sun
with her hand; and she stood by the edge
holding her face upward waiting
while the last light found her cheek
and her hair, and then on over the trees.

You could hear the great sprinkler arm
of water find and then leave the pavement,
and pigeons telling each other their dreams
or the dreams they would have. We were
deep in the well of shadow by then, and I
held out my hand, saying, "Tina, it's me—
Hilary says I should tell you it's dark,
and, oh, Tina, it is. Together now—"

And I reached, our hands touched,
and we found our way home.

Rhyme

Rhyme, like regular rhythmic patterning, is not used as often in today's poetry. However, experimenting with rhyme can help you become attuned to the music of words. It can also help you become more innovative in your use of words, because, in deciding to use a rhyme scheme, you add a new challenge to your crafting of the poem.

You should be aware of several types of rhyme.

masculine rhyme	• one syllable rhymes with another syllable *sit* and *bit*; *heart* and *smart*
feminine rhyme	• two syllables rhyme *rattle* and *battle*; *blemish* and *Flemish*
triple rhyme	• three syllables rhyme *victorious* and *glorious*
near rhyme or eye rhyme	• words rhyme to the eye but not the ear *moves* and *loves*
end rhyme	• rhymes occur at the end of two or more lines of verse *As I was going up the* stair *I met a man who wasn't* there.
internal rhyme	• rhymes occur within a line of poetry *Who shall be* king *of the little kids'* swing? *(Dennis Lee)*

Many forms of verse depend on certain arrangements of rhymes, called the *rhyme scheme*. Rhyme schemes are based on the last sound in each line of a poem. To identify the rhyme scheme of a poem, give the sound at the end of the first line the letter *a*. The sound at the end of the second line gets the letter *b* if it doesn't rhyme with line 1, or the letter *a* again if it does rhyme. The next new sound gets the letter *c* and so on. For example, here is the rhyme scheme of a limerick (author unknown):

There was a young lady from Niger	*a*
Who smiled as she rode on a tiger	*a*
They came back from the ride	*b*
With the lady inside	*b*
And the smile on the face of the tiger.	*a*

Many special verse forms are based on the type of rhyme scheme each demands. For instance, the Shakespearean sonnet has a rhyme scheme of *abab cdcd efef gg*. The Italian or Petrarchan sonnet has a rhyme scheme of *abba abba* for the first eight lines, and either *cde cde* or *cd cd cd* for the final six lines. Other rhymed verse forms include heroic couplets (rhymed couplets in iambic pentameter) and the villanelle, a poem of nineteen lines with a rhyme scheme of *aba aba aba aba abaa*. An example of a villanelle is Dylan Thomas's "Do Not Go Gentle into That Good Night."

Metrical Variation

Keep in mind that the purpose of using rhythm and sound is not only to make the poem pleasing to the ear, but also to echo the sense, or meaning, of the poem. Thus, as an obvious example, if your poem is describing a traffic jam, you would not use a lilting rhythm and euphonious sounds. Through manipulating meter and line length and through using the devices of sound, you can influence how quickly or slowly a word, phrase, or line is read. You can create pauses or emphasize words that are important in meaning. Following are some generalizations about sound in poetry:

- A short line that follows longer lines will usually cause the reader to read slowly or to pause in order to give the line as much time as the one before it. This causes the reader to dwell on the picture in this line.

- A long line will usually cause the reader to read rapidly in order to fit the line into an established pattern. This results in a sense of lightness, speed, or vigorous activity.

- Changing a foot from the basic pattern emphasizes the thought of the word that receives the change.

- Two or more stressed syllables in succession emphasize the thought of each word and their relation to each other.

- Great irregularity in any one line (especially several stressed one-syllable words) often expresses strong emotion.

- A sound device can also emphasize certain words and phrases. (See the next section for more information on devices of sound.)

Research the various traditional verse forms. Choose one, or come up with your own verse form that uses a regular rhythm and rhyme scheme. (If you are new at this, iambic meter is likely the best choice for your rhythm, as it most closely resembles English speaking patterns.) Write a poem in the form you choose. What is difficult about writing in a regular pattern? What are the advantages? When you have finished your poem, give it to a partner to identify the rhyme scheme and meter.

Other Sound Devices

Here are other sound devices that you may use as tools when writing your poems.

Onomatopoeia—the use of a word to imitate natural sounds, such as *meow, sizzle,* or *crackle*

Assonance—the repetition of a vowel sound in two or more words in a line of poetry, such as *lake* and *wail*, or eerie and *deep*
"Lightning blinks, striking things in its midst with blinding light." (Christian Bök)

Alliteration—the repetition of the initial letter or sound in two or more words in a line of poetry
"whirring as wound wires whir" (Felice Holman)

Consonance—the repetition of a consonant sound in two or more words in a line of poetry
"His dark nose twitches, flares, scans/ the air for a scent" (Ree Young)

Euphony—sweet, melodious sounds, a pleasing arrangement of sounds
"from fires alight in rooms below/the stillness holds...." (Fran Newman)

Cacophony—harsh, discordant sounds
"All day cars mooed and shrieked / Hollered and bellowed and wept." (James Reaney)

Repetition—the use of a word, phrase, or line more than once in a poem. Repeating something adds emphasis to it. A ballad, for example, uses a *refrain*, a short stanza that is repeated throughout the ballad.

As you develop your ear in writing poetry, you can experiment with these devices. Use them sparingly, because overusing a device can have the effect not of power or beauty, but of silliness. For example, overuse of alliteration produces tongue-twisters (such as "Peter Piper picked a peck of pickled peppers"). Tongue-twisters are entertaining, but not poetic.

APPLICATION

1. Analyze a poem that uses devices of sound extensively. Do more than a treasure hunt for techniques; rather, identify how the sounds reflect or develop the sense and meaning of the lines. Some poems that should be easy to find are:
   Gerard Manley Hopkins, "God's Grandeur"
   Edgar Allan Poe, "Annabel Lee"
   John Keats, "Ode to Autumn"
   Edna St. Vincent Millay, "Love is not all"
   Joy Kogawa, "Rush Hour Tokyo"
   A J. M. Smith, "The Lonely Land" (page 199)

2. Write out a favourite poem of yours in prose form. (Try to choose a poem with strong rhythmic elements.) Then exchange the prose form versions with a partner and break the poem you receive into lines without looking at the original. Justify your line break choices by considering rhythm, sound, and line length.

3. Write a descriptive poem about a noisy place or activity (for example, a baseball game, a small child's birthday party, a crowded school bus, or a concert). Choose words that will let your reader/listener *hear* the subject/setting.

4. In each of the following paired quotations, the named poet wrote the version that more successfully adapts sound to sense. As specifically as possible, account for the superiority of the better version.[34]

   a) Your talk attests how bells of singing gold
      Would sound at evening over silent water.

      Your low voice tells how bells of singing gold
      Would sound at twilight over silent water. (Edward Arlington Robinson)

   b) A thousand streamlets flowing through the lawn,
      The moan of doves in gnarled ancient oaks,
      And quiet murmuring of countless bees.

Myriads of rivulets hurrying through the lawn,
The moan of doves in immemorial elms,
And murmuring of innumerable bees. (Alfred, Lord Tennyson)

c) The hands of the sisters Death and Night incessantly softly wash
again, and ever again, this soiled world.

The hands of the soft twins Death and Night repeatedly wash
again, and ever again, this dirty world. (Walt Whitman)

Image

A poet sees the world in careful detail; nothing is too ordinary or insignificant to miss the poet's attention. Centuries ago in Japan, poets began writing haiku: three-line poetry. The first line contains five syllables; the second, seven; and the third, five. Haiku poems traditionally use nature as their subject and present one or two images without explaining their meaning explicitly. Examine the following poem by Soseki:[36]

Over the wintry
forest, winds howl in a rage
with no leaves to blow.

In the early 1900s a movement called Imagism began in the United States and England. Drawing from the traditions of Asian poetry, the imagist poets focused on using precise words and concrete details to describe their subjects. Furthermore, they let the word picture that they created speak for itself; that is, they did not explain what the images represented. For example, in William Carlos Williams's often-anthologized poem "The Red Wheelbarrow" (page 212), Williams does not tell us what depends on the wheelbarrow or what the red wheelbarrow or white chickens represent.[37]

The Red Wheelbarrow

so much depends
upon

a red wheel
barrow

glazed with rain
water

beside the white
chickens.

Williams wrote poems about ordinary things and experiences, using ordinary language. He draws our attention to the significance, the excitement, and the beauty of simple, everyday subjects.

Ezra Pound, another imagist, disliked many of the qualities of nineteenth-century poetry. He avoided regular rhythm and rhyme schemes, flowery language, and lengthy description of feeling or meaning. Instead, he focused on describing honest, ordinary feelings (including negative feelings) in plain language and few words. For instance, his two-line poem "In a Station of the Metro"[38] was originally 30 lines, but Pound pared the poem down to all that he considered necessary for his intent.

The apparition of these faces in the crowd;
Petals on a wet, black bough.

James Barry presents the following "Tenets of the Imagist Movement":

1. Express the topic directly—either from the objective or subjective point of view.

2. Present the topic in images (word pictures). Use vivid, colourful images and not vague, cerebral generalities.

3. Employ the exact word, not the nearly exact word.

4. Write using the language of the senses. Appeal to colour, sound, taste, touch, and smell.

5. Make the poem brief and economical, without any unnecessary words. Concentration is the essence of poetry.

6. Use free verse rhythms—cadence based on the natural rhythms of speech.[39]

Imagist poems are not simple, even though the language is. If you read them carefully, they demand your thoughtful participation, since the meaning is suggested, but not explained. Because the imagists are still strongly influencing poetry today, a familiarity with their work will help your own writing of poetry. Many of the examples you have read in this chapter rely primarily on imagery to develop their themes. See, for example, "The Lonely Land" (page 199).

Image poems can focus on things (like William Carlos Williams's red wheelbarrow), persons, settings, or even incidents. When writing image poems, you want to present enough information to help the reader draw the same conclusions as you, but don't draw the conclusions for the reader. Note how the following poem by Sharon Page[40] (which won the Canadian Youth Poetry Competition—Senior Division in 2000) characterizes a person and shows the speaker's feelings about the person through images.

Water Buffalo + Emily = Love

Emily Fraser loves water buffalo
because they don't use toilet paper
or shampoo or put violets
in film canisters
like she does for Mother's Day.

In kindergarten the fort I made with her
was in the blackberry bushes
(water buffalo stake out their territory)
fascinating tunnels along the neighbour's fence
where we hid
a collection of dolls' shoes
and bottle caps.
At the end of recess
we got bloody fingers on prickles
(water buffalo don't use bandaids).
(They don't like mustard or
Barbie backpacks.)

Emily draws pictures of them
in her journal
blobs of brown crayon
against deserted hills and zebra grass.
Beat up a kid once
for the blue felt
(water buffalo lock horns over hollows of muck).

At parent-teacher interviews
Mrs. Steida suggests therapy.

In the following excerpt from a poem "Shawnandithit (Last of the Beothuks)" by Joan Crate,[41] notice how you can use a person as an image for something else. In this poem, Shawnandithit, the last of the Beothuks, becomes an image for a lost civilization. (The Beothuks were an Aboriginal nation from Newfoundland. They all died through conflict with the European settlers and through contact with the diseases that the Europeans brought. The last known Beothuk, Shawnandithit, spent the final five years of her life with a European family and died of tuberculosis in 1829.)

And so Shawnandithit, with Mother and sister dead
and none of your people left beating against winter,
it is your turn, the last Beothuk, broken
and barren, beautiful as loose feathers on stone.
In the whitemen's steaming kitchen, you falter, look
to the wall, the clock you can't read, then sketch
them stories of lingering death, marriage ceremonies
and hunting parties, love, and your lingering death.

A companion poem, "The Blizzard Moans My Name," uses contrasting settings—the European settler's kitchen and the stormy night outside—to show the conflict between two ways of life as well as the loss of one way of life.[42]

I sit here by the cookstove,
feet pushed too close, try to quench
the burning bark dazzle of unfreezing toes

and I will not answer

I will stay in this sultry kitchen,
Gaze outside glass at my home, the night,
The terrible snow, and try not to hear

the howl that feeds me empty, strokes me cold

Fingers scratch at the upholstered chair,
pull at springs. My throat parches with blood
and I drink tea from a china cup, nod gratitude
to the woman with skin starting to tear
like the paper they hand me to draw on.
No matter how many meals she cooks for me
it is not enough to fill.
No matter how many scented shawls she wraps
around my shoulders, it is not enough to thaw

wordless voices splintering ice through my lungs

I chew on a chocolate biscuit, sweet
lie in my mouth. I will stay
in this crackling log house and hide
from the ghosts who call my name—Shawnandithit—
turning me to storm

and all their destined love.

Note that the poet never states directly how she feels or tells the reader how to feel about the situation she describes. However, the poignancy of the details creates empathy for the speaker's isolation and a powerful sense of loss that her way of life is gone.

APPLICATION

1. Find some contemporary poets or songwriters that write in the imagist tradition. Analyze their work, identifying the images they use, and describing what makes their word choice exact and how they appeal to the senses.

2. Choose an abstract word (for example, *love, loyalty, hatred, kindness, mercy,* or *motherhood*). Write a poem that uses concrete images to suggest the essence of the abstract word you have chosen. You may either use one image or several different images. Do not use rhyme or a regular rhythm.

3. Write a 10- to 20-line poem about a place. Select details to create a clear word picture. Try to express both feeling and idea through the imagery. Avoid *telling* the reader what to think or feel. Use free verse.

4. Write a poem that describes a sensory experience. Use images so that the reader can see, smell, hear, taste, or feel what you're describing. For instance, instead of saying that the ice cream was "delicious," describe its sweetness, its smoothness on your tongue, and so on.

5. Choose some small object or entity for close observation: a stone, a fungus, a wristwatch, an onion, a ladybug, a sewing needle, a drop of pond water, or a piece of your own hair as seen under a microscope; a scab, a toenail, or an ice cube ... a candy-bar wrapper, a pine cone, a leaf, a frog, or a foam cup. Whatever you choose, give it your closest attention. Describe in writing all your sensory impressions of this object, all the details you can muster. You can start with prose or write your observations in loosely broken lines, whichever seems easier. Next, generalize from the things you observe to some meaning drawn from your observations. For example, describe a rock in great detail. Then make a generalization about life, or time, or the human condition, based on that description. Don't be afraid to overdo it. You can cut back in revision. Finally, experiment with making your prose or poetry rough draft into a polished poem.[43]

Figurative Language

No doubt you are already using figurative language in your poetry, especially if you've been writing poems based on images. The following are the most common devices:

The poem is a way of tapping that source of [unconscious] power and strength and putting things simultaneously together which are apparently quite different. To me this is what distinguishes poetry from most prose, which is linear and sequential. In poetry many things are going on at the same time and these layers of time and density of language make the poem uniquely poetic.

DONALD HALL[44]

- simile: a comparison between two unlike things, made explicit by the words *like* or *as*
  "My heart is like a singing bird" (Christina Rossetti)

- metaphor: a comparison between two unlike things
  "If you were a scoop of vanilla / And I were the cone where you sat" (X.J. Kennedy)

- personification: giving human qualities to inanimate objects
  the sun smiled

- hyperbole: exaggeration or overstatement
  back-breaking work

- understatement: deliberately downplaying the statement, saying less than is true; the result is usually witty

- irony: contrast or incongruity between what is said and what is meant, or between expectation and reality

- allusion: a reference to something in another work of literature or art or to an historical event

- symbol: a person, place, or thing that represents something more than itself

These definitions and examples are deceptively simple. Good poets use these devices in rich and layered ways. A metaphor can be extended throughout a poem; the entire subject of the poem can be a symbol for something else; an ironic tone can completely undermine the literal meaning of the speaker's words; a carefully chosen allusion can be the key to understanding the poem. To learn how to use these elements effectively in your own poetry, you will have to experiment. Dabble, muddle, and play. Use the suggested activities below or make up your own assignments to work with these elements regularly in your writing. Though you have studied poetry before, read each poem again as a fellow poet, to see how other poets use these devices, and try their techniques.

 **APPLICATION**

1. Write a poem that uses imagery (or use a draft from an earlier writing exercise). Extend the images in the poem by using similes or metaphors.

2. Write a poem that uses a series of metaphors and/or similes to describe its subject. See Sylvia Plath's poems "Mushrooms" and "Metaphors," Michael Ondaatje's "Sweet Like a Crow," or X.J. Kennedy's "What We Might Be, What We Are" as examples.

3. Write a poem that alludes to a famous painting or work of art.

4. Write a poem about writing without mentioning writing.

5. Write a poem about an abstract idea or feeling. Instead of naming the feeling or idea, use a symbol or symbols to express your thoughts.

Line Breaks in Free Verse Poetry

We have talked little yet about form in free verse poetry. Where the lines break and how the poem looks on the paper can also add to its meaning and effect on the reader. Paul Claudel[45] wrote "The poem is not made from these letters that I drive in like nails, but of the white which remains on the paper." How you choose to arrange your lines depends on a number of things. The following essay by Glen Kirkland[46] provides some guidelines and examples:

Line Divisions in Free Verse Poetry

One of free verse poetry's best features—irregular line lengths—puzzles some readers and frustrates some writers. The critical question is this: what are the reasons for dividing a line in one specific place and not in any other place? An examination of some poems and excerpts will reveal that writers can have one or several reasons for dividing a line in a particular way.

At the most basic level, a writer may divide lines into sense units, usually clusters of words that contain sufficient thought to be sensible to the reader. Lines, then, tend to be clauses or phrases that can be read in an easy sweep of the eyes. Often, such lines end where the reader might draw a breath if reading aloud, or where a form of punctuation occurs or is implied. The following poem illustrates this:

Morning Mask

Framed in cold silver,
his morning mask is distant,
slack—even dead—
as he tugs tighter
the slim, austere
knot of boredom
and jackets himself
in the wooly warmth of
predictability.

The small boy
who buried treasures,
rescued prisoners of war,
and shot savage tigers
saves only his money now.

He sips the tedium of his days
like tepid tea, and—
surrounded by killing quiet—
fills his emptiness with words:

"This may not be much,"
   he tells himself,
"but at least I will have
   a comfortable death."

While some lines in "Morning Mask" were divided for special emphasis, which we will discuss later, most were divided into sense units for comfortable, clear reading. Two observations will make this even more apparent: first, the number of articles, prepositions, and conjunctions on the left margin of the poem indicates that several lines have been divided into grammatical units; second, the number of punctuation marks on the right margin of the poem reveals that several lines have been divided where a reader might draw a breath or pause in reading.

In addition to dividing lines into sense units, writers of free verse may divide lines in order to give special emphasis to significant words or images, or to enhance the impact of the poem. For example, note the placement of the key words and the importance of the shorter lines in this poem:

Departure

leaving home
I stand with my dead
grandmother's suitcases in hand
coat slung carelessly over my shoulder
the car loaded down with
all my possessions
packed in boxes tied doubly
with string
(like a refugee from some
old movie)

my father coughs
shakes my hand
and offers me
a last-minute yellow screwdriver
with interchangeable heads

my mother kisses me
and says
as long as I have a sense of
humor
I will
survive

in the doorway now
I smile awkwardly and mutter
goodbye

my mother asks
again
have you
got
everything

yes
I say
I've got it
all

and frightened suddenly
I want to paint my name
in huge red letters
on the ceilings and walls
of every room
carve my initials in
the coffee table
and leave a life-sized reproduction of myself
asleep upstairs

The placement of the key words and images in this poem reveal other reasons for dividing a line in a particular way. "Departure" is about relationships, and the words that identify the poem's characters tend to fall on the left margin (I ... grandmother's ... my father ... my mother ... I ... I ... my mother ... I ... I), where they receive emphasis in reading. Other words and images are emphasized by their isolation in a short line (leaving home ... survive ... goodbye ... everything ... all). If we examine those, we see that they underline the overwhelming impact of making a break from one's family.

The emotional significance of the moment is emphasized, too, by the shorter lines. The speaker is preparing to leave home for perhaps the rest of his life, and he realizes that as he lingers in the doorway. The shorter lines in the middle of the poem help to convey the inability of the characters to express adequately what they feel in such an emotional moment. The longer lines at the end read more rapidly, thereby conveying the rush of emotions that suddenly overtake the speaker. Clearly, then, the line divisions in a free verse poem can make an important contribution to the poem's impact.

The previously mentioned reasons for dividing lines at a particular point addressed general practices that apply to several lines. Specific, individual lines might be divided at a point that brings out meaning that might otherwise be missed. For example, this excerpt describes a lonely old woman:

> Sitting in winter sunlight,
> surrounded by plants and family
> photos
> frilly doilies and china dogs …

As we read the second line, we expect, for a brief moment, that she has family with her. As we read on and complete the next line, we realize she is surrounded by family photos. This reversal emphasizes more strongly the old woman's loneliness and her attempts to fend it off by surrounding herself with comforting objects. If "photos" had been left on the same line as "family," that effect would have been lost.

A second technique used to bring added meaning to specific lines within a poem is more typographical in nature. Occasionally, a writer can arrange lines to create a concrete, visual effect that helps to communicate the meaning of those individual lines. This excerpt illustrates that well:

> … sometimes
> I feel like
>
>   old clothes
>   piled
>   in a corner

The arrangement of the last three lines suggests isolation and creates a visual image of the old clothes by piling the lines one on the other. While this device can add life to a poem, a caution should be noted. Overuse of this technique can make a poem tedious and "gimmicky."

These are but a few of the reasons a writer might give for dividing a line at a specific point. Because free verse is such a flexible form, poets have been able to divide lines for more subtle effects. A line break may work to suggest a gesture or expression, such as a frown; it may mark a shift of emotions, surprise a reader, create irony, or simply manufacture a pun. There is no limit to the imaginative use of line divisions to add impact to a free verse poem.

APPLICATION

Work with a partner. Take a free verse poem that you have written, and write it out as prose (without its line breaks). Trade the prose version of the poem with a partner and divide one another's poems into lines. Then, in writing or in conversation, justify the choices you made. Refer specifically to the reasons given in Kirkland's essay. (If you disagree with how your partner breaks the lines of your poem, you can change it back after this activity. However, try to identify the reasons for your choices as well.)

THE WRITER'S PROJECTS

Investigating the Writer's Craft

1. In a small group, research an historical period, movement, or genre in poetry, such as the romantic period, beat poetry, Imagistic poetry, ballads, dub poetry, haiku, and so on. Prepare a presentation on your topic. Include visuals (for example, use a bulletin board), and use lots of examples.

2. Research a poet, reading about his or her life, major influences, favourite subjects and themes, and style. Read at least 50 of his or her poems. Then, imitate that poet's style in two or three poems of your own. (*Sleeping on the Wing: An Anthology of Modern Poetry with Essays on Reading and Writing* gives many specific suggestions of how to use a poet's work as a starting place for your own. See The Writer's Reading List on page 224 for bibliographic information.) Also write a greeting card in the style of the poet you choose. The subject of the greeting card should be appropriate for the poet—would he or she send a "missing you" card, a "congratulations on your marriage" card, a bon voyage card, or something different? Write several paragraphs to explain what elements of the poet's attitudes, experience, and craft you are using in the greeting card.

3. Research a poet. Then choose a partner who researched a different poet. Create a dialogue between the two poets that focuses on the differences and similarities in their backgrounds, subjects, and styles. Perform the dialogue for your class.

Practising the Writer's Craft

1. Write some "found poetry." Take a page from a text or technical manual. From the words on that page, create at least two poems. Each poem must have a different theme or purpose.

2. Write a rhetorical poem, that is, a poem that attempts to persuade its audience using emotional appeals, reason, and other persuasive techniques. Your tone can be anything from heartfelt sincerity to comical to ironic. You may want to include facts, examples, testimonials, and so on. Urge the audience to reject opposing viewpoints. Choose one or more dominant arguments on which to focus your appeal. Your poem may use a formal stanza pattern or may be rendered in free verse. Use the poetic devices you've learned. Here are a few possibilities to get your ideas flowing:
   - Plead with a lover not to leave you.
   - Be a product in the supermarket and beg a consumer to buy you.
   - Appeal to someone for forgiveness.
   - Urge someone to see the beauty in life, nature, and so on.
   - Be a book, film, or video game and convince someone to use you.

3. Find a poet with a very distinctive style. Write parodies of two or three of the poet's works, exaggerating the features of his or her style.

4. Write a series of poems (minimum of three) about or from the point of view of an historical figure. You may want to choose someone we know little about and create the missing "history." Use narrative elements and imagery to reveal character. You can examine Joan Crate's poems about Shawnandithit (pages 214 to 215) or Margaret Atwood's *The Journals of Susanna Moodie* for examples.

5. Create an illustrated poetry book—a combination of poetry and visual art. Write an original poem of 20 lines or more, or two to three shorter poems that are thematically linked. Create or find visual images to accompany the poem(s). You can use your own drawings, paintings, photographs, or computer-generated visuals. Then organize your book. The poem(s) can be broken up over several pages or appear on one page with artwork on the page across from it. For examples of illustrated poetry books, see *The Journals of Susanna Moodie* by Margaret Atwood and Charles Pachter[47] or *The Cremation of Sam McGee* by Robert W. Service, illustrated by Ted Harrison.[48]

THE WRITER'S READING LIST

The Writer's Craft

> Dean, Nancy. *Voice Lessons: Classroom Activities to Teach Diction, Detail, Imagery Syntax, and Tone.* Gainesville, FL: Maupin House, 2000.

> Drake, Barbara. *Writing Poetry.* Toronto: Harcourt Brace Jovanovich, 1983.

> Koch, Kenneth and Kate Farrell. *Sleeping on the Wing: An Anthology of Modern Poetry with Essays on Reading and Writing.* New York: Vintage Books, 1982.

Examples of the Writer's Craft

> Anglesey, Zoe, ed. *Spoken Word Poetry.* New York: Ballantine, 1999.

> Barry, James, ed. *Themes on a Journey: Reflections in Poetry.* Scarborough, ON: Nelson, 1989.

> Cameron, Bob, Margaret Hogan, and Patrick Lashmar. *Poetry In Focus.* Toronto: Globe/Modern Curriculum Press, 1983.

> Davies, Richard and Jerry Wowk. *Inside Poetry.* Toronto: Harcourt Canada, 2003.

> de Roche, Joseph, ed. *The Heath Introduction to Poetry.* 2nd ed. Toronto: D.C. Heath, 1984.

> Geddes, Gary, ed. *Twentieth Century Poetry and Poetics.* 4th ed. Toronto: Oxford University Press, 1996.

> Janeczko, Paul B., ed. *The Place My Words Are Looking For: What Poets Say About and Through Their Work.* New York: Simon & Schuster Books for Young Readers, 1990.

> Koch, Kenneth and Kate Farrell. *Sleeping on the Wing: An Anthology of Modern Poetry with Essays on Reading and Writing.* New York: Vintage Books, 1982.

> Perrine, Laurence and Thomas P. Arp. *Sound and Sense: An Introduction to Poetry.* 8th ed. Toronto: HBJ College, 1992.

Endnotes and Credits

Chapter 5

1 W. Somerset Maugham, quoted in Jon Winokur, *Writers on Writing*. Philadelphia: Running Press Book Publishers, 1990, 229.

2 Emily Dickinson, quoted in Winokur, *Writers on Writing*, 224.

3 Elizabeth Drew, quoted in Winokur, *Themes on a Journey: Reflections in Poetry*; James Barry, ed. Scarborough, ON: Nelson, 1989, 66, 67.

4 Bronwen Wallace, "Shyly Slipping a Poem from the Purse," in *Arguments with the World: Essays by Bronwen Wallace*; Joanne Page, ed. Kingston, ON: Quarry Press, 1992. Reprinted by permission of Quarry Press.

5 This activity is adapted from a writing prompt in Jack Heffron, *The Writer's Idea Book*. Cincinnati, OH: Writer's Digest Books, 2000, 142.

6 Stephen Spender, quoted in Winokur, *Writers on Writing*, 234.

7 Excerpted from "A Poet's Advice to Students" by E.E. Cummings. Copyright © 1955, 1965 by the Trustees for the E.E. Cummings Trust. Copyright © 1958, 1965 by George J. Firmage, from *A Miscellany Revised by E.E. Cummings*, edited by George J. Firmage. Used by permission of Liveright Publishing Corporation.

8 Margaret Atwood, quoted in Barry, ed., *Themes on a Journey*, 204.

9 Margaret Atwood, "you fit into me," in *Power of Politics* (Toronto: House of Anansi, 1971, 1996). Reprinted with permission.

10 Eve Merriam, "New Love." From FRESH PAINT by Eve Merriam. Copyright © 1986 Eve Merriam. Used by permission of Marian Reiner.

11 From John Ciardi, *How Does a Poem Mean?* Boston: Houghton Mifflin, 1959, 846–850.

12 Unknown author, "Friendly Obstacles." The Inspirational Place Web site, www.theinspirationplace.com/poems/p25.htm.

13 Ciardi, *How Does a Poem Mean?* 850. Reprinted by permission.

14 Laurence Perrine and Thomas A. Arp, eds., *Sound and Sense: An Introduction to Poetry*, 8th ed. Toronto: HBJ College, 1992, 234–235.

15 Unknown author, "Keep Believing in Yourself." Cyber Quotations Web site, www.cyberquotations.com/poems/keep_believing_in_yourself.htm.

16 Langston Hughes, "Mother to Son." From THE COLLECTED POEMS OF LANGSTON HUGHES by Langston Hughes, copyright © 1994 by The Estate of Langston Hughes. Used by permission of Alfred A. Knopf, a Division of Random House, Inc.

17   Unknown author, "Out in the Fields with God." About.Com Web site,
      http://womenshistory.about.com/library/etext/poem1/b1p_unknown_out_fields.
      htm. This poem has appeared with different titles ("The Little Cares that Fretted
      Me" and "Out in the Fields of God" are two examples) and has been attributed to
      both Elizabeth Barrett Browning and to Louise Imogen Guiney.

18   Bobbi Katz, "October Saturday," in *The Place My Words Are Looking For* by Paul B.
      Janeczko. New York: Simon & Schuster, 1990. Copyright © 1990 by Bobbi Katz.
      Used with permission.

19   "Disappointment" by Jean Hillabold. First published in *Heading Out: The New
      Saskatchewan Poets*, Coteau Books, edited by Anne Szumigalski and Don Kerr,
      © 1986. Reprinted by permission of the author.

20   Haiku by Kaneko Tota from *Modern Japanese Haiku: An Anthology by Makoto Ueda*.
      Toronto: University of Toronto Press, 1976. Reprinted by permission of University of
      Toronto Press.

21   Unknown author, "Wisdom for the Road." Cyber Quotations Web site,
      www.cyberquotations.com/poems/wisdom_for_the_road.htm.

22   "The Rocky Road" by Michael Bennett and Douglas Romanow. Used by permission.

23   Joel Conarroe, quoted in *Six American Poets: An Anthology*; Joel Conarroe, ed. New
      York: Vintage Books, 1993. Quotation cited in Fairfield Review Web site,
      http://www.fairfieldreview.org/fairfield/tfrquotes.nsf/8525625300698706852 55
      91800506d8f/b04e734dc39f61a9852564f80051eb20?OpenDocument.

24   Samuel Taylor Coleridge, quoted in *Writers on Writing*, 235.

25   Eve Merriam, quoted in Janeczko, *The Place My Words Are Looking For*, 65.

26   Excerpted from "David" by Earle Birney. From *The Collected Poems of Earle Birney*.
      Used by permission, McClelland & Stewart Ltd. *The Canadian Publishers*.

27   A.J.M. Smith, "The Lonely Land," in *Poems: New and Collected* by A.J.M. Smith.
      Toronto: McClelland and Stewart. Reprinted by permission of William Toye, Literary
      Executor.

28   Patrick Lane, quoted in *Where The Words Come From: Canadian Poets in
      Conversation*; Tim Bowling, ed. Robert's Creek, BC: Nightwood Editions, 2003, 73.

29   Meguido Zola, "Canadian Indian place names," in *Here Is a Poem*. The League of
      Canadian Poets, 1983. Reprinted by permission of the author.

30   amuna baraka-clarke, "united colours of benneton." Reprinted by permission of
      the author.

31   Excerpted from "Hurricane" by Dionne Brand. From *Earth Magic*, copyright © 1979
      by Dionne Brand.

32   William Stafford, *You Must Revise Your Life*. Ann Arbor, MI: University of Michigan
      Press, 1986, 44.

33   Stafford, "One Time." Copyright 1982, 1998 by the Estate of William Stafford.
      Reprinted from *The Way It Is: New & Selected Poems* with the permission of
      Graywolf Press, Saint Paul, Minnesota.

34 This activity is from *Sound and Sense*, Eighth Edition. Edited by Laurence Perrine and Thomas A. Arp. Toronto: HBJ College Publishers, 1992, pages 205–6.

35 William Burroughs, quoted in Winokur, *Writers on Writing*, 4.

36 Soseki, Haiku, in *Modern Japanese Haiku: An Anthology by Makoto Ueda* by Makoto Ueda. Toronto: University of Toronto Press, 1976, 37. Reprinted by permission of University of Toronto Press.

37 "The Red Wheelbarrow" by William Carlos Williams. From *Collected Poems: 1909–1939*, Volume I, copyright © 1938 by New Directions Publishing Corp. Reprinted by permission of New Directions Publishing Corp.

38 "In a Station of the Metro" by Ezra Pound. From *Personae*, copyright 1926 by Ezra Pound. Reprinted by permission of New Directions Publishing Corporation.

39 Barry, *Themes on a Journey*, 81.

40 "Water Buffalo + Emily = Love" by Sharon Page. From *Vintage 2000*. League of Canadian Poets. Vancouver, BC: Ronsdale Press, 2000.

41 Joan Crate, "Shawnandithit (Last of the Beothuks)," in *Native Writers and Canadian Writing*; ed. W.H. New. Vancouver: University of British Columbia Press, 1992, 40. Reprinted by permission of the author.

42 Joan Crate, "The Blizzard Moans My Name" in *Native Writers and Canadian Writing*; ed. W.H. New. Vancouver: University of British Columbia Press, 1992, 18. Reprinted by permission of the author.

43 From *Writing Poetry* 1st edition by Drake. © 1983. Reprinted with permission of Heinle, a division of Thomson Learning: www.thomsonrights.com. Fax 800-730-2215.

44 Donald Hall, quoted in Fairfield Review Web site, http://www.fairfieldreview.org/fairfield/tfrquotes.nsf/85256253006987048525562f001195f6/6d55fc1de36df6e e852564f9006ba748?OpenDocument.

45 Paul Claudel, quoted in Winokur, *Writers on Writing*, 221.

46 Glen Kirkland and Richard Davies, *Inside Poetry* (Toronto: Harcourt Brace Canada, 1987), 326–330. All poems and excerpts in this essay written by Glen Kirkland.

47 Margaret Atwood and Charles Pachter, *The Journals of Susanna Moodie*. Toronto: McFarlane Walter and Ross, 1997.

48 Robert Service, *The Cremation of Sam McGee*. Ted Harris, illustrator. New York: Greenwillow Books, 1987.

Writing for the Workplace

Since business writing is practical, an effective business style is not fancy but functional. It's simple and straightforward.

MARGOT NORTHEY

Chapter 6: Business Writing

Appendix C: Beyond the Print Résumé

Business Writing

*Be natural.... Business jargon too often is cold, stiff, unnatural.
Don't put on airs. Pretense invariably impresses only the pretender.*

MALCOLM FORBES[1]

LEARNING GOALS

▸ demonstrate an understanding of the writing skills and knowledge required for business careers

▸ organize information and ideas effectively to suit the form, purpose for writing, and intended audience of business communication

▸ select appropriate techniques, diction, voice, and style and use them effectively to communicate ideas and experiences in business communications

▸ assess the content, organization, style, and impact of drafts and final versions of work produced by peers, providing objective and constructive suggestions

▸ revise drafts to produce effective written work by refining content, form, technique, diction, voice, and style

WHAT IS BUSINESS WRITING?

Business writing occurs when you are writing to a business, from a business, or for a business. There are many exciting jobs that writers perform within a company. They write manuals, documents, brochures, newsletters, reports, and presentations. They create scripts for presentations and write articles for in-house publications. There are some types of writing that are required in just about all jobs in the business world. Letters, memorandums, e-mail, perform-ance reviews, reports (informal and formal), résumés, and proposals are just a few. This chapter focuses on the most common business writing that you are likely to do—letters, memos, e-mail, reports, résumés, performance reviews, and computerized presentations—as well as some less common types—proposals, technical writing, and press releases.

No matter what you write, all business writing should be clear, specific, accurate, and courteous.

Clear: The purpose of your writing should be clear. Often, unless you are conveying bad news, the purpose will be included in the first paragraph. Busy people don't have time to read an entire letter or report before they come to the point.

Specific: Whatever the purpose of your writing, you must include details. If you are writing to tell someone he or she has not been hired, you should give an explanation. If you are complaining about a product or service, you must provide specific details. You need to recognize what must be included, and delete any extraneous information. Depending on what you are writing, you should include photocopies of pertinent documentation.

Accurate: Even if you think it might be to your advantage, don't stretch the truth or include inaccurate information. Be sure research you have completed is accurate and can be verified.

Courteous: A person can write a strongly worded letter and still be courteous. Even under the worst of circumstances, you need to be conscious of your tone. If you are writing in anger, give yourself 24 hours to calm down and then reread what you have written. Remember, once your words are in print or spoken aloud, they cannot be taken back.

Purpose and Audience

The tone of business writing will depend heavily on purpose and audience. An informal tone in a letter announcing the layoffs of several employees is not appropriate, just as a formal memo inviting staff and their families to a company picnic is out of place. In business, it is essential for you to know your audience and consider your purpose as you are drafting your writing. If you are unsure about the tone, have at least one other knowledgeable person revise and edit your draft before you write your final version.

Appearance

The appearance of your writing is extremely important. In many cases, your writing may be the first impression you make. You should always word-process your work. If you don't have a computer at home, libraries, Internet cafés, and schools generally have computers that you can use. Save everything on disk.

Format and Layout

Just about every type of business writing has a specific format. Generally, companies and organizations have their own letterheads, interoffice memos, and standard elements and format for reports, making it easier for employees to achieve a consistent and professional look in their communication. But just to be sure, always check with someone who knows about standard practices before sending out or publishing your business communication.

If you have your own business, you should create the office standard so all your communications look professional. Or, if you are an individual writing to apply for a job or for other business communication, you may create your own letterhead.

Use a full block-style layout (with all lines justified left) and choose a serif typeface that is easy to read. Serifs are the short horizontal strokes at the bottom and top edges of letters. (Times font style in 11 point is currently one of the most readable fonts.)

Résumés are the exception to this general rule. A creative layout and interesting look will often stand out amongst all the other résumés. Be careful, however. You should consider elements and principles of good design if you are going to create an out-of-the-ordinary look.

Stationery

Unless you represent a business whose approach is avant-garde or on the edge, use good quality white or off-white paper with a matching envelope. Follow this guideline to apply for a job, to seek information from a company or organization, or to conduct other business.

Of course, if you are an employee, companies generally provide letterhead, company envelopes, and standard memos.

Grammar and Spelling

As you are writing, you may not want to stop to check and correct your grammar and spelling. But when you check afterward, having good resources is important. At the least, you should have a dictionary, a thesaurus, and a writing handbook. Many of these resources are available with your word-processing program or on-line.

No matter how well you write, however, you will need an editor to read your work and give you feedback on usage, grammar, and spelling. Electronic aids can assist you but, in the end, at least one other pair of eyes is invaluable.

Use a spell checker when using a computer to compose your writing. If you are writing manually, use an electronic spell checker or a dictionary. Remember that, although spell checkers are useful tools, they do not correct homophones (for example, *their, they're,* and *there*). So if you had intended to use the word *their*, but had typed *there*, the spell checker will not catch this error. Similarly, it will not catch words that you misspelled but that exist in the English language. For example, you may have intended to type the word *lot* but instead typed *pot*.

Grammar-checking programs are excellent tools if you know how to use them. If you don't understand basic grammatical constructions, you may not find them useful. If you are a very good writer and you purposefully include the passive voice and some sentence fragments, you will constantly get error messages. However, it is always a good idea to put your work through a grammar checker, even if it catches one or two errors you didn't intend to make.

Reread your work several times, even if you have an editor. If possible, leave your writing for a while and then return to it. Putting some distance between drafts helps give you perspective on what you're writing.

THE WRITER'S WARM-UPS

1. You believe you should have received a higher mark on your last assignment. You think perhaps you should put your complaint in writing. Write a letter of complaint to the teacher.

2. Write a paragraph starting with the following statement: The accomplishments I am most proud of are....

3. Find a job opening in the classified section of a newspaper for which you believe you are qualified. Prepare for an interview by creating a two-column chart: one column for your strengths and the other for your weaknesses.

4. Come up with a new product that you think our society can't live without. Write a script for a business presentation in which the speaker has to pitch the new product.

5. Write a letter asking a teacher for a recommendation. Be sure to explain what you will be using this recommendation for.

6. Write an opening paragraph for a letter of complaint in which you start with a positive tone.

7. Write a summary of a major paper you have written for another school subject. Make it brief (200 words), but thorough.

8. In the most positive way you can (without being unclear or saccharine), deliver, in writing, a piece of bad news regarding layoffs in the office to a business colleague.

9. Write a press release for the local newspaper detailing a fundraising activity you have held (or will hold) in your school.

10. Write a proposal to your principal outlining the need for a new piece of equipment for your school.

 THE WRITER'S TOOLKIT

Business Letter Format

There are several ways to set up a business letter. The two most common are full block style and modified block style.

Full Block Style

Most businesses choose the full block style, mainly because it is easier to format. Every line starts at the left margin and paragraphs are not indented. Each paragraph is separated by one line space.

A common punctuation style in business letters is *open punctuation*. In such a style, there are no punctuation marks at the end of any line that is above the message (the salutation) or below the message (the complimentary closing). There is an exception to the rule: if the last word in the line is an abbreviation (Blvd.), it should be punctuated with a period. Another punctuation style that is used in letters is *mixed punctuation*. Like open punctuation, this style limits punctuation marks. However, unlike open punctuation, a colon appears after the salutation and a comma after the complimentary closing. (The first two sample letters on pages 235 and 237 use open punctuation, while the sample letter on page 240 uses mixed punctuation.)

Sample Full Block Style Using Open Punctuation (With Letterhead)*

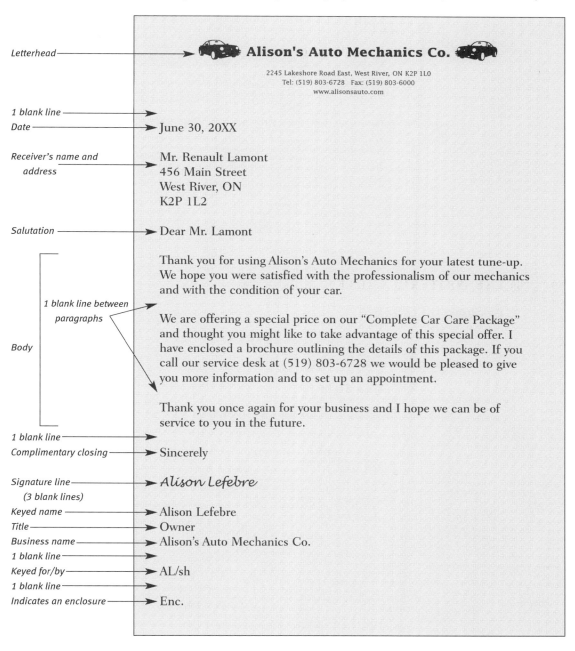

Letterhead

Alison's Auto Mechanics Co.

2245 Lakeshore Road East, West River, ON K2P 1L0
Tel: (519) 803-6728 Fax: (519) 803-6000
www.alisonsauto.com

1 blank line

Date → June 30, 20XX

Receiver's name and address →
Mr. Renault Lamont
456 Main Street
West River, ON
K2P 1L2

Salutation → Dear Mr. Lamont

Body

Thank you for using Alison's Auto Mechanics for your latest tune-up. We hope you were satisfied with the professionalism of our mechanics and with the condition of your car.

1 blank line between paragraphs

We are offering a special price on our "Complete Car Care Package" and thought you might like to take advantage of this special offer. I have enclosed a brochure outlining the details of this package. If you call our service desk at (519) 803-6728 we would be pleased to give you more information and to set up an appointment.

Thank you once again for your business and I hope we can be of service to you in the future.

1 blank line

Complimentary closing → Sincerely

Signature line (3 blank lines) → *Alison Lefebre*

Keyed name → Alison Lefebre
Title → Owner
Business name → Alison's Auto Mechanics Co.
1 blank line
Keyed for/by → AL/sh
1 blank line
Indicates an enclosure → Enc.

---

* If you use a blank page without letterhead, the format will be almost exactly the same. The only difference is that the sender's company or organization name and address will need to be keyed. There will still be one blank line between the name and address and the date.

Modified Block Style

A modified block style is similar to a full block style. The differences are the following:

- The sender's business name and address (if not using a letter-head), and the date may start at the centre. They should align with all elements below the message (complimentary closing).

- Paragraphs may be either indented or not.

Much of business communication is in the form of letters. For the purpose of this chapter, we have grouped the types of letters that you may be expected to write into two categories:

- employment letters (including cover letters, letters of recommendation/reference, and letters declining a job offer)

- general letters (letters of introduction, letters requesting information, letters refusing a request, and letters of complaint)

Employment Letters

Cover Letter

The cover letter is the first impression you make on a potential employer. It is often the key to getting your résumé read or to getting an interview.

REMINDER!

Your cover letter must be the following:

Clear
- *State the job you are applying for.*
- *State how you heard about it.*
- *Briefly explain what qualifies you for the job.*
- *Provide information on how you can be contacted for an interview.*

Specific
- *Outline some skills and qualifications that set you apart.*
- *Speak in the language of the job—use technical terms if they are appropriate.*

- *Keep it short and to the point—your résumé should say the most about you.*

Accurate
- *Do not include anything that isn't true.*
- *Reread, revise, and edit.*
- *Have someone else offer revision and editing suggestions.*
- *Ensure your writing is error-free.*

Courteous
- *Your tone should be businesslike but not so formal that it is stilted or boring.*
- *Let your voice come through.*

Sample Cover Letter

Greg Polanski
234 Maple St.
Natsuki, SK
P3F 5F2

March 25, 20XX

Brenda Kahn
Human Resources Manager
Olympic Pool and Spa
47 West Haven St.
Burton, Alberta
R2W 5N7

Specific contact name ➝ Dear Ms. Kahn

1 blank line ➝

Where he heard of the job ➝ I am responding to the advertisement in *The Globe and Mail* (March 25) for Junior Sales Associate in your Burton showroom. I am transferring to Burton from Natsuki, Saskatchewan, and am interested in applying for the job.

Experience with pools and people ➝ For the last three summers, I have been lifeguard, instructor, and coach in a competitive swim program for children ages 8–16. In addi-
Responsibility ➝ tion to working with children and their parents, I was responsible for
Technical expertise ➝ setting up and maintaining the filtration system, as well as managing the chemicals necessary for keeping the water healthy and safe. As a co-op student last year, I worked at Narraway's Honda dealership as
Customer service ➝ an assistant mechanic. In that role I learned how to talk to customers,
Personal skills ➝ work with other mechanics and perform regular car maintenance, such as oil changes and tire rotations. These past experiences plus my ability to learn quickly and work independently would be assets in a sales position at Olympic Pool and Spa.

I will be moving permanently to Burton on April 7, but can be available for an interview on 24 hours notice. I can be reached at my
Contact information ➝ cellular phone number (306) 705-3333. I look forward to hearing from you in the near future.

Best regards

Greg Polanski

Greg Polanski

Letter of Recommendation/Reference

As you get older, gain more job experience, and work with more people, you may be asked to write a letter of reference for a person seeking employment. If you feel you cannot recommend the person for a position, you must decline or explain that you will write one but you must include information that may not enhance the person's chance of getting the job. Do not lie on a reference letter. It is unfair to the company who is looking for a good employee.

If you feel you can write a reference for a person, ask for the following information:

- whether the letter should be general or specific

- the name of the individual to whom the letter is being sent

- the position being applied for

- a job description

- specific skills required for the position

Have the person make a list of accomplishments during the time you have known him or her so that you can refer to one or more of them in the letter.

REMINDER!

Your letter of recommendation/reference must be the following:

Clear
- *State when you worked with the individual you are recommending, for how long, and the position(s) the person held.*

Specific
- *Provide specific examples of skills or attitudes the individual exhibits.*

Accurate
- *Ensure that the dates, names, and positions you provide are correct.*
- *Do not stretch the truth about the person.*
- *Be sure your writing is error free.*

Courteous
- *Because you want the person you are recommending to be hired, your tone will be courteous.*
- *If you have some reservations about the individual, state them clearly but avoid negative prefixes like "un-" ("unemployable") "non-" ("non-team player"), or "ex-" ("ex-employee").*

When you have finished a draft of your letter, you may want the person for whom you are writing the letter to read it and make suggestions for revision. In some cases, the letter is supposed to be confidential, in which case, you will simply submit it after revising and editing it.

Note: Many people are under the impression that if someone uses you as a reference, everything you say will be positive. This is not necessarily so. You should always be asked if you will act as a reference. It should never be a surprise. The person asking you for the reference letter might want to know what you will say and, in that case, you should be honest. Sometimes, you will be asked to fill out a standard form instead of writing a letter. If you feel you cannot adequately describe the individual using just the form, write additional information and staple it to the form if permitted.

Sample Letter of Recommendation/Reference

CITY OF
NATSUKI

Department of Recreation
425 Main Street
Natsuki, SK
P3F 5F2
Tel. (306) 845-9034
Fax. (306) 845-9000
E-mail. emilyjohnston@cityofnatsuki.com

March 25, 20XX

Brenda Kahn
Human Resources Manager
Olympic Pool and Spa
47 West Haven St.
Burton, AB
R2W 5N7

Dear Ms. Kahn:

Purpose of the letter → I have been asked by Greg Polanski to write a letter of reference on his behalf. I have known Greg for three years. He has worked for the City of Natsuki Parks and Recreation Department as a lifeguard, swimming instructor, and coach for the past three summers. His move to Burton will be a great loss to this program.

Specific examples of skills and personality → Greg works extremely well with the public. Even his youngest and most timid students look forward to their lessons because of his gentle and encouraging support. Parents feel confident when they leave their children with him. He is constantly learning new teaching techniques and upgrading his qualifications. He is now a Level 2 swim coach.

Skills and attitude → Greg took on added responsibility last year when he volunteered to learn daily maintenance routines. He comes in early to vacuum the pool, backwash the filters, test the water, and make necessary adjustments to the chemical balance.

Closing and contact information → Greg has an outgoing personality. He is both a self-directed worker and a team player. I feel Greg will make a positive contribution to your company. If you have questions please don't hesitate to call me at (306) 845-9034 from 9 A.M. to 5 P.M. or e-mail me at emilyjohnston@cityofnatsuki.com.

Best regards,

Emily Johnston

Emily Johnston
Director of Recreation

Letter Declining a Job Offer

You may choose to decline an offer of employment. The way you phrase this letter is very important. You never know when you might apply for another position at the same business, so keep the letter positive even if you have negative reasons for declining.

REMINDER!

Your letter declining a job offer must be the following:

Clear
- *Make sure the company understands you are turning down the job.*

Specific
- *If possible, include a reason for declining the offer.*

Accurate
- *Be truthful without being hurtful or slanderous.*
- *Ensure your writing is error free.*

Courteous
- *Write promptly.*
- *Be positive without being saccharine.*

Sample Letter Declining a Job Offer

Greg Polanski
234 Maple St.
Natsuki, SK
P3F 5F2

April 10, 20XX

Brenda Kahn
Human Resources Manager
Olympic Pool and Spa
47 West Haven St.
Burton, AB
R2W 5N7

Dear Ms. Khan

Goodwill message → Thank you for taking the time to interview me for the sales position at Olympic Pool and Spa. I enjoyed meeting you and the rest of the interview team.

Purpose of letter and reason for declining offer → I regret that I will have to decline your offer of employment. I have accepted a supervisory position with Burton's Parks and Recreation Department and feel this position best matches my qualifications and previous experiences.

Closing → Thank you once again for the opportunity to meet you and learn more about your company.

Sincerely

Greg Polanski

Greg Polanski

General Letters

Letter of Introduction for University Entrance or Scholarship

Many students graduating from high school will be required to write letters of introduction either to enter a specialized program or to apply for a scholarship. In both cases these letters have to convince the recipient that you are the best candidate.

REMINDER!

Your university entrance or scholarship letter must be the following:

Clear
- *Make your request clear.*
- *Name the program or scholarship for which you are applying.*

Specific
- *Explain why you are making the request.*
- *Detail what qualifies you for the program or the scholarship.*
- *Think of qualities you have that set you apart from other candidates.*

Accurate
- *Be truthful: do not embellish your personal qualities or achievements.*
- *Show how you are going to use whatever you have requested.*
- *Ensure your writing is error free.*

Courteous
- *You are making a request: be as courteous as you can without being too ingratiating.*

Sample Letter of Introduction for a Program in Journalism

Chandula Ahmed
4425 Cherry Blossom Lane
Acadia, NS
B3X 2T9

January 31, 20XX

School of Journalism and Communication
Carleton University
1125 Colonel By Drive
Ottawa, ON K1S 5B6

Attention: Journalism Program

Reason for letter → I am applying for a position in the School of Journalism and Communication Program.

Education → For the past four years I have attended Bedford High School. For all four of those years I received averages of over 85 percent.

Related job experience → I worked for the school's newspaper, *Acadian*. In Grade 12, I became editor-in-chief. Four years of multi-tasking—filling in for both reporting and production staff, meeting tight deadlines, and working through the night to finish editions while still doing my schoolwork—has prepared me for the demands of a journalism program. As well as being published in the *Acadian*, I have had articles published in *The Herald* and have had several letters to the editor published in *The Globe and Mail*.

Career interests → I am interested in full-time journalism and eventually would like to combine freelancing with travel to Australasia, South Asia, and the Middle East.

Closing → Accompanying this letter are samples of my work from both the *Acadian* and *The Herald*. I look forward to setting up an interview with you in the near future. I can be contacted at the following number: (902) 649-0356.

Sincerely

Chandula Ahmed

Chandula Ahmed

Enc.

1. Research some scholarship or bursary opportunities for post-secondary education. Choose one scholarship or bursary for which you could be eligible and write a letter of application to the sponsor.

2. Many colleges and university programs require letters of introduction from prospective students. Choose a program and write a letter of introduction.

Letters of Request

Letters of request fall into two categories: letters that benefit the sender and receiver (for example, a request for product information) and requests that benefit only the sender (for example, a request for a donation of free coffee from a coffee shop for a charitable event).

REMINDER!

Your letter of request must be the following:

Clear
- *Make your request clear.*
- *Provide dates, times, and contact names, if applicable.*

Specific
- *Explain why you are making the request; if the request only benefits you, then explain in more detail why you are making the request (background, what others are doing for you, and so on).*

Accurate
- *Be truthful: tell how you are going to use whatever you have requested.*
- *Ensure your writing is error free.*

Courteous
- *You are making a request: be as courteous as you can.*

Sample Letter of Request (Benefiting Only the Sender)

F. Linkslater
576 Jakes Ave., Apt. 1324
Vancouver, BC
V2T 1B6

January 26, 20XX

Ethel Smart, Manager
Classics Coffee Shop
56 Main Street
Vancouver, BC
V0G 9B2

Dear Ms. Smart

Statement of goodwill → I have been a regular customer at Classics Coffee for the last year. I find your customer service excellent and your coffee delicious.

Request and clear explanation → On Saturday, February 10, our community choir, Singing Voices Chorus, is holding a large garage sale at the community centre two doors from your shop. All proceeds will go toward the recording of our CD. To attract more customers, and because it has been so cold recently, I recommended serving coffee during the sale. Would it be possible to donate two large urns of regular coffee to our sale? We will supply the cups, milk, and sugar, but I know that the customers would enjoy a decent Classics Coffee instead of the inferior product we produce at the centre. If you agree to supply the coffee, we will send a representative to pick up the urns at 8 A.M. just before the sale starts.

Thanks and contact information in closing → Thank you for considering our request. I can be contacted at (604) 683-4291. I look forward to hearing from you whether or not you will be able to make this donation. We are sure the sale is going to attract many buyers, but they will be happier buyers if they are able to have a Classics Coffee.

Sincerely

F. Linkslater

F. Linkslater
Treasurer
Singing Voices Chorus

Letter Refusing a Request

Refusal letters are difficult to write because they contain bad news. But, like rejection letters sent to job applicants, they can be done in a pleasant manner.

REMINDER!

Your letter refusing a request must be the following:

Clear
• *Make sure the requester understands that you are not going to fulfill the request.*

Specific
• *If possible include a reason for denying the request.*

Accurate
• *Be truthful without being hurtful.*
• *Ensure that your writing is error free.*

Courteous
• *Write promptly.*
• *Be courteous even if the request is unusual.*

Sample Letter Refusing a Request

February 1, 20XX

F. Linkslater
576 Jakes Ave., Apt. 1324
Vancouver, BC
V2T 1B6

Dear Mr. Linkslater

Words of goodwill —▸ Thank you for your letter requesting the donation of coffee for your chorus's garage sale. I have been fortunate enough to hear your choir perform and understand how important it is for you to be raising money for your CD.

Refusal and reason —▸ Unfortunately, we will not be able to fulfill your request. We are inundated with similar requests every day and I feel if we agreed to one, we would have to agree to all. In this economic climate it is not feasi-

Alternative suggestions —▸ ble for us to do this. Perhaps we could post an advertisement of your sale on our window and on our store's bulletin board. We could also keep some flyers on the counter. If any of these suggestions are an option, have one of your members drop by with posters and flyers and we will make sure they are available to all our customers.

Closing and goodwill —▸ Thank you for thinking of Classics Coffee. I hope your sale goes well and I look forward to hearing the CD when it is available.

Your truly

Ethel Smart

Ethel Smart
Manager

CLASSICS COFFEE SHOP
56 Main Street, Vancouver, BC V0G 9B2
Tel. (604) 222-1234 Fax: (604) 222-1000
www.classicscoffee.com

Letter of Complaint

It is not unusual to feel dissatisfied with a product you have bought. When this happens, you can lodge a complaint. Go to the retail outlet where you bought the product. If you are a business that has purchased something through another company, go directly to the customer service department in that company.

Many times, speaking directly to a person who has some authority can result in a refund. It is important for you, as the consumer, to have all the information needed to make that refund possible: dates of purchase and delivery, receipts, invoices, packing slips, and so on. If you are not satisfied after a face-to-face discussion, sending a letter may be the solution.

REMINDER!

Your letter of complaint must be the following:

Clear
- *State what you want from the company (a refund, credit note, exchange).*

Specific
- *Provide all dates (purchase, delivery, previous complaints, names of sales associates, or managers).*

Accurate
- *Be truthful: do not embellish your story or fill your letter with emotive words.*
- *Ensure your writing is error free.*

Courteous
- *Your tone should be courteous, but not ingratiating; if you have sent several letters, your tone may become more curt, but never rude or threatening.*

Sample Letter of Complaint

Janice Woo
111 53rd Avenue
Edmonton, AB
T2A 3H1

January 31, 20XX

Ned Phelps
Manager of Customer Service
Kim's Clothing Company
500 11A Street
Edmonton, AB
T6A 1B7

Dear Mr. Phelps

Purpose →

I have been shopping in your department store for several years now and have always been pleased with the quality of the products you sell. Recently, however, I purchased a pair of shoes that I wish to return for a full refund.

Complaint with clear explanation →

On December 21, 20XX, I bought a pair of Schneider sandals to wear on my vacation (copy of bill enclosed). I wore them for two days, and the heel strap broke. On January 6, 20XX, when I returned to your store, I attempted to exchange them for a new pair. The manager, Chris Shoehorn, explained that, because the shoes were on sale, I did not qualify for an exchange.

Thanks and contact information →

The sandals were defective. They should not have broken after only two wearings. I would like to return them to the store for a full refund. Please call me at 555-4103 or e-mail me at janice.woo@networks.com to arrange for this return or to discuss the problem with me. Thank you.

Closing →

Sincerely

J. Woo

J. Woo

Enc.

If you are not satisfied with the outcome of your first letter, you will have to write again. While still being courteous, you will need to word your second and subsequent letters more strongly. Remember, strong does not mean rude.

APPLICATION

1. Write a letter of complaint to a real company about a product you own or an experience you have had. Ask at least two people to offer revision and editing suggestions. Send your final version to the company.

2. Imagine you are a member of the student council. A group of students within the school has asked for money to support their "club." The group, however, is not a recognized school club and is not eligible for funding. Write a letter of refusal that will clearly state the council's position and provides an explanation to the group.

3. Imagine you are the principal of a school in Kitchener-Waterloo, ON. The environmental club has requested funds for a trip to Ottawa for a three-day conference on global warming. Write a letter to the club explaining that you cannot fund the entire trip, but are willing to pay for the bus and the registration.

Memos

Memos are another common form of business writing. Memos differ from letters in that they are generally sent within the same organization and tend to be less formal. They could be written and circulated to staff members in hard copy form or they could be sent by e-mail. Memos serve many functions:

- announcements of meetings, of new policies or procedures, or of new employees

- confirmation of meetings, of conversations, or of dates and times

- requests for information, for assistance, for a meeting, or for a report

Because memos are the organization's lifeline they must adhere strictly to the "rules" of good communication. There is no "right" way to set up a memo, but if you use the following model, you can't go wrong.

Sample of a Typical Memo

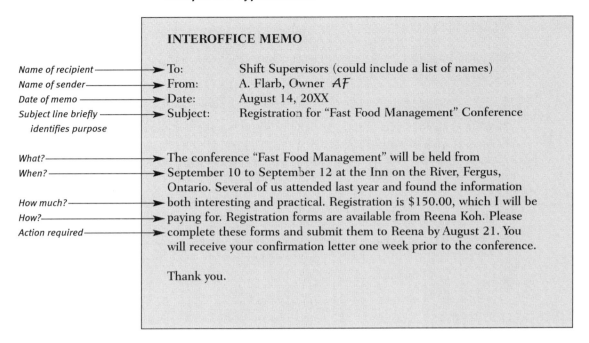

INTEROFFICE MEMO	

Name of recipient → **To:** Shift Supervisors (could include a list of names)

Name of sender → **From:** A. Flarb, Owner *AF*

Date of memo → **Date:** August 14, 20XX

Subject line briefly identifies purpose → **Subject:** Registration for "Fast Food Management" Conference

What? →
When? → The conference "Fast Food Management" will be held from September 10 to September 12 at the Inn on the River, Fergus, Ontario. Several of us attended last year and found the information

How much? → both interesting and practical. Registration is $150.00, which I will be

How? → paying for. Registration forms are available from Reena Koh. Please

Action required → complete these forms and submit them to Reena by August 21. You will receive your confirmation letter one week prior to the conference.

Thank you.

REMINDER!

Your memo must be the following:

Clear
- *State the purpose of the memo in the subject line.*

Specific
- *Include all the information necessary for the recipients to take the required action.*

Accurate
- *Provide the correct times, dates, locations, and so on.*
- *Ensure your writing is error free.*

Courteous
- *Depending on the purpose of the memo, the tone will change; as always, it is essential to be courteous (even though you may be writing to colleagues with whom you are familiar), but some memos may be more formal than others.*
- *Sign memos whenever possible; it creates goodwill.*

1. Write a memo informing an employee of the most recent budget cuts and how these will affect that employee.

2. Write a memo inviting members of your class to a reading you are giving.

3. Write a memo to your writing group informing them that they have not received funding from the local library.

E-mail

In today's business environment, e-mail has largely replaced hard copy memos, and letters. Here is some "e-mail etiquette" that you should keep in mind:

- Keep your e-mail brief and to the point. People in the workplace are busy and receive many e-mail messages each day and will not have the time to read a novel. As well, prolonged reading on the computer screen tires the eyes.

- Always include a clear and brief subject line, telling readers the purpose of your message.

- State your point immediately.

- If you have to include something lengthy (a proposal, a long agenda, minutes of a meeting, and so on), do so in an attachment.

- If you send an attachment, be sure to tell the recipient the name of the attachment (document name).

- Make sure you "attach" the attachment; double check before you click on Send.

- Be sure the attachment is in "plain text" or "rich text format" so that it can be easily read.

- Avoid writing personal e-mail to family and friends on company e-mail.

- If the e-mail you are sending has a serious purpose and audience, avoid using short forms like "u" for "you" or "4" for "for"; avoid emoticons, such as ☺ and :-), and other graphical symbols.

- Check business e-mail for spelling and grammar.

- Take the time to reread, revise, and edit your business e-mail.

- "Flaming" (capitalizing all the letters) is a way of yelling on e-mail; flaming is not acceptable business writing, mainly because it is not courteous. Find ways of reacting that are calm and tactful. If you are really angry or upset by something, don't respond immediately. Leave some time before writing and sending your response.

Remember: E-mail is not as confidential as you may think. Carefully consider what you are saying and whether or not e-mail is the appropriate vehicle.

APPLICATION

1. From your own experiences, make up an additional five rules for using e-mail in a business setting.

2. Discuss whether or not sending personal e-mail and using the Internet for checking stocks, bank records, sports scores, and so on is appropriate during business hours on company computers.

3. Write a plot line for a story in which office e-mail is a central issue.

Reports

The purpose of a report is to provide information. For this reason, information in the report must be presented clearly and logically, using headings (if the report is long), graphs and visual aids (if the report contains a lot of research information), and clear and objective language.

The two types of reports that you may be involved in writing during your working career are informal reports and formal reports.

Informal Reports

The informal report is the more common of the two types of reports that you may write during your working career. The length of the informal report varies depending on its purpose and scope, but generally it is one to eight pages in length. Since it is often written in a memo or letter, the subject of the report is contained in the "Subject" line. The writer may or may not use headings to organize the information. Below is an example of a report, in memorandum form, outlining a problem.

Sample Informal Report in Memo Format

INTEROFFICE MEMO

To: Albert Chu, Manager
            Audio Visual Services
From: Nadine Khan, Vice President of Sales *NK*
Date: March 29, 20XX

Subject: Audio Malfunction

During a presentation I was conducting this morning in Boardroom C the audio system malfunctioned. Although all connections appeared to be secure, there was no amplification.

I borrowed the portable system from Boardroom B, but realized that, over the next three days, there are presentations in both rooms for which audio equipment will be needed.

I would like the system in Boardroom C repaired or a portable system provided before 9 A.M. tomorrow, March 30. If we need to rent a system on a short-term basis while repairs are being completed, please send the requisition through Maria Johnson.

Progress and activity reports describe how a project is evolving. They will often contain headings, such as Progress, Problems, Timelines, Costs, and Summary or Conclusions. Following is a progress report on a writing project:

Sample Progress Report in Letter Format

Write at night

83 Park Blvd., Toronto, ON M4G 6N2
Tel: (416) 777-1234 Fax: (416) 777-1000
www.writeatnight.org

April 7, 20XX

Mr. Ernest Eden-Smith, Project Manager
Hands-on Publishing Company
437 Church Avenue
Toronto, ON M3G 8S2

To: Mr. Eden-Smith

Subject: Grade 12 Literacy Textbook Progress Report

This report, as required by our contract, covers the progress of the Grade 12 Literacy Text. I am currently on schedule as outlined in our original agreement.

Progress
I have completed the introductory chapter on Types of Literacy including the bibliography and suggested glossary terms. As well, I have completed the chapters on Media Literacy and Visual Literacy. These chapters, along with their corresponding activities, have been submitted to Ms. Nancy Park electronically.

Problems
I have chosen several illustrations for the Visual Literacy chapter but am having difficulty securing copyright for these images. It would speed up the completion of the text if your in-house copyright department could seek some of these copyrights on my behalf. I have included a list of images and their sources with this report.

Timelines
As per the schedule, I will submit three more chapters electronically to Ms. Park by April 25. The final chapter and the Toolkit will be submitted by May 5.

Conclusions
Other than the copyright difficulties, I am proceeding as planned. Working with Ms. Park has been a positive experience. I look forward to her continued editorial advice.

Sincerely

Ana Lassiter

Ana Lassiter
Author, Write at Night
Enc.

Longer informal reports generally include an introduction (or background), a body (including headings if the information breaks down in this way), and a conclusion. If there is research involved, the writer will also include references and a bibliography.

A Note About Headings

When you use headings in your report, ensure that they all have parallel structure (the same grammatical structure for all headings that have the same function), as shown in the sample report, to make your report appear cleaner and more professional. You may choose to use either nouns for all your headings (as in the sample report) or participle forms of verbs for all your headings. For example, in a report on how a designer creates an effective layout, your titles might look something like the following:

Headings Using Nouns	Headings Using the Participle Forms of Verbs
Titles	Choosing Titles
Fonts	Varying Fonts
White Space	Creating White Space
Graphics	Using Graphics

Formal Reports

Formal reports are generally written to someone in another organization or to an individual within the writer's own organization with whom the writer has little contact. Formal reports are less common than informal reports and few employees have to write them unless they are in consultative positions. These reports are much longer and contain more research information than informal reports.

Many businesses have a standard way to write formal reports. If you have not been given a specific format, the one that follows will be a good start:[2]

Front matter

Title page

Abstract: a brief summary of the report; includes enough information to allow a reader to determine whether or not this report would be beneficial to read

Table of contents

List of figures (diagrams, charts, graphs)

List of tables

Body

Executive summary: a more detailed summary than the abstract, the executive summary goes into the procedures and recommendations as well as the basic content of the report. It is written for the person who doesn't have time to read the whole report but who needs basic knowledge of its content.

Introduction: includes the background to the report

Text (including headings such as Procedure, Data Collection, etc.)

Conclusions

Recommendations

References

Back matter

Bibliography

Appendixes

Glossary

Index

APPLICATION

Go to the library and read a formal report on a subject that interests you or on a subject that you have to research for another course. Compare the parts of that report to the ones listed here. Account for any differences.

Performance Reviews

Some of you may have received a performance review. However, if you run your own business or you are supervising other employees, you will likely be required to write one.

Following are some topics that you can discuss with your employees prior to the review, in order to gather information.

Communication skills

- listening to understand and learn from others
- reading, understanding what is read, and using written materials (graphs, charts, visual materials, and so on) to complete the job successfully
- writing clearly and effectively in the required format so that others can understand what you have written
- voicing opinions clearly without overpowering others
- applying understanding of the sender/receiver communication model

Thinking skills

- thinking critically, acting logically
- evaluating situations, using good judgement, and applying effective decision-making skills when faced with a problem
- using technology and information systems effectively
- applying any specialized knowledge that you have to the project

Learning skills

- learning independently
- learning something new from the project
- improving on skills learned during previous projects

Attitudes and behaviours

- completing the project with confidence
- feeling a sense of self-esteem from working through the process and completing the project
- having honesty and integrity
- having a positive attitude toward learning and personal growth
- persisting with the project in order to complete it

Responsibility

- setting goals and priorities and working toward them

- planning and managing time effectively

- being accountable for your actions

Adaptability

- recognizing and respecting the differences and talents of others

- identifying and suggesting new ideas and ways to get the job done—displaying creativity

Working with others

- understanding the project and working as a group member toward completing it successfully

- understanding the dynamics of the group and working effectively within it

- planning and making decisions with the group and taking responsibility for outcomes (both positive and negative)

- respecting the thoughts and opinions of others

- having a give-and-take attitude within the group to achieve results

- working as a group member when appropriate and as an individual within the group when appropriate

- taking various roles in the group (leader, recorder, reporter, worker, decision maker) when appropriate.

Performance reviews can have a great effect on a person's future: whether he is kept on, whether he is given a raise, whether he is promoted, or whether he will be hired by someone else.

REMINDER!

Your performance review must be the following:

Clear
- *The reader (including the employee) should know whether or not this is a positive review.*

Specific
- *Provide specific information pertaining to the categories of skills you or your company uses.*
- *If the review is simply a checklist, add information on the bottom or on the back for anything that may be ambiguous.*

Accurate
- *Information must be accurate; whether the review is negative or positive, you must include details to back up your evaluation.*
- *Ensure your writing is error free.*

Courteous
- *Being courteous is easy when a review is positive. When an employee has performed poorly, it is more difficult; try to find a positive thing to say, no matter how minor it may seem. Do not, however, make that positive remark overpower the negative ones, especially if this person is going to be let go for incompetence.*
- *Keeping a negative report formal will make it sound less personal and thus less hurtful.*

APPLICATION

1. Write a performance review for yourself based on the last writing assignment you completed for this class.

2. Write a performance review for a club or team in your school. Be sure you have all the facts.

3. Create a performance review checklist for a job about which you have some knowledge.

Résumés

A résumé is a summary of your personal, educational, and job experiences. When a manager or human resources officer reads your résumé, it should be clear why he or she should give you an interview and, ultimately, hire you. As you have studied résumés in your career education courses, this section of the chapter will focus on the variety of ways you can categorize your personal and employment information and the language you should use to make the best first impression.

Many students think that a generic résumé is appropriate for all job applications. This isn't true. Different jobs require different skills. You need to consider what information is needed to prove you have the skills and experience necessary for a particular job, and then tailor your résumé to emphasize those skills and experience and to suit the job for which you are applying.

Order and Information

The order in which you present the information on your résumé will determine the first impression you make on your potential employer. What do you want that employer to know first? What is the most important aspect of the job? Do you have particular skills that set you apart? Do you have specialized training or education that many people don't have? Do your past job experiences give you an edge over others who might be applying for the same job? Have you won awards, written academic papers, or made presentations that have given you a reputation for excellence? Does your cadet training or volunteer or community work showcase the enthusiasm you bring to your work? Examine the job description carefully and choose four or five categories of information that you think are most appropriate. Rank the categories according to their importance to the job and to the impression you want to make. Rearrange your résumé several different ways to experiment with the messages inherent in the various orders.

No matter which categories you decide to include or how you plan to arrange them, there is a limit to how long an employer has to read your résumé. A long narrative résumé may not get the attention that a shorter point-form résumé might. A rule of thumb is to keep your résumé to two pages or less.

Following, listed alphabetically, are some categories you might consider using on your résumé. Obviously you are not going to use all of them. Use the ones that suit the job and your strengths.

Categories	Description
Activities	interests outside work hours
Areas of expertise	aspects of the job or specific applications for which you have extra training or experience; this is particularly important for jobs involving technology
Awards and recognition	recognition for special achievements
Certifications	certificates above and beyond secondary or post-secondary education, usually in a specialized area
Community service/ volunteer work	any unpaid position that assisted members of a community (Distress Line volunteer, Girl Guide/Scout leader, volunteer swimming instructor for disabled children)
Computer/technical strengths	specialized equipment and programs
Education	if in high school, do not list your elementary school history
Experience	job experiences
Goals	position you are seeking and how this position will help you reach a future goal
Licences	special licences such as a licence to drive a school bus or transport trucks equipped with air brakes
Military service	include paramilitary training such as cadets
Personal summary	summary of your talents and personality
Presentations	workshops or presentations you have given
Professional affiliations	unions, federations, professional societies, boards of directors
Professional writing	publications, reports, papers
Strengths/skills	specific strengths and skills you possess that are necessary for the job

References

The inclusion of references is a personal decision. Many job applicants simply indicate "references on request" on their résumés. Some employers will ask you to fill out a list of references' names and contact numbers on a separate sheet on which they will record each individual's comments.

Language and Tone

Sometimes it's hard to write a résumé because you may feel that you are bragging, but the résumé is a sales tool and you must sound confident. An employer won't want to hire a person who can't recognize his or her own strengths. Be positive. Be confident. If you are concerned about the tone, have another person review your résumé for you. If possible try to find a person working in the field in which you are hoping to be hired.

When writing your résumé, use active verbs whenever possible. Here are some examples:

arranged	established	managed
assessed	evaluated	oversaw
assisted	facilitated	performed
composed	fixed	prepared
computerized	founded	presented
consulted	handled	promoted
contributed	hired	provided
coordinated	illustrated	recruited
created	implemented	set up
delivered	increased/decreased	structured
designed	initiated	supervised
developed	installed	trained
employed	maintained	worked
		wrote

Parallel Structure

When you list your experiences or skills, be sure to keep your structures parallel. Look at this "experience" section for a student applying for a part-time restaurant position:

Don't

Experience

Sales Associate: La Cienaga Clothes

- supervised two junior sales associates
- cashing out
- work well on a team

Maintaining the parallel structure makes the writing crisper and cleaner.

Do

Experience

Sales Associate: La Cienaga Clothes

- supervised two junior sales associates
- cashed out and closed Friday and Saturday nights
- contributed to the spirit of the sales team

APPLICATION

1. Choose three jobs from the classified ads and write one résumé for each.

2. Choose one job and write several résumés using different categories and arrangements in order to arrive at the best one. Have a classmate read all the résumés and choose the one that best matches the job and best showcases your talents.

Computer-Enhanced Presentations

Often at work, you will need to create computer-enhanced presentation slides or visuals to accompany reports that you are presenting orally. You first need to come up with the words that will appear on the slides. Then you need to figure out how you might use backgrounds, animations, charts or graphs, and sounds to enhance the words on your slides. Following are some tips for creating your slides:

- Organize your research ahead of time so you know what information you want to include.

- Be concise.

- Limit the information on each slide—include just enough to allow you to talk about the point.

- Keep each slide simple: a cluttered background with large graphics and a great deal of information will make your slide hard to read.

- Use the effects available on the program (sound, movies, animation, various types of dissolves, and so on) to enhance the words on your slides and engage your audience, but don't let them overshadow the points you are making.

- Ensure that your typeface is large enough to be seen from the back of whatever room you are presenting in.

- Use the same or similar typeface throughout: vary the size or style (bold, italic, shadow, outline) to emphasize titles or key points.

- Use a serif typeface: serifs are the little horizontal strokes at the bottoms and tops of uppercase letters. Serifs lead the reader's eye to the following letter, making reading easier.

- Ensure that all words and graphics on your slides convey a tone appropriate to your purpose and audience.

- Start with a title slide that states the topic and your name.

- End with a slide that indicates the end of the presentation.

APPLICATION

Choose a topic you are interested in researching. Narrow the focus so that you have about five minutes of information you would like to present to the class. Using one of the presentation software programs, create a computer-enhanced presentation for the class.

Proposals

A proposal is a document that is written to persuade someone to follow a specific plan of action. Proposals may be either internal (written to people within the company) or external (written to people or organizations outside the company). Internal proposals are often in the form of a memo, whereas proposals that go outside an organization are often written like formal reports.

The types of proposals you are likely to write may involve recommending a change or an improvement in current practices. A proposal may also suggest a new idea. Every proposal has an opening that states the purpose of the proposal. The body details the plan being proposed, including materials required, costs, and a blueprint for how the plan will be carried out. The conclusion (authorization) restates the recommendations and offers to set up a meeting time or provide more information on request.

You may be writing to one person or to a committee. Either way, it is important to understand who will be reading your proposal. Knowing your readers' biases, their previous knowledge of the subject, and what specific examples to use will allow you to make your proposal more persuasive. While you want your readers to buy into your proposal, you need to use language that is objective and positive, without disparaging competitors. The information you provide must be truthful.

Suppose you are involved in the arts and you feel that the artistic talents of the students in your school, John Jenkins Secondary School, need a higher profile. You might write a proposal to the school's arts department for an "Evening at J.J.'s Coffee House" at which students would perform original works (poetry, fiction, music, drama). Following is a sample proposal for this plan, written in a memo format:

Sample Proposal

Name of recipient → **To:** Ms. Painter, Head of Arts

Name of sender → **From:** Leila Kearney, Arts Council Representative

Date → **Date:** November 12, 20XX

Subject line briefly → **Subject:** An Evening at J.J.'s Coffee House: Profiling the Arts
identifies purpose

Reason for proposal → **PURPOSE**

In the last two years at our school, the arts have not had a very high profile with students or staff. We have many talented students who would like to let the rest of the school (staff and students) and the community (students' relatives and friends outside the school) know that the arts are thriving here at John Jenkins Secondary School. It is important to bolster the arts. We need the arts to maintain our culture and our civilization, no matter what we study or which careers we choose.

The proposal → **THE PROPOSAL**

In view of the importance of the arts, I would like to propose "An Evening at JJ's Coffee House," an evening at the school in which students read their poetry, scripts, or stories, perform music or dance, or display their artwork.

Description of the concept → **Description of "An Evening at J.J.'s Coffee House"**

The "coffee house" would provide an informal forum for student performers to read their creative works, sing, or play instruments. It would also be a place for students to display their paintings, sculptures, and other works of art.

Performers would have 10-minute time slots for their performances.

A performance schedule would be posted so audience members could plan which performance they would like to see and when. They could move around at will, in and out of the room.

Outside the room where the performances are to be held, artwork would be on display with visual artists painting, sculpting, designing their graphics on computers, and so on.

The audience could purchase coffee, tea, juice, soft drinks, and baked goods. There would be servers to take orders at each table, collect payment, and serve food and beverages.

The coffee house evening is proposed to run on Wednesday, February 12, from 7:30 P.M. until 9:30 P.M.

Specifications and details of all requirements

REQUIREMENTS

Space

The coffee house could be held in the cafeteria or in the drama studio. The former is a large space and could seat many people. However, its size makes it difficult to capture the coffee-house atmosphere. The drama studio is smaller. While it would mean a smaller audience, it is more intimate and provides a more authentic atmosphere.

An area adjacent to the performance area needs to be set aside for artwork and artists. We have to reserve whichever space we decide on, since many other groups use the school in the evenings. Specifically, Tuesdays and Thursdays have to be avoided, as night classes run during these evenings.

Furniture

To create a coffee house, we need 26 square or round tables. The library has 6 that are suitable but we would have to rent 20 more. Whether we use the cafeteria or the drama studio, chairs are easily accessible.

Equipment and Supplies

We need sound equipment, lights, a raised platform on which the students would perform, display boards, computers, and art supplies.

Since sound equipment is available in the school, we need only a student volunteer to operate the equipment. Several members of the AV club have agreed to volunteer their time. As well, Mr. Sanderson has offered to act as the AV troubleshooter.

A portable spotlight could be rented for the evening if we use the cafeteria. If we use the drama studio, studio lighting is sufficient.

Risers that the school uses for the annual commencement are suitable for a stage.

Six portable display boards for artwork could be borrowed from the Board of Education; three computers from the computer department; and easels, paint, and other art supplies from the art department.

Food and Refreshments

Baked goods could be prepared ahead of time by student volunteers and set up in an area designated for refreshments. All food will be labelled with ingredients. No peanut products will be allowed.

The school has three large urns that could be used for coffee and tea. Soft drinks, juices, milk (at least one litre of which will be lactose free) as well as sugar and sweetener would be purchased for the event. Plastic glasses, paper cups and plates, napkins, and stir sticks would also be purchased.

STAFFING

Staff (teachers and administrators)—The principal needs to determine the supervising staff.

Staff (students)—Students are needed for the following jobs:
- Refreshments: 10 students (6 serving tables; 4 preparing orders)
- AV/ lighting: 2 students
- Stage setup and management: 4 students
- Computer setup: 1 student
- Security for art area: 3 students

Cleanup is to be done by volunteer students and caretaking staff.

COSTS

Spotlight:	TBA
20 tables: 20 @ $5.00	= $100.00
Refreshments	= $200.00
Plates, etc.	= $ 50.00
Caretaking staff	= $150.00
Total cost	= $500.00
Ticket price	= $ 6.00 per ticket
Beverages	= $ 1.00 per beverage
Food	= $ 0.75 per piece

Possible funding: Student Council pop machine funds

All funds made from the event will go into the Students' Art Council.

AUTHORIZATION

A night highlighting the arts would allow many students to showcase their talents as well as provide an entertaining evening for staff, parents, and students of John Jenkins Secondary School. The more people we can convince that arts are an important part of our education and that the arts can benefit us all, the healthier our arts programs will be.

I would like to meet with you and with the Arts Department to discuss this proposal and answer any questions you might have. Please let me know when we could meet. I look forward to talking to you in the near future.

REMINDER!

Your proposal must be the following:

Clear
- *State the purpose of your proposal immediately.*
- *Explain why your proposal is needed.*

Specific
- *Give details of your plan.*
- *Use technical terms where necessary, but remember that some of your readers may not have as much technical knowledge as you do.*
- *Keep your proposal to the point.*

Accurate
- *Research your facts.*
- *Reread, revise, and edit.*
- *Have someone else offer revision and editing suggestions.*
- *Ensure your writing is error free.*

Courteous
- *Your tone should be businesslike, but not so formal that it is stilted or boring.*
- *Let your voice come through.*

Brainstorm a list of ways you could improve your school, your job, or a club or team to which you belong, for example, by creating an outside eating area for the school, improving team spirit, going on a special trip with your club, or fundraising to pay for new team uniforms. Write a proposal outlining your strategy for putting that improvement in place.

Technical Writing

How many times have you bought a piece of equipment that needed assembly only to find that the accompanying instructions are unclear, confusing, or simply indecipherable? A good technical writer (or excellent translator of technical language to plain English) could have made your job go much more quickly and smoothly.

The technical writer's job is to make technical information accessible to audiences ranging from those highly knowledgeable about a subject to those who know little or nothing about it. The technical writer must be able to read and understand technical information first and then write about that information clearly and effectively for a specific purpose and audience.

What Technical Writers Write

Technical writers can be found in manufacturing, hi-tech, scientific, medical, and government industries. They write any of the following:

- Web pages
- on-line and print documentation
- product information
- instructions and instruction manuals
- technical reports
- corporate communications

- proposals (internal and external)
- policy and process documents
- public service campaigns
- educational programs
- presentations
- grant proposals

Skills and Knowledge That Technical Writers Need

Besides clear writing skills, technical writers need to have other skills to help them communicate information. Technical writers work with engineers, technologists, computer specialists, and scientists, along with a host of other technical experts to gather information. They must have excellent verbal communication and group work skills. They conduct their own research, including interviews and literature searches, both on-line and in libraries. They must be fast learners since they are generally dealing with a variety of complex topics.

It is advantageous for technical writers to have a background in science or business and in simple computer programming. Becoming proficient with desktop publishing and design software is also an asset.

The Language of Technical Writing

Technical writing is clean and utilitarian. Crafting beautiful sentences and using figurative language is not as important as getting the information across to the reader. Figurative language would only be used to clarify a concept.

When writing for a lay audience (those who are unfamiliar with the subject), avoid technical jargon. In instructions or manuals for the average audience, use parallel structure to help the reader understand and follow the directions. For example, in the following instructions for setting up a printer,[3] all the sentences are imperative, each beginning with a verb and ending with a noun. They use a parallel structure to tell the user clearly how to set up the printer. Notice also the writer's use of illustrations to help clarify each step of the instructions, as well as the symbols to draw readers' attention.

HOW TO SET UP THE PRINTER

Note: If you need help as you set up your printer, see "Troubleshooting" in the *Printer ABC Guide*.

1. Unpack the printer.

Remove the printer from its packaging. Check that you have all these items:

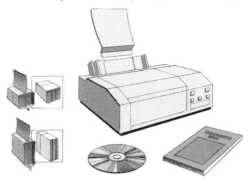

Put the printer near your computer and an available outlet. Avoid areas with high temperature or humidity, in direct sunlight or dusty conditions, and near electromagnetic interference.

2. Attach the paper support.

Attach the paper support into the slots at the back of the printer.

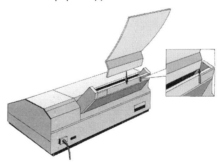

3. Install the ink cartridge.

   1. Plug the printer's power and cord into a grounded outlet.
   2. Open the front cover.

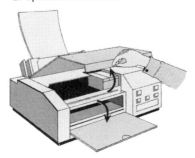

3. Press the power button to turn on the printer. The power light will flash. The ink cartridge holder will move into loading position.

! Don't use an outlet that is the same circuit as a large appliance. This may disrupt the power to the printer, erasing its memory and/or damaging its power supply.

4. Disengage the arm of the ink cartridge holder.

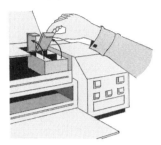

5. Remove the ink cartridge from its package.

6. Slide the ink cartridge (label facing out) into place, and engage the arm.

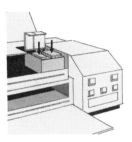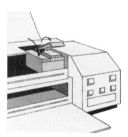

! If ink gets on your hands, wash them with soap and water. If ink gets in your eyes, flush them immediately with water.

7. Close the front cover.

4. Load the paper.

Load a stack of white paper, with the printable side facing up. Don't load the paper higher than the right-edge guide or the printer won't be able to grip it.

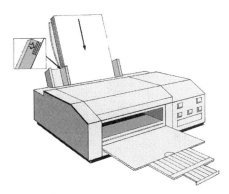

5. Connect the printer.

    1. Turn off the printer and the computer.

    2. Connect the USB cable that came with your printer: one end to the printer jack, the other end to your computer. Make sure the connection is secure, then turn on your printer and computer, and run a "test" sheet.

REMINDER!

Technical writing must be the following:

Clear

- Use parallel structure and uncluttered language.
- Simplify technical terms where possible.
- Use illustrations, charts, and graphs to assist in the reader's understanding.

Specific

- Include only the information that is needed.

Accurate

- Research your facts.
- Have an expert read your work for accuracy.
- Reread, revise, and edit.

Select a piece of technical equipment with which you are familiar (for example, a digital watch, a DVD player, or a digital camera) and write a set of instructions for using it. Have a classmate read the instructions to determine whether or not they could be followed.

Press Releases

Press releases are an essential form of communication for all organizations. They are used to make announcements about an organization, raise its profile, create a positive image, or correct misinformation. Much like a news report (see Chapter 2, page 38), the first paragraph of your press release contains the essential information (who, what, where, when, and why). Subsequent paragraphs should contain the details, with the less important details going at the end of the release.

The reader of a press release always wants to know why the information is important to him or her, so ensure that your press release is aimed at a specific audience. The writing in a press release, although designed to interest a reader in an event or an announcement, should sound neutral (not to be confused with boring). Avoid using adjectives and adverbs that may make your release sound biased.

Be informative. Include details. If you are writing a press release about a recent charity drive at your school, describe the charity, the events that students took part in to raise money, how much was raised, and what that money will be used for. Include quotations from teachers, parents, or the charitable organization to showcase your accomplishments.

If you use quotations, make sure you have permission to use them. Photographs add interest to your press release, so include them when they are practical. Permission will also be needed for any photographs used.

Sample Press Release

FOR IMMEDIATE RELEASE
MARCH 28, 20XX

CONTACT: MS. S. LOUKS
PRESIDENT: JOHN JENKINS SECONDARY SCHOOL
STUDENT COUNCIL
(905) 930-7297

STUDENTS RAISE $25,000 FOR BRAIN TUMOUR RESEARCH

Red River, MB, March 28, 20XX—Over the last two weeks, John
Jenkins Secondary School, the newest secondary school in Red River,
raised $25,000 for brain tumour research. This is the second year that
the school's charity drive, "March Madness," has been held.

"The students have been planning these activities for months. Every
student was involved," said school principal Tina Psaila. Funds were
raised from "Two Loonies a Day" parking charges (both staff and
students), "Collect Your Pennies," and a "Donuts, Pizzas, and
Lollipops" sale. "I've never eaten so much in my life," one Grade 12
student said.

The charity events started with a presentation given by the Brain
Tumour Society, followed by a student-made movie that showed highlights from last year's drive.

The money raised will be used for research into developing new treat-
ments for people with brain tumours.

REMINDER!

Press releases must be the following:

Clear
- *Use uncluttered language.*
- *Avoid descriptive adverbs and adjectives.*
- *Put the most important information first.*
- *Use pictures to increase readers' interest.*

Specific
- *Include only the information that is needed.*

Accurate
- *Do not embellish the facts.*
- *Have the person in charge of the event or appointment read your work for accuracy.*
- *Reread, revise, and edit.*

APPLICATION

Write a press release for an event you have held or are going to hold in your school or in another organization to which you belong.

THE WRITER'S PROJECTS

Investigating the Writer's Craft

1. Research other types of business communication (speech writing, grant writing, brochure writing) that do not appear in this chapter. Using the format of this chapter, write additional "lessons" for those types of business communications. Publish them in your classroom.

2. Interview a teacher, principal, and/or vice-principal about the types of business communications they have to write during the year.

3. Interview a variety of workers about the types of business communications they have to write on the job.

4. Investigate the role of editors in the publishing industry or other businesses.

Practising the Writer's Craft

1. In a small group, re-create a day in the life of a person in a position of responsibility. Interview at least two people who hold positions of responsibility about the types of writing they do on a daily basis. Choose five situations in which that person would have to exercise good business writing. Write five different types of business communication that could come from those situations. They should vary in purpose, audience, and tone. Take those pieces through the writing process.

2. Create a portfolio of a variety of types of business writing that you have done in the past or are doing currently either in the workforce or in other classes.

THE WRITER'S READING LIST

Block, Jay, A. *101 Best Résumés to Sell Yourself.* New York: McGraw-Hill, 2002.

Brusaw, Charles T., Gerald J. Alred, and Walter E. Oliu. *Handbook of Technical Writing*, 5th ed. New York: St Martin's Press, 1997.

Canadian Legal Forms and Agreements. Burnaby, BC: C.G.T. Legal Forms, 2002.

Guffey, Mary Ellen and others. *Business Communication: Process and Product*, 3rd ed. Toronto: Nelson Thomson Learning, 2001.

Lamb, Sandra E. *How to Write It: A Complete Guide to Everything You'll Ever Write.* Berkeley, CA: 10 Speed Press, 1998.

Northey, Margot. *Impact: A Guide to Business Communication*, 5th ed. Toronto: Prentice Hall, 2002.

Rogers, Douglas B. *Write of Way*. Toronto: Pearson Canada, 2002.

Thill, John V. and others. *Excellence in Business Communication.* Canadian Edition. Toronto: Pearson Canada, 2002.

Endnotes and Credits

Chapter 6

1 Malcolm Forbes, quoted in Francis A. Corcell, "Why Don't Accountants Write Well?" Massachusetts CPA Review, Winter 1995, 13–15.

2 Adapted from Charles T. Brusaw and others, *Handbook of Technical Writing*, 5th ed. New York: St. Martin's Press, 1997, 224.

3 These printer installation instructions are based on a combination of instructions from printers made by various manufacturers.

Beyond the Print Résumé

Crawford Kilian

If you have a personal Web page, you may use it "proactively" when seeking employment. Here, you can post your résumé, along with a portfolio, to attract potential employees. In the following pages, Crawford Kilian discusses some strategies for writing and designing résumés and creating portfolios for your Web page. They are a little "trickier" than the traditional print documents....

For one thing, a lot of people are ahead of you. One particular web site, the Monster Board, has an estimated 300 000 résumés in its data base; its Canadian affiliate reportedly gathered 45 000 résumés in its first year of operation. The Monster Board claims that 80 000 job seekers come to its site each day. And it's only one of hundreds of sites that try to match up jobs and people. If your résumé is going to stand out, you'll need to do things better than most people.

MAKE A GOOD FIRST IMPRESSION

When we write web documents, we bring some habits from print. They don't always apply in hypertext, however, and this is especially true of the résumé....

So if you're using the web to market yourself, how do you organize your electronic résumé?

You have a couple of options. You could make it a long, scrolling document, or a stack of short pages linked to a front page. The scrolling document is technically easier to create, since it's just one file and it keeps everything unified. When your readers open your résumé, the first thing they see is whatever you think is your strongest qualification. They can then scroll down through the rest of the résumé, learning more about you.

If you create a stack of pages, the front page is really just a table of contents, a set of buttons that link to an education page or a work-experience page. This gives your readers the chance to decide for themselves what's most important about you from their point of view:

your recent training, your work experience, or your specific work skills.

Maybe, however, the employer has an old modem, and skipping from page to page is painfully slow. That could be annoying. An alternative could be to create a set of links at the top of a single page: education, tour guide experience, volunteer experience, work skills. The employer can then rappel down your pages, hopping straight to the section of most interest—with a button in each section that will lead back to the top of the page for another hop.

Choose the organizational structure you think will create the least trouble for employers. Within each section, display your information as you would in a regular print résumé: for example, job title, summary of duties, perhaps the name of your supervisor and your reasons for leaving....

SURPRISE: REDEFINE YOURSELF AS DIFFERENT

In print, you can set yourself apart from the herd by presenting an unusual layout, by adopting a different tone (maybe very informal), or even by using a distinctive font or pale lavender paper. On the web you can do the same things, but they may backfire. Unusual layouts may just look awkward on your employer's particular browser and platform. A page designed for a big monitor may look terrible on a small one. A knockout special effect (or even access to the page itself) doesn't even happen if the reader lacks a particular plug-in. The background colour you chose so carefully may never show up if the reader's browser has the wrong settings, and your classy font may not show up either if your reader doesn't have the font on his or her computer....

On the web, the reader largely decides how a page will display.... So it's in content that you'll be able to set yourself apart from your competitors by giving the employer a pleasant surprise or two.

Plain English will be the first such surprise. Many job-seekers on the web are technical and scientific workers, businesspeople, and bureaucrats. They're used to writing a thick, kludgy, verbose English even though they say they hate such a style in their colleagues' writing. Where such a technical style is critical to accuracy, it's perfectly OK to use it—but don't use a technical style when you don't need to.

Plain English gives you several advantages in presenting your qualifications in a web-based résumé:

(a) *Pleasure.* Readers can actually understand, at once, what you're telling them. Most will find this a welcome change, and since good writers of plain English are scarce, you've added yet another qualification to your skill list.

(b) *Speed.* Remember that the monitor slows down reading speed. Plain English, concisely written, will help readers get the message faster.

(c) *Nonverbal confidence message.* Plain English tells the reader you're confident in yourself and your understanding of the field in which you work. You're not trying to impress by using business English or bureaucratese or technobabble. Sure, you know those dialects, and you can use them when necessary, but you're not talking shop in your résumé—you're making a sales pitch for yourself. The more people who understand you, the more potential employers you have.

Your web résumé has other nonverbal messages. These messages are critical for the way they support or undercut your verbal message.

Suppose you're presenting yourself in your text as a capable web designer—but your own site organization is clumsy and confusing, with unappealing graphics and spelling errors in the text. Which message will your readers believe, the verbal (what you say on your site) or the nonverbal (how you say it)? The nonverbal, of course....

Probably the best surprise you can offer a potential employer is the nonverbal message that you know your area of expertise, you enjoy using that expertise, and you're not trying to impress anyone with irrelevant information. If you judge your on-line résumé by the three principles of good web writing (i.e., Orientation, Information, and Action),[1] and it passes, chances are your potential employer will be very pleasantly surprised indeed.

CREATE A PORTFOLIO ON YOUR SITE

Many job seekers turn up for a hiring interview with a portfolio that demonstrates their skills: reports written for previous employers, copies of ads they've written or designed, photos they've taken, letters of commendation, and awards. These can be an effective way of showing, not just telling, potential employers what you can do for them.

Your web site can serve as a portfolio that employers can consult even before they call you in for an interview. Consider some of the items you could include in your portfolio:

- Reference letters

- Awards

- Evaluations by previous employers

- Degrees and certificates

- Course descriptions or outlines (both for courses you've taken and courses you've taught)

- Writing samples: technical reports, business plans, proposals, ad copy, news releases, novels in progress, poetry

- Graphic samples: photos, video clips, line art

- News stories (whether by you or about you)

- Links to organizations or individuals

Some of these elements need careful thought. For example, do you want to include a scanned graphic of your college degree, or of an award you won as a freelance writer? Maybe, but from the employer's point of view, will the jolt of seeing the graphic be worth the wait? Are the writing samples really relevant to the job you're seeking, or just the kind of thing you enjoy doing for yourself?

If you provide an e-mail link to a reference or previous employer, has that person given you permission to do so? After all, you're asking the person to go to the trouble of replying to queries about you— maybe a lot of them—and it's simply courtesy to check first to see if that's OK.

PROVIDE USEFUL SERVICES

Your web résumé should supply a benefit to potential employers even if they don't hire you. Maybe you're an accountant who's helped design a new spreadsheet; let your readers link to a demo version of the spreadsheet.... Your were a cook in a local steakhouse? Give us a great barbecue sauce recipe. (In all these examples, I assume you own the rights to what you're offering!)

If you've got the skills to be worth hiring, you know something useful that you can give away. By doing so you build goodwill and likely reach potential employers who will never see your web site—but they may well see a copy of your spreadsheet ... or recipe that has been forwarded to them by someone else, and get in touch with you because they like what they've seen of your work....

MAKE RESPONSE EASY

Your readers may well hop from page to page in your résumé. If they like what they see, getting in touch with you should be as easy as you can make it. This is really a design question inspired by the "you" attitude. For example, each page should have a link titled something like E-mail Me. Click on it, and an e-mail form pops up, pre-addressed to you....

Ease of access, by the way, sends another nonverbal message: I'm thinking of your needs and making life as easy as I can for you.

Another thoughtful touch: In addition to your on-line résumé, whether scrolling or chunked, provide a version that employers can print out for themselves for easy reference. Keep it simple and short—not more than three pages and preferably one or two. Normally such a version would not contain elaborate formatting, links, or other web-dependent effects: just words and white space, laid out for easy readability.[2]

Endnotes and Credits

Appendix C

1   Orientation refers to background information about the site and navigation aids that help readers move around the site. Kilian states that an effective orientation is one that follows two secondary principles: minimalism and coherence. Information refers simply to the message on the site and must be both clear and correct. Action is what a Web page owner wants his or her reader to do after reading the information on the site. To encourage the reader to act, the site must have a positive attitude and a "you" attitude (i.e., thinking of the needs of the reader and presenting information "in terms of the reader's advantage").

2   Excerpted from "Personal Pages, Résumés and Self-Marketing" by Crawford Kilian. *Writing for the Web* by Crawford Kilian, 1st edition © 1999 Crawford Kilian. Reprinted by permission of International Self-Counsel Press.

Writers on Writing

I think the best thing about being a writer is that we get to make up things and tell the truth at the same time.

KYOKO MORI[1]

The Same Ticking Clock   Carol Shields

My friend Sarah was worried about her five-year-old son, Simon. "I hear voices in my head," he told her, "and they're talking all the time."

It took her a few days to figure out that the buzzings in his brain were nothing more than his own thoughts, the beginning of that life-long monologue that occupies and imprisons the self.

It's here in the private, talky cave of our minds that we spend the greater part of our lives—whether we like it or not. And mostly, it seems, we do like it—"The soul selects her own society"—but there are times when the interior tissues thin and when the endless conversation grows unbearably monotonous, when it seems to be going back and forth across the same grooves of experience, the same channels of persuasion, and we long for release. Long, in fact, to become someone else. Even the most fortunate of us lead lives that are sadly limited; we can inhabit only so many places, follow so many lines of work, and can love a finite number of people. We're enclosed not just by the margins of time and by the accident of geography, but by gender and perspective, and by the stubborn resistance of language to certain modes of meditation.

Our own stories, moreover, are not quite enough; why else are our newspapers filled with Dear Abby and Ann Landers, with problem columns for golden-agers, for adolescents, mid-lifers, parents, consumers, patients and professionals? It's not for the solutions that we devour this often execrable journalese, but for a glimpse of human dilemma, the inaccessible stories of others. Even the smallest narrative fragments have the power to seduce. School children read in their arithmetic books about Mary Brown who buys three pounds of turnips at twenty cents a pound and a kilo and a half of cheese at five dollars a kilo. How much change will she get back from a twenty-dollar bill? The answer arrives easily, or not so easily, but leaves us hungering after the narrative thread—who is this Mary Brown, what will she do with all that cheese, and what of her wider life, her passions and disappointments? A phrase overheard on a bus or perhaps in a single name scratched on a wall have the power to call up the world. We want, need, the stories of others. We need, too, to place our own stories beside theirs, to compare, weigh, judge, forgive, and to find, by becoming something other than ourselves, an angle of vision that renews our image of the world.

Of course we draw on our own experiences, though only a few writers draw directly. We want to imbue our fictions with emotional truth, but does this require that we stay imprisoned in the tight little outline of our official résumés, that we must write about the prairies because that's where we live, that we cannot make forays into the swamps of Florida or Mars or Baloneyland, that we must concentrate our steady eyes on the socio-economic class we come from and know best, that we must play it safe—because this is what it amounts to—and write about people of our own generation? A lot of energy has been lost in the name of authenticity; we fear far too much that critical charge—"it doesn't ring true"—and worry too little that it may not ring at all.

"When I write I am free," Cynthia Ozick argues in one of her essays, collected in her book *Art and Ardor*—and she means utterly free, free to be "a stone, or a raindrop, or a block of wood, or a Tibetan, or the spine of a cactus." Our circumscription is largely of our own making, and at least a portion of it flows from a peculiar reluctance—whether caused by a stance of political purity or a fear of trespassing or "getting it wrong"—to experiment with different points of view, and, in particular, with shifts of gender.

We all know that a fully furnished universe is made up of men and women, and that women writers are often called upon to write about men, and male writers about women. Writers go even further at times, not just writing about the other sex, but speaking through its consciousness, using its voice. The question can be asked, and often is, how successful is this gender-hopping? Does any truth at all seep through? Maybe more than we think. Oscar Wilde had the notion that we can hear more of the author's true voice in her or his fictional impersonations than we can hear in any autobiography. (Not that he bothered with the niceties of gender pronouns.) "Man is least himself," he said, "when he talks in his own person. Give him a mask, and he will tell you the truth." A mask, he said, but he might also have said, a skirt. Or a small pointy beard.

This is not to say that crossing gender lines consists of trickery or sleight of hand, nor is it a masquerade as Anne Robinson in her book, *Male Novelists and their Female Voices*, would like us to think; and certainly not an impersonation as Oscar Wilde suggests. To believe this is to deny the writer the powers of observation and imagination and also to resist the true composition of the universe, real or created, in which men and women exist in more or less equal numbers.

Nevertheless it is still considered a rare achievement for a man to have created a believable and significant woman, and a woman a believable and significant man. We point to these gender trips as exceptions, as marvels. Isn't it amazing, we say, that Brian Moore could get inside the head of Judith Hearne and make us believe in her? And Flaubert—how remarkable that he was able to comprehend the temperament of a French housewife, her yearnings and passion! And there must be a couple of others out there—aren't there? Jane Austen gave us a few men who were worth waiting four hundred pages for, although there's a chilliness about even the best of them. Charlotte Brontë uses the male voice in her novel *The Professor*, but the tone is painfully awkward. In writing the male character, Brontë says, she was working under a disadvantage; when writing about women she was surer of her ground. Joyce Carol Oates once remarked that she did badly with male narrators because for her the angle of vision was restricted, and too much feeling and self-awareness had to be sacrificed.

A few years ago women could point to their own lack of experience in the world of men, but this situation has been extraordinarily altered by legislation and by a revolution in thinking. What has also been altered is the kind of experience that can legitimately be brought to art—birth, motherhood, the rhythms of the female body, a yearning for love, and the domestic component of our lives—which serious literature had previously suppressed. But the news is out: we all, male and female alike, possess a domestic life. The texture of the quotidian is rich with meaning, and the old problem-solution trick is beginning to look like a set-up, a photo opportunity for artificial crisis and faked confrontation. Acknowledgment of that fact leads us to the hypothesis that we are all born with a full range of sympathy toward both men and women—yet something, somewhere, gets in our way and makes us strangers. This is puzzling since, despite the inequities of the power structure, men have always had mothers, sisters, wives, daughters, just as women have had access, albeit limited, to the lives of fathers and brothers, husbands and sons. We have been living under the same roofs all these years and listening to the same ticking clock.

It seems baffling, then, that in this day there should be so few men and women writing well about the other sex and even sadder that they are not writing *for* the other sex. The world we are being offered as readers is only half-realized, a world divided down its middle. As readers we are being mislead; as writers we are cheated. I wonder sometimes if the loneliness writers complain about isn't a result of scraping a single personality, our own, down to its last nuance.

What is needed is permission to leave our own skins, worrying less about verisimilitude and trusting the human core we all share. Of course our experiences are necessarily limited—this is part of the human conundrum—but observation and imagination may lead us to what we intuitively know, and have known all along.[2]

Inspiration? Head Down the Back Road, and Stop for the Yard Sales ANNIE PROULX

The Irish singer Christy Moore clips out "Don't Forget Your Shovel," a song I like not only for its tripping rhythm and sly social commentary but for its advice to the diggers of the world, a group to which I belong.

A whole set of metaphoric shovels is part of my tool collection, and for me the research that underlies the writing is the best part of the scribbling game. Years ago, alder scratched, tired, hungry, and on a late return from a fishing trip, I was driving through Maine when a hubbub on the sidewalk caught my eye: milling customers at a yard sale. I stop for yard sales.

Pay dirt. I found the wonderful second edition unabridged *Webster's New International Dictionary* with its rich definitions and hundreds of fine small illustrations. On a collapsing card table nearby sat *Harper's Dictionary of Classical Literature and Antiquities, The Oxford Companion to English Literature*, and other weighty reference works, discards from a local library and the best catch of the trip.

I am an inveterate buyer of useful books on all possible subjects. Collectors pass up ex-libris books, but I need reading copies. And because I often fold down page corners and scribble in margins, it is best to keep me away from first editions.

On the jumbly shelves in my house I can find directions for replacing a broken pipe stem, a history of corncribs, a booklet of Spam recipes, a 1925 copy of *Animal Heroes of the Great War* (mostly dogs but some camels); dictionaries of slang, dialect and regional English; a pile of Little Blue Books (none are blue) from the 1920s featuring titles like *How to Be a Gate-Crasher* and *Character Reading From the Face*. One of these, *Curiosities of Language*, treats us to the tortured orthography our grandparents thought hilarious:

> There was a young man, a Colonel,
> Who walked in the breezes volonel;
> He strolled in the aisles,
> Of the wooded maisles,
> And, returning, read in his jolonel.

This digging involves more than books. I need to know which mushrooms smell like maraschino cherries and which like dead rats, to note that a magpie in flight briefly resembles a wooden spoon, to recognize vertically trapped suppressed lee-wave clouds; so much of this research is concerned with four-dimensional observation and notation. These jottings go into cheap paper-covered notebooks that I keep in a desultory fashion, more often onto the backs of envelopes and the margins of newspapers, from there onto the floor of the truck or onto the stair landing atop a stack of faxes and bills.

The need to know has taken me from coal mines to fire towers, to hillsides studded with agate, to a beached whale skeleton, to the sunny side of an iceberg, to museums of canoes and of windmills, to death masks with eyelashes stuck in the plaster, to shipyards and log yards, old military forts, wildfires and graffiti'd rocks, to rough water and rusty shipwrecks, to petroglyphs and prospectors' diggings, to collapsed cotton gins, down into the caldera of an extinct volcano and, once or thrice in the middle distance, in view of a snouty twister.

I listen attentively in bars and cafés, while standing in line at the checkout counter, noting particular pronunciations and the rhythms of regional speech, vivid turns of speech and the duller talk of everyday life. In Melbourne I paid money into the hand of a sidewalk poetry reciter to hear "The Spell of the Yukon," in London listened to a cabby's story of his psychopath brother in Paris, on a trans-Pacific flight heard from a New Zealand engineer the peculiarities of building a pipeline across New Guinea.

The grand digging grounds are still the secondhand bookshops. Every trip ends with boxes of books shipped back, dusty old manuals on the hide business or directions for the dances of Texas with footprints and dotted lines reeling across the pages. But bookstores are changing. Recently I rattled the latch of a favorite in Denver before I saw the sign announcing that it was forever closed, but the inventory could be "accessed" on the Internet. Another dealer, a specialist in local histories, operated from his living room for years and put out an interesting catalogue from time to time. Both the catalogue and a visit to his bookshelves are things of the past, rendered obsolete by chilly cyber-lists.

I rarely use the Internet for research, as I find the process cumbersome and detestable. The information gained is often untrustworthy and couched in execrable prose. It is unpleasant to sit in front of a twitching screen suffering assault by virus, power outage, sluggish searches, system crashes, the lack of direct human discourse, all in an atmosphere of scam and hustle.

Nor do I do much library research these days, though once I haunted the stacks. Libraries have changed. They are no longer quiet but rather noisy places where people gather to exchange murder mysteries. In bad weather homeless folk exuding pungent odors doze at the reading tables. One stands in line to use computers, not a few down for the count, most with smeared and filthy screens, running on creaky software.

I mourn the loss of the old card catalogues, not because I'm a Luddite, but because the oaken trays of yesteryear offered the researcher an element of random utility and felicitous surprise through encounters with adjacent cards: information by chance that is different in kind from the computer's ramified but rigid order.

This country swims with fascinating pamphlets. In a New Mexico greasy spoon I pick up a flyer that takes St. Paul sharply to task on the subjects of hair style, clothing and women. A hundred miles later I read a narrow sheet with advice on how to behave in the presence of a mountain lion. ("Do not make direct eye contact.... Try to appear as big as possible.")

Food and regional dishes are important research subjects. Some you can order in restaurants, but others exist only in out-of-print cookbooks and must be prepared at home, like a duck roasted inside a watermelon, a dish called Angel in a Cradle, or another called the Atlanta Special, which sounds like a train, although the ingredient list begins, "1 beaver (8 to 10 pounds)."

I like to drive in the West, making a slow drift over caliche and gravel roads, volume cranked up and listening to music (this, too, is research), usually regional subtexts of alternative genres. But two that I never tire of hearing are Glenn Ohrlin singing "Barnacle Bill, the Sailor," in his two-tone voice, and the good ol' boy Texas country-and-western yodeler Don Walser with the Kronos string quartet, sliding a heartaching "Rose Marie" straight at me.

The truck wanders around intersecting roads as tangled as fishing line. At times topographic maps, compass bearings or keeping the sun at my shoulder are better direction guides than signs, usually nonexistent or bullet-blasted into unreadability. The rules of road drift are simple: Always take a branching side route, stop often, get out and listen, walk around, see what you see. And what you see are signs, not direction signs but the others, the personal messages. We live in a world of signs.

I am amazed when people mourn the loss of the Burma Shave jingles. Better stuff is all around us, in public restrooms, in phone booths, on rocks, stapled to telephone poles, struck on lawns. I remember a large billboard that stood for many years on a back-country road in Colorado. The community used it as a kind of enormous greeting card, welcoming home a son on leave from the Navy, congratulating a child on her fifth birthday, inviting neighbors to a party.

The signs of urban panhandlers seem to indicate that many of them took creative-writing courses. These messages are always printed in neat capital letters: "WILL KILL FOR FOOD," "BIG DUMB UGLY BUM NEEDS YOUR HELP," "MY MOTHER LOVED ME BUT NOW SHE'S GONE."

The digging is never done because the shovel scrapes at life itself. It is not possible to get it all, or even very much of it, but I gather what I can of the rough, tumbling crowd, the lone walkers and the voluble talkers, the high lonesome singers, the messages people write and leave for me to read.[3]

Why Not Put Off Till Tomorrow the Novel You Could Begin Today? ANN PATCHETT

My life is a series of ranked priorities. At the top of the list is the thing I do not wish to do the very most, and beneath that is everything else. There is vague order to the everything else, but it scarcely matters. The thing I really don't want to do is start my fifth novel, and the rest of my life is little more than a series of stalling techniques to help me achieve my goal.

This essay, for example, which I asked to write because all of the other essays I have thought of are now finished, will easily kill a day. I have already restored my oven to the level of showroom-floor cleanliness, written a small hill of thank-you notes (some of them completely indiscriminate: "Thank you for sending me the list of typographical errors you found in my last novel"), walked the dog to the point of the dog's collapse. I've read most of the books I've been meaning to read since high school.

The sad part is, when there is something I very much don't want to do, I become incredibly fast about shooting through everything else. This week I have cleaned out my sister's closets. And then my mother's.

For a long time before I start to write a novel, anywhere from one year to two, I make it up. This is the happiest time I have with my books. The novel in my imagination travels with me like a small lavender moth making loopy circles around my head. It is a truly gorgeous thing, its unpredictable flight patterns, the amethyst light on its wings. I think of my characters as I wander through the grocery store. I write out their names like a teenage girl dreaming of marriage.

In these early pre-text days my story has more promise, more beauty, than I have ever seen in any novel ever written, because, sadly, this novel is not written. Then the time comes when I have to begin to translate ideas into words, a process akin to reaching into the air, grabbing my little friend (crushing its wings slightly in my thick hand), holding it down on a cork board and running it through with a pin. It is there that the lovely thing in my head dies.

I take some comfort that I've done this before, that eventually, perhaps even today, I will write the opening pages. Somewhere around Page 80 I will accept that I am neither smart enough nor talented enough to put all the light and movement and beauty I had hoped for onto paper, and so I will have to settle for what I am capable of pulling off. But the question then becomes: On what day do you format a new file on the computer and type that first sentence? I don't actually sell the book until I've finished writing it, so I don't have a deadline to compel me. And if I'm careful with the money I've got, it could last me for a while.

Suddenly, five novels seem ungainly. The thought of it convinces me how boring I've become, and I start to wonder why I never went to medical school. I imagine Elizabeth Taylor choosing a dress in which to marry Richard Burton. Did she believe that this time everything would be different? That this time she would be true until death did them part? I marvel at such hopefulness.

Starting a novel isn't so different from starting a marriage. The dreams you pin on these people are enormous. You are diving into the lives of your characters, knowing that you will fall in love with all of them, knowing (as surely Elizabeth Taylor knew) that in the end the love will finish and turn you out on the street alone.

From the vantage point of a novelist trying to get inside the novel, it makes the most sense to me to shoot for something along the lines of "A Man Without Qualities" or "Remembrance of Things Past," a genuine tome that will keep me busy for the next 30 years or so. But that doesn't work either, because as soon as I'm comfortably inside my book I inevitably long to get out. The farther into the story I get, the harder and faster I write. In short, I become a malcontent dog, either scratching to get in or scratching to get out.

It should be noted that there are two blissful things about writing novels: making them up and seeing them finished. The days I spend in either those two states are so sweet, they easily make the rest of the process bearable. The novel in my head is all mapped out and ready to go, but in these final minutes before departure I feel the rocking waves of doubt.

In trying to start a novel, I dream about the novels I wish I had written, the ideas I should have had. A book about a boy in a boat with a Bengal tiger? Surely I would have come up with that one had Yann Martel not written *Life of Pi*. Surely with a little more time I would have come up with something as important and beautiful as Carol Shields's *Unless*. And yet, the books I most long to plagiarize are my own.

Every time I start a new novel, I think what a comfort it would be to crawl back into the broken-in softness of the old one. Would it be completely unreasonable to write another book about opera and

South America? Would reviewers say I was in a rut? Honestly, how often do reviewers actually read the preceding novels? Of course when I was starting *Bel Canto*, I was longing for just one more book about a gay magician, and so on, backward.

Despite the hand wringing, housekeeping and the overdrive of unnecessary productivity, there will come a point very soon when I will begin, if for no other reason than the stress of not beginning will finally overwhelm me. That, and I'll want to see how the whole thing ends. Sometimes if there's a book you really want to read, you have to write it yourself.[4]

Maximize Your Writers' Group Experience

RAYMOND OBSTFELD

For some, writing is its own reward and release. But for many of us, the recognition and pleasure of having our work read and enjoyed by others is a key part of the experience.

Membership in a writers' group can spur you to write more and write better or, if the group is dysfunctional, make you vow never to put pen to paper or fingers to keyboard again. The goal, of course, is to avoid the latter.

A good writers' group will provide three crucial benefits:

Feedback. We all need someone outside the world we've created to look at our work and make sure others will see on the page what we see in our heads. Many bestselling writers belong to groups, though the groups typically consist of three or four close friends and fellow writers.

Discipline. Most writers are prolific in their minds, creating many masterpieces. But when it comes to the actual writing, we are one lazy bunch. A writing group is like a literary chain gang, forcing each member to stay writing to have something to submit when it's his or her turn to be critiqued.

Competition. Seeing the person next to you turning in ten great pages makes you want to do the same. Reading a powerful passage by another writer in the group is different than reading a powerful passage in a published book. You feel that if the person sitting next to you can write that well, so can you, with a little work.

Get started

Finding writers' groups is fairly easy. Often, it's as simple as attending a writing class, meeting students whose work you respect and whose personalities complement yours and inviting them over to form a group.

There are other ways. Post a notice asking for interested writers to show up at a coffeehouse or restaurant to discuss forming a group (it's better not to have any meetings with strangers in your home). Such notices can be posted in your apartment building, housing complex, school, coffeehouse, athletic club or church. You'd be surprised at how many secret writers there are out there, anxious for an excuse to show their work to others. There's also plenty of discussion online.

Starting a group is the easy part. Maintaining it is the hard part.

Avoid pitfalls

Writing groups often have a short life span, despite the best intentions and oaths of loyalty sworn by the participants at the group's inception. I've been called in as a consultant to many groups that were once healthy, vibrant gatherings, but are now on their deathbeds. There is a cure, but first you must diagnose what's wrong with your particular group. Let's look at the two major symptoms.

Hostility. (Usually manifested by clenched teeth and deep sighs during meetings and muttering to oneself on the drive home after each meeting.) What usually happens: The participants start fighting among themselves, either outright or in their heads. They don't respect the comments of some group members who may seem too harsh or completely off-base. For example, if you write science fiction and no one in the group reads science fiction, their comments may seem useless. Sure, they could comment on general things such as characterization or style, but other comments may seem damaging to your work because of their ignorance of the genre.

Lack of focus. (Usually manifested by a few people talking all the time, often using the manuscripts as an excuse to discuss their opinions about the world and their own lives.) This occurs when there are significantly different levels of writing ability in the group and/or different levels of commitment to writing. If most of the people are serious about their work and are striving to improve, then having two or three members who consider writing a hobby or an excuse to meet other people can demoralize everyone. This has nothing to do with how nice a person is: A very sweet and kind person can unknowingly kill off a promising writing group.

The result of these symptoms is that the writers soon write less and don't show up at the meetings as often. Other things start to take priority, and pretty soon they've stopped writing altogether.

Make it run smoothly

The more organized a group is, the better its chances of survival. Here are five ways to get organized:

Scheduled meetings: Avoid the "Let's call each other later in the month and set up the meeting" syndrome. This wastes time and makes the group seem too casual. Meetings can be used as goals ("I will have 20 pages done by the next meeting"), but irregular meetings are like an irregular diet or exercise plan—self-defeating.

Regular attendance: Participants must commit to the group. Those who continually miss meetings need to be replaced. Such a cavalier attitude can become contagious, and soon everyone is skipping meetings. It may be difficult, but pull the offenders aside as soon as they start missing and say, "I realize you have a busy schedule, as we all do, so maybe you should rejoin us when things slow down for you."

Writing level of members: Some groups have prospective members submit a writing sample before they're accepted. Some also have prospective members sit in on a session first, to hear what kind of insights and comments they might offer. This helps eliminate the person who simply likes everything or loathes everything but can't articulate why.

Leaders: Select a leader who is responsible for running the meetings. This leadership can change at each meeting or it can be the same person each time. But meetings go much more smoothly and efficiently when one person keeps the discussion focused and cuts off digressions.

Read manuscripts before arriving: Some groups have their members read their manuscripts aloud to the group. This is a bad idea. True, you get the rhythm of the words (especially helpful with poetry). But your audience will read your work. Manuscripts for critique should be handed out at the previous meeting. Members should write directly on their copies any praise or suggestions for improvement. Each member should summarize their reactions on a manuscript cover sheet. When the group discusses a manuscript, the leader should ask for these general comments.

After everyone has given his or her reactions, begin a page-by-page analysis:

> **Leader:** "Anyone wish to comment on page one?"
>
> **Bill:** "I liked the opening paragraph. It hooked me immediately and made me care about what was happening to the narrator."
>
> **Susan:** "I agree. But this metaphor in the third paragraph needs to be polished. It's a bit confusing."
>
> **Leader:** "Anyone agree or disagree?"
>
> **Jim:** "Yeah, I didn't get the metaphor either."
>
> **Leader:** "Anyone else? Okay, what about page two?"

This systematic approach actually moves much more quickly than the freewheeling approach. And, because it's specific, the writer will better remember the comments. When the session is over, each member should hand his or her copy of the manuscript back to the author, who can take the stack home and decide which comments to follow and which to discard.

Some authors are nervous about this method because they're worried about copies of their work floating round for someone to steal. Relax. Your ideas are pretty safe. Your chances are much better of dating George Clooney or Nicole Kidman.

Get excited about writing

When a writing group works well, the members can't wait to show up. They look forward to seeing each other and respect each other's opinions about the manuscripts. This doesn't mean they always agree, it just means that they believe the person gave a thoughtful and sincere analysis.

When a group really works, the writers go home inspired to write more and better. When members do that, they'll keep coming back.[5]

Interview with M. NourbeSe Philip

ANDREA GRIFFITH

I was one of the lucky few who participated in a recent writing work-shop with M. NourbeSe Philip and was energized by her insight, suggestions and wisdom.

Andrea Griffith: *unherd Magazine* is geared towards unpublished poettes. As an editor, I'm very interested in how you, a former lawyer, were able to develop your writing skills. Apart from just practice, were there any other factors, influences or activities that profoundly affected or improved your writing skills?

M. NourbeSe Philip: One of the things I always say to younger writers, new writers is that it is important that they read a lot. That is probably, in some ways, more important than the writing itself. You really have to immerse yourself in language to understand how it really works and to see when it's working and when it is not working. One of the ways of doing that is going back to what we call the "old forms." The sonnet. The billionelle. The pantun. All those things. Play around with them. See what it is. In each of those forms, see what makes the poem compelling, because you can bring some of those things into modern poetry.

As I was telling you, I once did an experiment, or exercise—this is what I also encourage new writers to do. Do exercises! And one of the good things about exercises, is that … because it is an exercise, you're not worried about publication, so the censor and the editor is off your back. It frees you up in a really profound way to let things flow. And, in fact, I think that quite often exercises can end up becoming really good forms of short stories for the very reason that you're not thinking, "*I'm writing the ultimate great poem here!*" Yes?

Language excites me. Period. So any way in which you can find to learn about language and how it is working, I urge. But the reading is really important. I think of the first questions I asked you when I met you was, "Who are your favourite poets?" because if you like that poem, it means that that poet is speaking to something in you. You recognize something. And if you look at the word "recognize" it means that you know it again—so you already know it. It doesn't mean that you are going to write like that poet, but that poet has something to teach you. There is something in what that poet is doing that is speaking to you.

AG: A lot of people will say they don't do exercises because they don't have time or the discipline. I think that the two go hand in hand. You can have a lot more discipline when you have time. How do you find the time to write? Do you find it difficult to manage time?

MNP: I think that all of us have that problem living in this part of the world. We seem to have more leisure time, but less time for everything. One of the things I always say is that poetry (I think more so than fiction or prose) requires attention. I think it is probably the most difficult of the written arts, and central to it is attention—both in terms of writing it, and in terms of reading it. And attention is what we don't seem to have in this world. You know we want the five-minute quick clip. We want it now. I think if you are committed to poetry, you are going to have to make the time and be quite ruthless. I think the time is important. I don't think learning about language comes easily.

And [language] is very dangerous. I say working with language is dangerous because unlike the other art forms we use language every day. It is what makes us human. It is what separates us from other animals. We don't use paint every day, we don't use stone every day. We may listen to music every day, but you see what I'm getting at? Even if we think of it in terms of what is happening today—in terms of this September 11th crisis—language is used to confuse us. It is used to persuade us. It is used for propaganda. The challenge for us as writers (and particularly as poets) is to take this medium that is so contaminated most of the time, and purge it of that contamination. So that when I read what you are writing, I see it as if for the first time. That's an amazing challenge. But, it can't come in the five-minute clip. It really comes only with attention. And there is no way around it.

AG: I know it is a typical question to ask, "Why do you write?" but I'm interested. Do you find that poetry helps you in any way?

MNP: When the writing (almost of its own accord) begins to move into poetry, that's when some sort of insight comes. When I was giving birth to my last daughter, the only thing that I could read was poetry. And I think it was because of those rhythms in poetry. I think it's connected to the breath, to how we are as humans. So, in that sense, I think that poetry is really central to our lives. And certainly, in terms of understanding my place in the world as a black woman coming from a former colony. It was my poetry that helped me to understand that. I didn't set out to the poetry to understand it. The poetry taught it to me after. But, I think I said to you when you came to the workshop, "At any point in time there are two poems. There's the one that you want to write and there's the one that has to write itself." I think it's in the poem that wrote itself where you learn most about what you don't know and what you thought you knew. I think that is a really important aspect of poetry, that it has to be a revelation to you even though you are the one who is writing it. Which may seem [a] contradiction in terms.

AG: I understand that. There's got to be some sort of newness to it.
MNP: Absolutely.

AG: That was one of the most profound things you said to me during the writing workshop. "There are two poems within a poem." And it made me realize again how essential editing is to writing. And I think that a good writer is their own best editor. How should a poette negotiate between the initial conception of what the poem should be and what it really should be, or what the page is saying? At some poet, you've got to look at what you've written, take a step back …
MNP: I think that each poet comes to that problem in a different way. Essentially, as you said, take a step back. Essentially, you are putting your ego out of commission, which is a very difficult thing for us ego-ridden Westerners…. As we went through that session, we also noticed that it is in those places where you think there's a problem, that are often in the most fertile places to look for what the poem is trying to say. It is the unconscious tripping you up, or the subconscious, or whatever it is. Yes? So you'll be going, and then think "Why is this not working? What is it?" And the answer is often not to pitch it. It's to try to work with it, winnow it, shake it. Move it around. Push it around to see "What are you trying to tell me here about the poem?"

AG: I find that most of the times when I feel there is a problem in the poem, there really is a problem. So a poette should really trust her instincts.
MNP: Yes.

AG: In doing this magazine, I found it was difficult to find women writers. I know they're out there, hiding in bedrooms, maybe writing under night lights. There may be two reasons why I had difficulty finding women poets. One, some young women aren't confident in their writing; and two, sometimes writers are afraid to put whatever they have out there because they are afraid of criticism. What can you say to new poettes about that fear?

MNP: What I've often said [is] that one of the best resources for a writer of poems is a friend, someone you trust. Someone whose instinct you trust and who is prepared to read your stuff. Often, you'll find that where you think the problem is, they'll also see it. And it doesn't come easily to find someone like that because you may have a friend who thinks everything you do is wonderful. That's not what you want. You want someone you trust, who you know isn't telling you this to hurt your feelings.

This is where a magazine like *unherd*, or even writing collectives [come in]. Groups of people, two or three women, who get together and say, "We're going to get together and show our work. We know each other, we trust each other and we are all working towards a similar goal. Can we collectively give each other feedback and inspire each other to then say 'Okay this is good enough, Andrea. Put it out there'?" I think that is one way of dealing with it is coming together. Either through something like the magazine, or on your own with two or three or five people. I know when I began writing there was a workshop going, a collective group of women, meeting, talking about their work. I think that can be really invaluable.

AG: Okay, I read this on the Internet so I don't know if it's true. "She Tries Her Tongue" was rejected fifty-five times? Is that even true?
MNP: Well, it wasn't 55. At least 20, 25 easily.

AG: How did you know that it was worth publishing?
MNP: I knew it was good. My body told me. And that's where we come to it again—the instinct. I just knew that this was poetry.

AG: That is so inspiring to other poets.
MNP: I just knew it.

AG: Even if someone says "no" to you, try again. But you should feel it in yourself. And that's where confidence comes in, and that's when instinct comes in.
MNP: Probably instinct more than confidence. It was very … primal. I knew I had done something. I didn't know what I had done, but I knew I had done something. And the fact that it is still in print some ten years after confirms that.[6]

Dying Metaphors Take Flight   Cathleen Schine

I have been thinking about metaphors lately, and I think you should think about them, too. I have been thinking that the dying metaphor deserves to live.

In his classic 1946 essay, "Politics and the English Language," George Orwell made a simple division: There is what poets do, the metaphor newly invented that "assists thought by evoking a visual image," and there is the dead metaphor, which no longer evokes any visual image at all. This dead metaphor has been around so long that it has reverted; it is now just an ordinary word.

"Brand-new" is one example. When I've thought about it, which is not very often, I've assumed it was an expression that had something to do with Madison Avenue thinking up new names for old products, or new products for old markets. But the dictionary says it probably derived from a "brand" that was a piece of wood burning on a stove and so meant, originally, fresh from the fire. And there's "deadline." A deadline is something I have never looked forward to. I just never realized why. It means a line around a prison beyond which a prisoner will be shot.

Even dead metaphors are poetry to poets. Randall Jarrell was a master at breathing life into these poor creatures, and what life! Here with the word "overtone," is one of thousands of examples from his novel *Pictures From an Institution:* "Gertrude thought children and dogs overrated, and used to say that you loved them so much only when you didn't love people as much as you should. *As much as you should* had a haunting overtone of *as much as I do*—an overtone, alas! too high for human ears. But bats heard it and knew, alone among living beings, that Gertrude loved."

But what about Orwell's third category, the dying metaphor, gasping uncertainly, neither ordinary word nor vivid image? Dying metaphors disgusted Orwell. Euphemism, vagueness or any kind of lazy, unthinking use of ready-made phrases covers up meaning, often brutal political truths. And dying metaphors are nothing if not euphemistic, vague, lazy, unthinking and ready-made.

Still, dying metaphors will always be with us, for metaphors must make their way from new-born to corpse somehow. They cloak not only the politicians' brutal designs; they cloak ordinary thoughts and intentions as well. But what do they cloak them with? Odd, intriguing figurative speech. Look beneath the metaphor to the true meaning of a statement. Clarity is intellectual morality. But then, for the sheer joy of it, look at the cloak itself, at the dying metaphors. They, too, are poetry, and we are the poets because of them.

I am often accused of "flying off the handle." What does that mean? It used to mean, to me, that some member of my family was insensitive, unsympathetic, uncooperative and unsupportive. Now, I see myself flying through the air, flung from the handle of an ax like a loose blade, sparkling steel cutting through the blue of the bright sky, soaring, noble and alone, toward the heavens! My life has been considerably enriched.

Some years ago, I experienced a metaphor epiphany while watching "Chariots of Fire." On the screen, one of the skinny young men in flapping white shorts drew a line in the dirt with his foot, then carefully stood, placing the toe of his primitive running shoe against that line. The music began pumping, the scrawny Brits in their underclothes ran like gods, emotions soared, mine among them— "Toe the line!"

I forget who won the race. But I'll never forget that moment—an awakening, a usage revelation. Unblock that metaphor! My mother, left with the dog when my brother and I went off to college, called me one evening, miserable, and said "The dog is … *dogging* my steps." Pause. "He's hounding me, too!" she cried out in excitement of her linguistic discovery. And so, understanding, she forgave.

"Toe the line" was one of Orwell's examples of a dying metaphor. It has so thoroughly lost its pictorial power, he wrote incredulously, that it is often written "tow the line." Until my "Chariots of Fire" epiphany, I, knowingly full well how to spell it, had nevertheless pictured its meaning as "tow the line." But it *was* a picture: a downtrodden, oppressed sort of fellow in a blue peasant blouse, a rope over his bent shoulder, hauling a barge heavy with its cargo of conventions, rules, expectations.

Now here's a question. In a recent newspaper article on women in film, a high-level female producer was quoted in this way: "You do have a responsibility to make movies that are commercial, and you do try to tow the studio line." Was she misquoted? Did she in fact say "toe the studio line"? Very likely. But perhaps, on the other hand (a lovely dead metaphor: "on the other hand"), perhaps she's never seen "Chariots of Fire" or read "Politics and the English Language." In which case, she might have imagined, as she spoke, a down-trodden, oppressed sort of female producer in high heels, a rope over her bent shoulders, hauling a huge barge heavy with studio conventions, rules, expectations.

I don't know the answer to my question, but I think that for many reasons, including all those downtrodden folk unnecessarily hauling all those barges when they could simply be standing with their toes neatly aligned, we should revive the dying metaphor.

I used to think a potboiler was a book that bubbled with trashy sex and intrigue. A beach book. Now I know the reference is not to the book itself but to the author's boiling pot, brimming with meat and potatoes earned through his hack labors, writing, you know—a beach book.

One can become overenthusiastic, it is true. I interpreted "Curses! Foiled again," to mean "Curses! My opponent's narrow, flexible sword has touched me again!" Then I looked up "foiled" in the dictionary. It means ... foiled. But so what?

The dying metaphor gives to the world a fresh and vivid sense of absurdity. We are sticks in the mud stabbing in the dark. Think what a stick in the mud really is. *Feh!* And think, now, what you yourself are. A living body of language: nosy, handy, tongue in cheek. You can have a belly full and go belly up, stomach one thing, palm off another. Headstrong, hotheaded. And best of all: cheek by jowl. Picture a cheek by a jowl. Very close indeed. We're homesick one day, suffering from cabin fever the next. We're windbags or razor-tongued. There is a preposterous, literal-minded grandeur to the deconstructed dying metaphor, a quality otherwise found only in Greek myths and Saul Steinberg drawings.[7]

Excerpts from *Fear and Loathing at the Laptop*   Sandra Martin

One of the differences between novels and real life is that nobody calls the cops when you kill off the fictional brother-in-law who is so boring he makes your back teeth ache. Unlike relatives, characters can be pruned back, transplanted or even chucked entirely. All you need is the courage to pull the plug and start all over again with another empty page.

That is the hard part. No matter how tedious or overbearing characters become, they are still there keeping you company in your imagination. Getting rid of them means admitting you have wasted months, maybe years. Like detonating a bad relationship, you may be better off but you are still alone and bereft.

"It happens to everyone," says Margaret Atwood. "Or at least it has happened to everyone I know." Over the years and the course of writing novels she has come to recognize three symptoms of character fatigue.

- The narrative grinds to a halt.

- You know a lot about people's lives and what they have done in the past, but they haven't done anything in the present. They eat breakfast a lot but you can't get them to do anything else.

- You develop a general feeling of malaise and despair when you will do almost anything other than sit down and write—working on your financial accounts, watching daytime television and realizing you have seen the same weather report twice, refolding all of the Christmas wrapping paper—and it is July.

The only writer I have ever met who claims never to rewrite is Bernice Rubens, the Booker-Prize winning author of *The Elected Member*. And even she admits it's because she spends so much time working out the plot and the characters before she puts pen to paper.

Most writers know instinctively when something is wrong. While they may delude themselves into doggedly hitting their computer keys for a few more agonizing months, eventually they—at least the ones whose books we read—do what needs to be done and send unruly characters packing.

"You have to make the decision yourself," says Guy Vanderhaeghe. "Editors may gently suggest but, at least in my case, there is a moment in which you find out that there is a character that is like a bad smell at a party. You know that this character has to be asked to leave and only you can do it."

Barbara Gowdy is unusual in that she shows her work early on in the writing process to her editor. "I have the confidence that I can create something," she says, "but I don't have the confidence that I can do it on my own or that I will even see how it can be done."

Here are some stories from the fiction-writing trenches about what it is like to stare a character or even an entire novel in the eye and blink.

Michael Ondaatje

The case of the disappearing greyhounds

Ondaatje wrote about 150 pages of *In the Skin of a Lion* from the point of view of Ambrose Small (the self-made millionaire owner of a string of theatres in Ontario, who vanished in December, 1919) before he realized that he was forcing himself to stay with a character "who was beginning to bore me."

Although Ondaatje had "piles of research" on Small—"his theatres, his Rosedale house"—as well as all the chapters he had already written, he abandoned the book and the question of what had really happened to Small.

Eventually, after working on some other projects, Ondaatje returned to the mystery of Small's disappearance, but this time he focused on "the minor characters who were obliquely linked to him: such as the girlfriend he left behind and the 'detective' who went searching for him." That "searcher" became Patrick Lewis.

"He had an iguana in the earlier draft, and that was all he brought with him into the new version," says Ondaatje. "I never looked at that early draft again and focusing now on those minor characters, some invented, some based on historical persons, I was never bored again. I suppose if you write dutifully, ponderously, that will be reflected in what you are writing.

"In the new version, Small was reduced to about eight pages though he is still the catalyst for the plot which brings all the characters together. Funnily enough, when I gave my finished draft to a friend to read he said, 'You know there is a really interesting character here, you should have more of him—Ambrose Small.' So I took a second look and put a bit more back."

The reborn version of *Lion* also had a whole subplot about greyhounds, including several racing scenes, which was a popular sport at the time in Toronto, and a climax up in Georgian Bay involving many more greyhounds. "I had at one point even gone to the Greyhound Museum in Abilene, Kan., (which is next to the Eisenhower Museum, and far more interesting)," recalls Ondaatje. "All these hounds got jettisoned, wisely I think, though I imagine that their scenes exist in the book whenever I think of it, rather like a phantom limb. I believe I left in one paragraph where Patrick stops and peers into a cage of greyhounds in Union Station. It wasn't a really necessary moment but I wanted some scent of them left in the book."

Michael Redhill

When you have to put the archivist in storage

About four years into the writing of *Martin Sloane*, his Giller-nominated first novel, Redhill dumped a character (an archivist named Elizabeth), a subplot, and about 200 pages of what he had conceived as a "collage" novel made up of interviews, transcripts and descriptions of artworks.

"Poor thing is sitting in a box somewhere," he says. "She had a love story, a partner who was worried about her obsessions and who eventually left her, and all sorts of resonances connected with Martin's disappearance, but it wasn't working, so she went."

Elizabeth was "standing in the way of me writing the story as it needed to be written," Redhill says. "As soon as I took her out, the book was there. All the stuff that was in the secondary level of the story moved into the foreground and Jolene became the main character and a lot of the interviews that the Elizabeth character had done turned into dialogue between characters."

That doesn't mean it was easy to pull the plug. "I knew something drastic had to happen for the novel to make the vertical leap it needed to make, but I had invested so much time in her and the story as I had imagined it, that I would just keep writing and then I would say I will go and work on something else today."

Like a lot of first novelists, Redhill was trying to do something that was too complicated. The whole thing "was bent under the burden of its own conception."

After killing off Elizabeth, he put the novel away for a year. "I was grief-stricken. I thought I was never going to finish it. I knew she couldn't be in the book any more, but that didn't mean I had any solution to what could, or should, be there in her place.

"And I was scolding myself for having wasted so much time when I could have been writing poetry and plays and who did I think I was anyway?

"After enough time had passed, I picked it up again and the original impetus that had made me want to write the novel was still there." Even so, he quit writing a couple more times and he also tried to withdraw it from publication after it had been accepted by Doubleday. "I lost my mind for a couple of years in the end there. I just couldn't see the forest or the trees by the time the book was approaching publication. I was just terrified."

Margaret Atwood

Even as compleat a writer as Atwood can get off on the wrong fictional foot. When she began writing *The Blind Assassin*, the main character, Iris, was freshly dead and one of her granddaughters had discovered the body.

"I couldn't get into the character of the old lady that way," explains Atwood, "and the granddaughter started to take over and the book became all about her."

After about 60 pages, she trashed that formulation. "I kept a few little snippets. Iris had some containers of bran cereal in which she hides her keys and that is in the final draft."

Atwood started again with the old lady very much alive, but still speaking in the third person. There were two other characters, a man and a woman, who became entangled with each other. The man had a father, whom Atwood quite liked, and newborn twins, of whom he was very fond. "He had just painted his attic a beautiful shade of tuscany," she recalls. "He was going to have a study up there and a ladder he could haul up when the twins got big enough to walk."

Things began to go awry, however. "When you start describing a lot of furniture, you know you are in trouble," says Atwood. Now she has "a whole family plus an affair living in a drawer," and Iris is speaking in her own voice.

With *Alias Grace*, she started with the right character but in the wrong person—the first instead of the third. "I had done about 100 pages," she remembers, "and I was on a fast train to Paris and two things happened at once. I got a blinding migraine headache and I realized I had to throw out that 100 pages and start again."

She had thrown out an entire novel, although before it was completely finished. "It was obvious that it wasn't going to be finished because it got very long and no events had taken place. There was a lot of landscape in it."

On the other hand, there is hope for the adulterous man living in a drawer with his offspring. "They may be revived," she says. It has happened before. She started *Surfacing* the first time in 1964, with a different character, dropped it into a drawer for seven years and picked it up again in 1970–71 and began again. "Saving characters," she says, "is like saving string. You never know when you may need that piece of string."

Paulette Jiles

Jiles has many books of poetry and memoir to her name, but she got so bogged down with the writing of *Enemy Women* (a first novel about a young woman named Adair who goes through enemy lines to rescue her father during the Civil War) that she started over again—twice.

"I couldn't come to grips with my character," she says from her home in San Antonio, Tex. At first, she created "a Scarlett O'Hara type" named Savannah with the result that the book "was very sentimental and very long." What made it worse was the fact that Jiles also hadn't figured out the plot.

"It was the most frustrating thing that has ever happened to me," Jiles admits. When she learned that women had been held by both sides as prisoners of war, she had the basis of her plot, but then she went to the other extreme and created a cold and passive character named Sarah. "It was impossible for her to carry the weight of a novel in which there was a lot of action."

Years were passing and Jiles was still "banging my head against a stone wall."

About this time, a friend, who teaches creative writing at the University of San Antonio, went on sabbatical and asked Jiles to substitute teach for her. "Working with her kids and trying to help them with their fiction," turned out to be a self-help project for Jiles. In rereading *Anatomy of Criticism* by Northrop Frye as part of her course preparation, she realized that her own problem stemmed from her confusion about the kind of novel she was trying to write.

There are two basic fictional narratives, she learned: the exploration of social and psychological circumstances, which are the kinds of novels that Jane Austen, Margaret Atwood, Carol Shields and Iris Murdoch write; and the prose-fiction romance or quest novel, such as Ernest Hemingway's *The Old Man and the Sea*, Mark Twain's *Huckleberry Finn* and more recently, Charles Frazier's *Cold Mountains*.

Jiles loves the first kind of novel, but she was trying to write the second type. Then she came across a book called *The Writer's Journey* by Christopher Volger, which "knocked me out." Although primarily for screenwriters, the Volger book dispelled her notion that quest novels were merely "bodice rippers" and convinced her she could try to write one with literary quality.

"I came to it after I had figured out what I was doing and after I had got my character, Adair," she says, "but he confirmed that I was right in everything I was doing and that I was closer to the folk tale than the novel of psychological exploration."

As for the two discarded heroines, Jiles found a happy home for Savannah, the sentimental one who is Adair's younger sister in the final version. Adair and Savannah are family names that belonged to the daughters of Jiles's great-great-grandfather who disappeared during the Civil War. "After I decided I am going to stop fighting this and I am throwing it away," she says, "I photocopied [the manuscript] and sent it to my aunts. I knew they would love it."

Sarah, the cold and passive sister who kept getting in the way of the action, was not so lucky. She was trashed. "I just got tired of her, so I threw her out," says Jiles. Relief was what Jiles felt after doing the deed. "It wasn't hard to dump them. The puzzle was how to make this work."

Susan Swan

"I teach creative writing and I spend a lot of time telling my students how you have to find the right voice and if you don't find the right voice, it is not going to work," says Swan. "And here I am—this is my sixth work of fiction—and I am no different from the novice creative-writing student."

Swan has been working on her next novel, tentatively titled, *What Cassanova Told Me,* since 1997. The novel has two narratives, one in the present day and one in the 18th century. The historical characters, Cassanova and Asked For Adams (the fictional daughter of the second president of the United States), materialized very quickly. But she has just realized, after more than four years of writing, that her contemporary characters—Winn Adams and her niece Joey, who are descendants of Asked For Adams—are wooden and all wrong. "It is like having stuffed dolls with their eyes missing. They really have no souls."

She is "chagrined" that she has been labouring with the wrong characters for so long. Having already done a dozen revisions, she figures she has another five or six months of work and probably three more revisions ahead of her. "I should have figured this out more quickly, but in some way I write to discover who my characters are," she says. "I don't have a blueprint in place before I start. I have a hunch of the story but I don't have it all figured out."

Swan's not completely sure why it took her so long to figure out the problem, but she thinks it is partly that she was writing Winn and Joey in the third person instead of her usual first person voice.

"In *The Wives of Bath*," she explains, "I initially told it in Polly's voice and I had to switch to Mouse, but this was relatively easy for me to identify because working in the first person is what I am most experienced in."

This time, she was working in the third person, so instead of recognizing that the characters were at fault, she blamed the voice in which they were speaking.

Swan keeps her corpses around. Her process, she says, is like a compost pile that fertilizes her other writing. In the past few weeks, she has been deconstructing Winn and Joey and incorporating some of their parts into her new present-day characters, Lee and Luce. "Even with the wrong characters—the stuffed dolls without eyes thing—they may have a shapely limb or a speech mannerism or a job that needs to be grafted onto the characters that are taking their place. A total exorcism isn't necessarily the best thing in my messy, organic process."

Guy Vanderhaeghe

Forget consigning unwelcome characters to the bottom drawer or the compost heap, says Vanderhaeghe, two-time Governor-General's Award-winning writer. Get them out of the house or the garden. It's a tip he picked up from Margaret, his artist wife. She torches canvases that aren't working.

Denying he is brave or ruthless, he claims it is cowardice that has made him throw out characters, subplots and even an entire novel. Just like a recovering smoker who won't keep cigarettes in the house, Vanderhaeghe says he doesn't want to be "tempted to tiptoe back to that drawer, yank the thing out and go down that bad path all over again."

Consequently, researchers will never be able to pick over the imagery and themes in Vanderhaeghe's unpublished first novel, *Going to Argentina*. "It was a really dumb idea, a vulgar picaresque with elements of allegory that was set in western Canada in the 1940s." He had been working on it for years, while he was employed as a schoolteacher in Herbert—as in Hoover—Saskatchewan. After his first collection of stories, *Man Descending*, won the Governor-General's Award in 1982, he sent *Argentina* to his publisher. "Then I got very twitchy."

He had an intuition that the collection of stories was much

stronger than the novel, and "when I looked at this bastardized intellectual romp, I said, "No, I don't think I want to publish this book." His publisher didn't seriously dissuade him and after a moment of terrible disappointment—"I sat in the bathtub for about four hours and got really wrinkled," he says—he was relieved.

In *Homesick*, the second novel that Vandergaeghe published, Vera, a character from rural Saskatchewan, goes to Toronto and marries a Jewish intellectual. Vanderhaeghe fell in love with this character—a self-educated autodidact. "He kept getting bigger and bigger in my mind and he began growing larger than his wife in the novel," explains Vanderhaeghe. He kept writing and then chopping because he knew the relationship between Vera and her husband was "torquing" things out of shape. Finally he bit the bullet and killed him off. "I always knew that this guy was going to die and she was going to become a widow," he says. "He just died sooner and less of their life was described in the book."

Barbara Gowdy

"I was about 100 pages into *Mr. Sandman* when I was told it was too flat. I had suspected it and it was corroborated by my editor, so I took an entirely different tack," says Gowdy, who admits she is completely suggestible. "I shouldn't show my work too early because I will believe what anyone says, especially my editor."

Like most people, she doesn't like hearing her work criticized, but she is also grateful for the feedback. For her it is akin to being diagnosed with cancer at a stage when it can still be treated. "I tend to think there is a basic vision or talent that comes with any art form," she says, "but a lot of it is craft and if it isn't working you kind of sense it." Besides, she has a hunch that she shows her work early when she has a sneaking suspicion that it isn't working.

"With *Mr. Sandman*, if my editor and a couple of other people I trusted had said, 'Are you kidding, this is fabulous,' I would have said, 'Oh great.' You have to show it to people you can trust, but even then, they can falter."

For her, writing is a lot like climbing a mountain: It's a long trudge. She had just done a major rewrite—15-hour days over six months—on her forthcoming novel, *The Romantic*, a rewrite that she didn't think was necessary, at first. "I thought I was at the peak," says Gowdy, "and she turned me around and told me the peak is over there, so I picked up my backpack and headed off."

The novel, which should be out next March, is about "how men and women love very differently, but I didn't realize that until I had three day-long conversations with my editor." So she revised one more time.

"When you stop working on a book is completely arbitrary," Gowdy says. "It is usually when you just can't stand it any longer." Grim as that sounds, Gowdy is grateful now that the hard slogging is done. "Just because you have spent a lot of time and worked hard, doesn't mean it is good," she says. "When a book is done, it is done like dinner. It is in the stores and you can't fix it. You can second guess it, but you can't do anything about it."[8]

What It Means to Be a Writer   SHARON RIIS

I am a country and western song
splayed and obvious
my breast bone cracked in two.

Or, I can forego the metaphor and simply say: I am a writer. The
currency of writing, *good* writing, whatever the form, is your own life;
your own visceral experience. I'm not referring to circumstances:
class, education, age, gender, genetics; but to deep, often buried,
sometimes unpalatable, occasionally terrifying emotion. Loneliness,
dread, joy, grief, despair, delight, torpor, desire, shame ... When
people say "write what you know" they're not talking about place but
about emotional experience. David Adams Richards needn't be
restricted in his writing to the Miramichi nor Suzette Couture to
Franco-Ontario. They are *good* writers. Give them a subject (marriage)
and an unusual setting (fourteenth-century Cambodia) and, with a
little research regarding time and place, and perhaps a brief sojourn in
Phnom Phen to experience the unholy humidity, they could deliver a
fabulous story, each utterly different from the other. The point is:
there's no such thing as generic life; every life is peculiar. When you
tell the truth, you can hang any story, any idea on it, in whatever
genre you like, comedy, satire, drama or adventure. The truth will be
recognizable by everyone, everywhere. You may even have a hit on
your hands.

Of course, unhinged emotion like an unhinged idea means less
than nothing. It just means that you're unhinged. Writers are first and
foremost storytellers. Ideas are a dime a dozen; a good story is a rare
and wondrous thing. But a good story isn't simply narrative. It's narrative driven by emotional truth, honed by a distinct point of view. The
point of view might make us uneasy, but if the emotion supporting it
is honest, then that's reason enough to accept the point of view as
authentic and therefore worthy of our attention. *The Night Porter*
comes to mind. Or, closer to home, *Leolo*. But I don't mean to single
out already celebrated films as examples of what I'm on about. A television series like "Straight Up" both entertains *and* cuts close to the
bone with its eerily real and disjointed depiction of late adolescence.
And "Traders" has found an audience not only because of its tight,
flashy style but because the characters are genuine enough that we
can believe in their authenticity. Their machinations are motivated.
It's not *simply* about greed. The writers are doing their job. Just
because we suck on our own bone marrow for sustenance doesn't

mean our stories have to be earnest or dead serious. The greatest comic writers in the world expose their nerve endings in their work.

Writers are isolated, obdurate, antisocial individuals with enormous egos, and sometimes no ego at all. We sit in our rooms and ruminate; occasionally we write something down. How then does such a lonesome charlie survive in the endlessly social, often glib world of film and television production? The short answer is that many don't. They don't have the temperament [or] the stamina. Those who do have discovered the very real excitement of collaboration; of having a producer or director *almost* as interested in your writing as you are; of having half a dozen individuals enter your peculiar world-view to try to make it better—clearer, more dramatic, more interesting—*with* you. And all this buoyant support is before production. If your script actually gets shot there are dozens, maybe hundreds, of people whose business it is to make your work sing. Not all collaborative efforts are charmed. But I've been writing scripts for sixteen years and only twice have the collaborations been a nightmare. Partly because of the banality of the producers in question, but mostly because we were approaching the material from different planets. The only thing to do in a situation like that is to bail out as quickly as possible. In order to be able to do so, it's important to steer clear of a big mortgage. It's also vital to have a life, tricky as that may sound …

Screenwriting is the most difficult form of writing there is. It's as succinct a medium as poetry and yet it must often do the narrative job of *War and Peace*. It requires us to write in images, to create meaning visually. The interior authoritative voice of prose is anathema to screenplays. Nonetheless we, as screenwriters, must have something to say. But we must show it, not tell it. And we must do so in 22 or 48 or 95 pages wherein we *never* repeat ourselves, for our worldwide audience is astonishingly literate.

A brilliant screenplay, like a brilliant play, poem or novel, is a work of art. But only potentially. A screenplay is not something in itself, but a map, a blueprint for something else entirely. That something else is dependent on a host of people. Those of us who've languished in development hell for any period of time, and that would be *all* of us, know this only too well. This may be especially true of long-form screenwriting. When a script stays unproduced, as most do, it doesn't quietly fold its tent and steal away; it treads water in the "slough of despond" inside your head, and clamours for release. The characters, central and secondary, harangue you for their day in the sun and there's little you can do about it. Well, you can always drink. And commiserate with their predicament because their predicament is *your* predicament.

Not only is screenwriting the most difficult form of writing, it's also the least respected. This is partly the result of a cavalier attitude among producers, agency drones and occasionally directors who think one writer is much like another. This is not so, though often I suspect we do end up *seeming* remarkably the same. This is probably rooted in the high costs of film-making and the bone-headed notion that the only way to make money is to produce a film that appeals to everyone. So terrific scripts are bled of all that makes them terrific. And terrific writers suddenly all seem the same. But good stories are always peculiar. They always have a strong central point of view. And if there's anywhere we should stamp our dainty foot and draw the line in all those story meetings, it's here. "Let me have my say. Help me say it better, clearer, but let me have my say!" When I started writing scripts way back when, I regarded almost everyone as an enemy. The producer, the networks, the agencies, the distributor, the script editor and sometimes even the director. But now I know better. *None* of these are enemies. We're all in it together. And these days, when I feel I'm crying in the wilderness, I realize that I simply haven't done my job yet. My first job being to include all the assembled players in my world-view. And I've come to understand that sometimes my world-view is enhanced and expanded when I take into consideration the peculiar slant of those around me. Lucky for me I'm a socialist.

So with the difficult form and the lack of respect, why on earth do we do it? Are we peculiarly masochistic, greedier than most or simply more sociable? There *is* money to be made. And the parties are a lot better than what the literary world offers up. Film and television are remarkably democratic mediums. If you've got talent *and* an obsessive, driven nature, you'll do fine. But I think the real reason we are drawn to the medium, as writers, is that the medium is *the* art form of our time. Believe it or not. We can all scorn that notion and list endless examples of bad TV and bad film. But there are lots of bad books and bad plays and bad poems too. The truth is that when our work is produced it is seen by hundreds of thousands more people than those reading a best-selling novel in this country. And that, fellow travellers, is power. We have the power to enlighten, unnerve, educate, expose, exhort, dismiss, *astonish*. We are a force to be reckoned with. Without the writer, there's no industry.

What every writer wants is to be brave in their work. What this requires in a collaborative medium is a brave producer, a brave director. And God knows … brave actors. Then the astonishing is possible. I wish you all, every one, courage.[9]

Adapting Lost in the Barrens *for Television*

KEITH ROSS LECKIE

I was approached by Atlantis Films to adapt the Farley Mowat novel *Lost in the Barrens* into a television movie. The exciting part of this was that they apparently had production financing in place and wanted to shoot the film in about three months time. I had worked on projects through months and years' worth of drafts hoping and praying that financing would eventually be found. But on this, with the money and crew ready and waiting, all I had to do was turn in a decent script and it would be shot. It was a wonderful gift to a writer. The other element was pressure. I find, as do many writers, that I work at my best and most focused when I'm under pressure.

A script did exist but it required a major rewrite and the writer had taken on other commitments and was unavailable. I was given the option and would receive the same fee to either rewrite the existing script or start from scratch. I decided not to read the old script and to start from scratch. I would always take this option if possible. It can often take less time and is always more satisfying.

Farley's book was written early in his career and *Lost in the Barrens* is not his strongest work. It's a simple action tale of two boys, a white (who has come up to northern Manitoba to live with his uncle) and a Native, who becomes separated from a hunting party and must use his wits and skill to survive several months against weather, starvation and predatory animals in the subarctic.

In trying to make this story better and more contemporary, my first consideration was the old three levels of conflict: (1) person against the environment; (2) person against person; (3) person against himself. Farley had lots of number one. The whole tale was man against the environment. So I started to work on ideas about the "person against person" conflict. In Farley's book, Jamie and his Uncle Angus are immediately great friends. I introduced some effective conflict between them, but most important was to introduce conflict between the boys. The boys represent the central relationship in the story. In the book, the boys are great friends at the beginning, middle and end. There is no arc to their relationship. So I started working on the boys' backgrounds. I used my experience with *Where the Spirit Lives* and had the Indian boy Awasin just returning to his people after four brutal years in an Indian residential school. He hates white people. As for Jamie, he has just been removed from an elite eastern boarding school where he was top dog and dropped into this primitive northern environment which he despises. This set-up provided lots of opportunities for "person against person" conflict between them.

Before I considered number three, "person against himself," the inner conflict, I thought some research was necessary into where they were going and what they were doing in the story. With an assistant from Atlantis I gathered a body of material on the Cree and Dene (Awasin's people), specifically on their hunting methods on the edge of the tree line and in the Barrens beyond. I found out some fascinating things about these people. They are among the most skilled and successful hunters in the world. As with the Inuit, hunting for them is a spiritual undertaking. They must purify themselves and achieve a "state of grace" and in this state on the eve of the hunt, they connect with the animals, their prey, and "will" them to come to them. Through prayer they express the hunger of their families and themselves and ask the animal to sacrifice itself. This was rich ground for me to embellish Farley's story.

I went a little further with research and was pleased to find some scientific studies done in the early seventies that contributed to the primary research. The study revealed that when a band of Cree hunters stalk a heard of caribou or elk, several of the old, sick, lame or young animals will turn from the herd and walk towards the hunters! They sacrifice themselves for the good of the herd. There is documentary helicopter footage available showing this very phenomenon. So, beginning as a sceptic, I found there is truth to the spiritual connection between the Cree hunters and the animals; "need" and "sacrifice." All wonderful stuff, and I used it not only in *Lost in the Barrens*, but in a later movie, *Trial at Fortitude Bay*.

Having found this strong hunting milieu, I went on to explore three, conflict level "person against himself," the inner conflict. The contrasting backgrounds of the boys, so effective for conflict level two, also gave strong opportunities for conflict level three. Awasin has been forced to live in a white-run residential school away from his band for four hunting seasons. He has lost touch with the skills of survival. He is not sure if he can survive in the wilderness any more, so his inner conflict is fear of failure. If he cannot remember the old lessons and regain his spirituality, the boys will die. As for Jamie, he believes he knows everything and can be taught nothing. He firmly believes that Awasin's spirituality is all silly mumbo-jumbo, so when it works and they are successful in the hunt—a caribou sacrifices itself to them and saves them from starvation—Jamie is forced to re-evaluate Awasin and to re-evaluate himself and his biases.

Whether I write original stories or adaptations, I am very much structure-oriented and work hard to create a structured framework before ever writing any actual scenes. I usually begin by sketching out a general three-act structure that accommodates the story: the "beginning, middle and end." Within this I then write each scene in paragraph form. This document (an extended treatment) can be as much as 50 pages on an MOW. This is perhaps more than many writers do but it is where the bulk of my work is done and usually it takes longer than actually writing the first draft. The benefits are great because at this stage you can rework the structure with great objectivity. You can ruthlessly slash and burn if you need to. It's in a form that allows producers and editors to see exactly what you're doing and give meaningful input. When this process has been thoroughly done and the scene-by-scene treatment is in great shape, then and only then do I attempt dialogue and a first draft. Dialogue is where I begin to make my emotional investment in the writing. Dialogue is where my characters come alive and I quickly lose my objectivity. If the structure is working, then I have the freedom to play around with the characters and I know I'll be all right.

There are some writers who start at Act One, Scene One and just write, not knowing where they will go. I know Paul Quarrington, a fine writer, writes this way. But for me it's important to know just where I'm going. I find it enhances the scenes as I write them. And to write dialogue right off the top can be a dangerous trap for a writer who hasn't got the structure working yet. They fall in love with a scene or even a strong sequence of dialogue and they will fight to keep it, compromising an objective analysis of the overall story.

Working and reworking a scene-by-scene treatment until it's as good as it can be before attempting a first draft can save many days and weeks rewriting at a draft level. And when the hard work is done, and you know the outline is solid and the story works, the act of writing the draft—giving life and voice to the characters—becomes the greatest freedom and pleasure for me as a writer. I believe this method saved me a lot of time on *Barrens*. My second draft was the production draft and this was only possible with a very strong, structured scene-by-scene treatment.

I went to Manitoba before writing *Barrens* because I believe more and more that writers have to go and experience the place they are writing about. I was once contracted to write a drama set in Africa though there was no money to send me there. The resulting script was very flat, lacking authenticity and probably the weakest thing I've written. Whether it be a wilderness environment or a murder site, the experience of being there is a tremendous inspiration to the writer, and producers must be made to realize this.

Probably the most important relationship for a writer is the one with the director. When you've rewritten the script five or eight or twelve times working with producers, network people, funding people and all their editors and the script has finally been green-lighted— just when you think, "Enough! It's perfect"—they bring on a director. There are some writers who will take their production fees and go home, but I believe this is the last and most critical stage of work for the writer to maintain control of his or her work.

When a director comes on board, emotions can be high because the director naturally wants to impose his vision on the script, the writer is feeling naturally defensive about his "baby" and this is the draft that will be shot and seen for all eternity. There are some directors who are "traffic cops" and they'll just shoot the script without really understanding the subtleties of the material. It's all just "blah-blah" to them. Then there are others who are "control freaks" and want to rewrite the whole script themselves. (This shows the ultimate disrespect for the script and the writer.) An ideal director is one who respects the script, wants to understand the writer's vision so he or she can make a better film.

On my first television movie in the mid-seventies, I had a producer who went to great lengths to keep me and the director apart. We actually had to have secret meetings! I think it is crucial for the writer to walk through the script with the director over the course of at least a couple of full, uninterrupted days, and it is the role of the producer to facilitate this process, bearing in mind that it was the scriptwriter whose work got him the green light. Some directors will resist this "mind-melding," but the good directors will ask for it. I talk the director through all the emotional beats, the character arcs and the narrative twists, and I'll answer all questions. We as writers live with those script elements every day and assume everyone must see them clearly on the written page, but a director's mind is full of visuals, locations, casting, schedules and budget. I remember once arriving on set to talk to the director just after a crucial scene was shot. We had not been through the script together. I'll never forget the chilling feeling when he said to me, "Oh, that's what you meant in that scene."

When I go through a script with a director, I accept that it is a give-and-take situation. I am obligated to keep open-minded to their new ideas and suggested changes. It must be a partnership. This "mind-melding" can be a long, hard process but invariably, it produces a better product. Ideally, the writer should be present for a "read through" by the cast. This is a wonderful opportunity for fine-tuning the script and staying in control of the material. It can make the difference between a good film and a great one.

Though time was tight, I had the opportunity of meeting and working with *Barrens* director Michael Scott in Toronto and Manitoba and wrote a production draft that incorporated many of his ideas. Mike is a warm, friendly guy, but he has strong opinions. After some give and take between us I left him to direct my script, satisfied we were seeing the same movie.

To be honest, I believe *Lost in the Barrens* might have needed just one more draft. There are some rough edges that still make me wince, but that's the case in every movie that I've had produced. *Barrens* did win an Emmy Award, and still has great circulation years later. And Farley says he likes it, which from Farley is high praise indeed.[10]

Creative Nonfiction   PEGI TAYLOR

What happens when writers have experiences that leave them lost for words? What can a writer do to convey, say, the grim ramifications of some foster care or even the inexplicable fads of teenagers? Fiction writers have always relied on devices like dialogue, point of view or metaphor. In the 20th century, many leading nonfiction writers looked to fiction for the resources to describe the indescribable. A group of journalists in the late 1950s and early 1960s started to experiment, more than any writers had before them, with just how many techniques they could snitch from fiction and still stick to the facts. Tom Wolfe's stylistically flamboyant pieces for the *New York Herald Tribune* justified his immediate inclusion in this club that came to be labeled "New Journalism." Calling himself "the Hectoring Narrator," Wolfe often would start his stories by insulting his subjects. "The Peppermint Lounge Revisited," a portrait of some New Jersey teenagers, begins:

> All right, girls, into your stretch nylon denims! You know the ones—the ones that look like they were designed by some leering, knuckle-rubbing old tailor with a case of workbench back…. Next, hoist up those bras, up to the angle of a Nike missile launcher. Then get into the cable-knit mohair sweaters, the ones that fluff out like a cat by a project heating duct. And then unroll the rollers and explode the hair a couple of feet up in the air into bouffants, beehives and Passaic pompadours.

The high-energy Wolfe became a spokesperson for New Journalism. In 1973, he wrote three essays that formed a manifesto at the beginning of *The New Journalism*, followed by his annotated anthology of what he considered the best of what New Journalism had produced. (The collection, for which Wolfe was co-editor, is out of print.)

Wolfe defined New Journalism as appropriating four specific fictional devices: "scene-by-scene construction"; recording the dialogue "in full"; and taking advantage of the third-person point of view, "presenting every scene to the reader through the eyes of a particular character."

Although Wolfe never refers to New Journalists as anthropologists or sociologists, he describes the fourth element as "Recording the everyday gestures, habits, manners, customs, styles of furniture, clothing, decoration, styles of traveling, eating, keeping house, modes of behaving toward children ... and other symbolic details that might exist within a scene."

As an example of a writer carefully amassing details to construct dramatic scenes as any novelist might, Wolfe included a selection from Truman Capote's *In Cold Blood*. Primarily a fiction writer prior to that book, Capote studied novelists like Gustave Flaubert, Jane Austen, Marcel Proust and Willa Cather in 1958 as he trained himself to produce "a narrative form that employed all the techniques of fictional art but was nevertheless immaculately factual." The following year he read about the murder of four members of the Clutter family in a small town in Kansas, with no apparent motives and almost no clues. He devoted the next six years to researching the crime, compiling 6,000 pages of interviews, and then wrote his stunning "nonfiction novel" that became an instant bestseller when it was published in 1965.

James Agee also influenced Capote's writing. In 1936, a magazine asked Agee and photographer Walker Evans to collaborate on an article about tenant farming in the U.S. by looking at a few families' daily lives. The project resulted in the 1939 landmark book *Let Us Now Praise Famous Men*. To bring readers into the tenants' homes, Agee commands readers in the second person to see what he sees: "Leave this room and go very quietly down the open hall that divides the house, past the bedroom door, and the dog that sleeps outside it."

Wolfe excerpts part of Norman Mailer's Pulitzer Prize-winning *The Armies of the Night: History as a Novel/The Novel as History* to show how New Journalists were manipulating point of view. Mailer chronicles his own participation in the 1967 March on the Pentagon using the third person. "Sin was his favorite fellow, his tonic, his jailer, his horse, his sword," writes Mailer about his own behavior at a party before the march, matching all the vividness of fiction. In the introduction to *The Time of Our Time*, a literary retrospective of his fiction and nonfiction, Mailer asserts, "There is little in this book, even when it falls under the category of nonfiction or argument, that has not derived ... from my understanding of how one writes fiction."

Hunter S. Thompson, who became touted as the "Gonzo Journalist" after he abandoned any reportorial distance to describe riding with the Hell's Angels in 1965, copied pages from the novels of William Faulkner and F. Scott Fitzgerald earlier in his writing career. Reading Jack Kerouac taught Thompson "that you wrote about what you did." Wolfe characterizes Thompson's frenzied accounts of his experiences as featuring "a manic, highly adrenal first-person style in which Thompson's own emotions continually dominate the story."

It takes tremendous craft for a nonfiction writer to dominate his subject. Wolfe, Capote, Mailer and Thompson could pull this off, but once they became celebrities in their own right, it became harder and harder for them to act as reporters. The instant they arrived to cover a story, their presence altered it. Other less-gifted writers who tried to copy them often failed when technique overwhelmed or even changed substance.

Sticking strictly to the facts and finding the most vibrant ways to convey those facts to readers continues to challenge nonfiction writers. "Most journalists experience a professional tug-of-war between the desire to tell a good story, and the desire to report thoroughly, analyze, and explain," Christopher Hanson wrote in a 1999 article in the *Columbia Journalism Review*.

[The] *New York Times* reporter Nina Bernstein was initially hesitant to let go of "conventional journalism" when she started to expand into a book her series of articles about foster care in New York. Published in 2001, her critically acclaimed *The Lost Children of Wilder: The Epic Struggle to Change Foster Care* chronicles both a '70s lawsuit meant to dismantle discrimination in New York's system and the lives of children, like Lamont Wilder, caught up in the foster care bureaucracy. During the drafting process, an editor persuaded Bernstein to engage in a tug-of-war and draw on fictional devices. Bernstein insists, similarly to Wolfe's defense of New Journalism, that composing a scene "takes enormous amounts of information to glean the telling detail."

"As I became more comfortable applying literary techniques to my store of notes," Bernstein recalls, "I think an unconscious but real influence was George Eliot's *Middlemarch*." Eliot brings to the reader an "empathic irony" through changing points of view. In following the fractured childhood of Lamont Wilder, who rarely lived in the same place for more than a year, Bernstein recounts the young boy killing a gerbil. To tell this story, Bernstein needed "to understand and identify with Lamont's actions, to feel what he felt and make readers feel it, or else this would be the point at which they distanced themselves emotionally from him." Based on information from many interviews, she draws readers in:

> It was dark in the latchkey room at school. The other children were watching a movie, but Lamont tiptoed to the back, where the gerbil lived in a metal cage. It twitched its whiskers at him, brown eyes

appealing for release. Carefully, Lamont slid the cage door open and took the gerbil out. It lay warm and soft between his hands, the pulse of its heart like undemanding love. It was content to have its fur stroked, and Lamont felt each caress as though he, not the gerbil, were being gentled. He cuddled the creature, seeking the comfort that eluded him all these months…. And the gerbil bit him, hard.

The unexpected pain was like the opening of a sluicegate on the boy's rage. In an instant, he dropped the gerbil to the floor and stamped it. If the animal cried out, no one heard it. Its small, broken body lay still on the linoleum floor beside Lamont's foot, its life extinguished by his overpowering anger. He ran from the room and hid in the boys' bathroom. Like the gerbil in its cage, he crouched in a corner and defecated on the floor.

Bernstein slowly describes the dim light and Lamont edging away from the group to pet the gerbil. She uses a simile, "the pulse of its heart like undemanding love," to establish the psychological weight of the moment for Lamont. The pace suddenly quickens, as the gerbil's teeth sink into Lamont's flesh, and the reader empathizes with his violent reaction.

For inspiration, Bernstein looked to some of the same fiction writers as New Journalists, including F. Scott Fitzgerald and especially Charles Dickens. The latter's satirical *Bleak House*, published in 1853, follows the legal delays, lasting for generations, of the suit of Jarndyce vs. Jarndyce, which uncannily parallels the multiple generations involved in the class-action Wilder suit that Bernstein analyzed. From the beginning, Bernstein says, "I knew that I was attempting a kind of modern-day nonfiction Dickens in scope and incident. I knew the narrative drive had to be strong enough to carry the weight of the history, law and politics that I wanted to include."

Adopting fictional devices opens up seemingly limitless possibilities for nonfiction writers, as well as making them more conscious of their craft. This consciousness has led to increased interest in literary nonfiction. In 1984, Robert Atwan sought a trade publisher to start an annual collection of essays for general readers. He could point to the success of Annie Dillard's Pulitzer Prize-winning *Pilgrim at Tinker Creek*. "Like the bear who went over the mountain," Dillard spent a year observing and describing the natural world, using more metaphors and similes than bees swarming around a hive thick with honey.

Houghton Mifflin published the first volume of *The Best American Essays* in 1986. From 1991 to 2000, *BAE* published 219 essays by

170 authors. Cynthia Ozick is represented six times, more than any other writer. Like most of the multiple contributors, including William H. Gass, Edward Hoagland, Jamaica Kincaid and John Updike, Ozick writes fiction as well as nonfiction. In the introduction to the 1998 *BAE,* for which she was a guest editor, Ozick distinguishes what she calls "the marrow of the essay from the marrow of fiction" and maintains, "Essays, like novels, emerge from the sensations of the self." Speaking of the essay like "a character in a novel or a play," she concludes, "Above all, she is not a hidden principle or a thesis or a construct: she is there, a living voice. She takes us in." Joyce Carol Oates, who collaborated with Atwan to edit *The Best American Essays of the Century,* lists some of the ways the essay takes us in, "employing dialogue, dramatic scenes, withheld information, suspense."

These editors applaud authors employing the tools of fiction in nonfiction. The tactic, however, is not without risk. A clear case in point was Edmund Morris's broadly criticized 1999 *Dutch: A Memoir of Ronald Reagan.* In order to narrate particular scenes, Morris wrote himself into the book as a fictional friend of Reagan's. Critics found this Doppelganger device confusing and distracting. An original member of the New Journalism club for her 1968 essay collection *Slouching Towards Bethlehem,* Joan Didion reviewed *Dutch* for *The New York Review of Books.* Unrelenting in her diatribe against Morris for shoddy research, Didion also assesses his insertion of fictional characters. "Literary conceits are tricky, hard work," she concludes. "When this kind of thing works, it works unnoticed. When it does not work, it swamps the narrative, and leaves the reader toting up errors or misapprehensions."

Fictional devices work in nonfiction when they enhance the narrative's realism. At 21, Dave Eggers started raising his 8-year-old brother after their parents died of cancer within two months of each other. In *The New York Times Book Review,* Sara Mosle calls Eggers' account of parenting under these conditions, titled *A Heartbreaking Work of Staggering Genius,* "a furious whirlwind of energy and invention." The book became a bestseller in hardcover and paperback partly for mimicking the antics of fiction writer David Foster Wallace. Eggers' memoir includes "Rules and Suggestions for Enjoyment of This Book" along with an "Incomplete Guide to Symbols and Metaphors." Under the surface of this play, Eggers engages in nonstop stream-of-consciousness—whether in the middle of lovemaking or after he summons the police to help calm a suicidal friend:

The other cop is writing things down in his pad. The pad is so small. His pen is really small, too. They seem too small, the pen and pad. Personally, I would want a bigger pad. Then again, with a bigger pad, where would I put it? You'd need a pad-holster, which might look cool but would make it even harder to run, especially if you have the flash-light attachment ... I guess you need a small pad so it'll fit on your utility belt—Oh, it would be so great if they called it a utility belt. Maybe I could ask. Not now, of course, but later.

This narrative verve and focus on the oh-so-particular slices through his humor and lets the reader see Eggers' full force. For a young man to witness both his parents die of cancer, every act of living becomes imbued with meaning. Eggers never writes directly about the impact of his parents' deaths. It is in his endless medita-tion on the minute that Eggers reveals his own indescribable pain and fear and longing.[11]

The Big Finish   DON McKINNEY

"Nobody ever writes about endings, " Bill Zinsser told me once, and while that statement is not strictly true, it comes close. Zinsser did include a chapter called "The Ending" in *On Writing Well*, one of the best books ever written on the craft of magazine article writing, but it's one of the shortest chapters in his book. The fact is that few people have thought much about the best ways to wind up an article. Long-time freelancer Max Gunther once asked a number of editors what kind of endings they liked, and got a lot of blank stares. "I know a good ending when I read one," was the almost universal response, but there were few useful suggestions.

One thought did predominate: A good ending is satisfying. It leaves the reader feeling that the subject has been covered, the main points have been made, and nothing more remains to be said.

Just as in a play or movie, the ending is what you leave the reader with; his final judgment about the success of the article may well be formed by the last paragraph or so. John McPhee, who many think is the best magazine writer of our time, places such importance on the ending that he claims to "always know the last line of a story before I've written the first one." I once asked freelancer Barbara Raymond how she was doing on an assignment and she said cheerfully, "I've got the lead and the ending and all I have to do is fill in the rest."

And while Jerome Stern, who directs the writing program at Florida State University, was not talking about magazine articles in his book *Making Shapely Fiction*, his point about endings works for nonfiction as well. "The closer and closer you get to the ending," he writes, "the more weight each word has, so that by the time you get to the last several words each one carries an enormous meaning. A single gesture or image at the end can outweigh all that has gone before."

During my years as an editor, whenever I picked up an article from a new writer I would usually read the lead and then skip over to the end; if the writer had started well and finished up strongly, I would know I was in good hands and would settle down to read with some sense of anticipation.

Having said all that, what is a good ending? What are the different methods you can use to bring your piece to a satisfying conclusion? "I always try to end sooner than the reader expects me to," Zinsser says. "The perfect ending should take the reader slightly by surprise."

While I agree that pieces should never be allowed to overstay their welcomes, I'm not sure that surprise is always necessary (although it can be wonderful when it works). But there are a great many ways to finish strongly, and I've made up an arbitrary list of ten of them. The catalog may contain a certain amount of overlapping, but whoever said magazine writing was a science?

The Circle Technique

This is probably the most popular, because nothing is more effective in giving the reader a sense that he has covered the subject than a return to a theme introduced in the lead. As Peter Jacobi, a long-time teacher, columnist and writing consultant, puts it, "The reader should be left satisfied, feel that he's read something finished, something with a point clearly made, something with a unity that has moved him from start to finish almost in a circular manner."

Dave Anderson, an award-winning sportswriter for *The New York Times*, has been using this technique for years. In a column written just prior to Nolan Ryan's five start after a recent no-hitter, Dave begins with a quote from former Baltimore shortstop Mark Belanger. It was 1973, and Ryan had pitched a no-hitter in his previous game; he was six outs away from another when Belanger slapped a ball between short and second for a single. "They told me that when I got to first base, Nolan looked at me," Belanger remembered. "Nolan tilts that head and gives you that look." And Anderson's ending: "Now the 44-year-old phenom has another chance ... But if one of the Blue Jays gets a hit, Nolan Ryan will tilt that head and give him that look."

In a profile of Cybill Shepherd in *Memphis* magazine a few years back, Ed Weathers began with Shepherd on the deck of her Memphis apartment overlooking the Mississippi, "wearing a 'Memphis Country Club Member—guest 1982' visor, aviator sunglasses and a black bikini ..." Several thousand words later Weathers is back on the deck, but this time it is late in the day: "The sky turns a deeper purple, and Shepherd turns contemplative. 'You know,' she says, 'I regret every sunset I miss here.' As she gazes across the Mississippi, the Memphis sun disappears, headed toward LA." Weathers has closed the circle, returning to where be began, and the reader feels a sense of completion.

The Summary

If the word *summary* brings up phrases like "as I have been saying" or "as we have seen," forget them. A good summary ending can take many forms, none of which begin with "in conclusion." Reading through a recent issue of *Reader's Digest,* I found several examples of summary endings in the form of quotes. At the end of an article on people who have been swindled in phony land deals, author Trevor Armbrister quotes an official of the federal Department of Housing and Urban Development: "If it sounds too good to be true, it probably is." This advice has been given a good many times, but it still makes a very apt ending.

Another *Digest* article, this one on the value of helmets for cyclists, concluded:

> "So many things are totally out of control in a motorcycle or bicycle accident," says Dr. Donald Leslie, a head-injury specialist. "A helmet is one thing you *can* control."

A splendid example of the summary ending that does not sound like a summary was used by Saul Pett in his Pulitzer Prize-winning article on the federal bureaucracy and how it got to be so big.

> The parts multiply like the denizens of a rabbit warren on New Year's Eve. Everybody, it seems, wants something or opposes something and, in the melee, bureaucracy grows larger and more shapeless and threatens to become, in itself, a government of too many people, by too many people, for too many people.

The Quote

The straight quote ending does not necessarily summarize the point of the piece, but it should reiterate its theme and tone. It's a good idea to look for an appropriate quote when you're typing up your notes; some comment that seems to sum things up in a snappy way. One I particularly like comes from a piece Richard Gehman wrote for us at *True* magazine many years ago. It was about the Dalton family, for many generations (even back to the time of Queen Victoria) the preeminent rat catchers of London. After what amounted to a short course in the history of the rat and how to catch him, Gehman concluded with a quote from Bill Dalton, elder statesman of the clan:

> He had grown so fond of rats over the years that sometimes, as he is sitting a lonely vigil in a dark room in the depths of this ancient city,

he begins to speculate uneasily over the future. "What I wonder," he says, "is this—suppose I'm a rat in the next world? What am I going to do to keep away from the bloody Daltons?"

The Anecdote

Just as you looked through your notes for a good quote to wind up your story, you might also look for a good anecdote, perhaps the second best if you plan to lead off with your best one.

A fine example of an anecdote ending, which also combines elements of the surprise and the ironic, was written by Joseph R. Judge in an article on early explorations of the New World and appeared in *National Geographic* a few years ago. After reporting that the first European settlements were Spanish, predating the English colonization by almost a century, he wound up this way:

> Thus it was when a Spanish caravel came into the Chesapeake in 1611, under pretext of searching for a lost ship, and captured a young English pilot named John Clark. Three from the caravel were stranded ashore and were jailed. One died of starvation; another, found to be English, was later hanged for treason. The third, Don Diego de Molina, survived four years imprisonment in Virginia, railing in letters smuggled home against English designs in a land to which Spain had such an ancient and honorable claim, and calling Jamestown "a new Algiers in America."
>
> Clark had been taken to Spain and interrogated, and in due course of time each man was returned to his native land. Clark returned to the sea and found work to his liking as first mate on a ship bound for America.
>
> Her name was Mayflower.

The End of Action

This is sometimes appropriate for a narrative, but not always. It, like the summary, gives a feeling that the last act has taken place and the events about which the article was written are over. In Joan Didion's classic collection of articles, *Slouching Toward Bethlehem*, she includes a wonderful memoir of coming of age in New York called "Goodbye to All That." After remembering what it was like for a young girl to come to the big city from California and try and make her fortune there, she ends:

> The last time I was in New York was in a cold January and everyone was ill and tired. Many of the people I used to know there had moved

to Dallas or gone on Antabuse or had bought a farm in New Hampshire. We stayed ten days, and then we took an afternoon flight back to Los Angeles, and on the way home from the airport that night I could see the moon on the Pacific and smell jasmine all around and we both knew that there was no longer any point in keeping the apartment we still kept in New York. There were years when I called Los Angeles "the Coast," but they seem a long time ago.

And is there any more perfect end of action than the closing lines of Melville's *Moby Dick*? (True, this isn't a magazine ending, but it's one I've never forgotten.) The whale has destroyed the ship, and she is about to sink. "Now small fowls flew screaming over the yet yawning gulf; a sullen white surf beat against its steep sides; then all collapsed, and the great shroud of the sea rolled on as it rolled five thousand years ago."

The Ironic Ending

In a marvelous essay called "Journalese, or Why English Is the Second Language of the Fourth Estate," John Leo crams in many of the worst examples of newspaper writing in one nifty closing paragraph, even including the cliché of the summary ending.

> In sum, journalese is a truly vital language, the last bulwark against libel, candor and fresh utterance. Its prestigious, ground-breaking, state-of-the-art lingo makes it arguably the most useful of tongues, and its untimely demise would have a chilling effect, especially on us award-winning journalists.

Irony should be used sparingly, but when the subject matter is appropriate, it can really drive home the point.

A combination of the anecdotal, the ironic and the quote ends Rex Reed's splendid profile of Ava Gardner, taken from his book *Do You Sleep in the Nude*? It had been a long afternoon of talking and drinking, and they are all going out to dinner.

> Ava is in the middle of Park Avenue, the scarf falling around her neck and her hair blowing wildly around the Ava eyes. Lady Brett in the traffic, with a downtown bus as the bull. Three cars stop on a green light and every taxi driver on Park Avenue begins to honk. The autograph hunters leap through the polished doors of the Regency and begin to scream ... They [Ava and her entourage] are already turning

the corner into 57th Street, fading into the kind of night, the color of tomato juice in the headlights, that only exists in New York when it rains.

"Who was it?" asks a woman walking a poodle.

"Jackie Kennedy," answers a man from his bus window.

The Surprise

Surprise endings are hard to find, and most articles, particularly long ones, don't lend themselves to this sort of treatment. Truman Capote pulled it off effectively in a piece called "Mr. Jones," which appears in his collection *Music for Chameleons*. Although Capote may have been best known as a novelist, he was an excellent reporter and matchless storyteller. Jones was a neighbor of Capote's in a small Brooklyn rooming house. He was both crippled and blind, with few friends and no known occupation, but no one thought him remarkable until the day he disappeared.

Then, ten years later, Capote was riding on a Moscow subway when he looked up and saw his former neighbor. "I was about to cross the aisle and speak to him when the train pulled into a station, and Mr. Jones, on a pair of fine sturdy legs, stood up and strode out of the car. Swiftly, the train door closed behind him."

What had seemed a simple sketch of a casual acquaintance suddenly turned into a spy story—and a memorable one.

The Poetic Ending

In this case, the writer is allowed to indulge in some flowery writing, perhaps even a bit of philosophy. It can be self-indulgent (be wary of this), but it can also leave an echo in the mind that the reader will not soon forget. One of the best I know is from E.B. White's classic essay on New York, originally written for *Holiday* magazine back in 1948 but reprinted dozens of times since. The New York he wrote about is gone, as is the great Mr. White, but his final image has stayed with me.

> A block or two west of the new City of Man in Turtle Bay there is an old willow tree that presides over an interior garden. It is a battered tree, long-suffering and much climbed, held together by strands of wire but beloved of those who know it. In a way it symbolizes the city: life under difficulties, growth against odds, sap-rise in the midst of concrete, and the steady reaching for the sun. Whenever I look at it nowadays, and feel the cold shadow of the planes, I think: "This must

be saved, this particular thing, this very tree." If it were to go, all would go—this city, this mischievous and marvelous monument which not to look upon would be like death.

The Echo Ending

This carries the circle technique to its ultimate extent by repeating a word or phrase frequently throughout the piece, so that it becomes almost a theme in itself. In Max Gunther's *Writing the Modern Magazine Article*, a truly excellent guide which is unfortunately out of print, he recalls an article he once wrote on the history and legends of gold. He dropped the word in frequently, in the form of one-word paragraphs, after many of his anecdotes, and closed with "It's the bloodstained metal. The metal that can make you rich. Or dead.

"Gold."

The Straight Statement

While this sort of ending does summarize the point of the article, beware of the simplistic "as we have seen" approach. Remember that your conclusion is the final thought you want to leave with the reader, the one that reemphasizes the point and answers the question: "Why did I read this piece?" I like to close with a thought that drives home the essence of what I have written. An example I'm fond of is from an article Sen. Eugene McCarthy wrote for *Geo* magazine. His subject was political campaigning, and he concluded:

> Defeat in politics, even relative failure, is not easy to accept. Dismissing the troops, as both Napoleon and Robert E. Lee learned, is not easy. Soldiers do not want to take their horses and mules and go back to the spring plowing. It is better to win.

In Conclusion ...

This list obviously does not include every possibility, but it should give you some ideas. The point to remember is that the ending is probably the second most important part of your article, after the lead, and you should be pointing toward it all the way through. A weak ending leaves a soft, squishy feeling about the article; a strong one will cover for a multitude of sins. When you've finished writing, and waited the requisite day or two before reading your work again, see if you haven't gone on longer than you really need to. The best ending may well be a few paragraphs back—maybe even a few pages!

I've quoted the estimable Mr. Zinsser frequently, so I think I'll let him have the last word: "When you've finished telling what you want to tell, just stop."[12]

THE WRITER'S READING LIST

Atwood, Margaret. *Negotiating With the Dead: A Writer on Writing*. Cambridge: Cambridge University Press, 2002.

Bowling, Tim, ed. *Where the Words Come From*. Roberts Creek, BC: Nightwood Editions, 2002.

Crouch, Leanna, ed. *One on One: The Imprint Interviews*. Toronto: Somerville House, 1994.

Dillard, Annie. *The Writing Life*. New York: Harper and Row, 1989.

Epel, Naomi. *Writers Dreaming*. New York: Vintage/Random House, 1994.

Frank, Anne, ed. *Telling It: Writing for Film and Television in Canada*. Toronto: Doubleday, 1996.

Gorman, Ed and Martin H. Greenberg, eds. *Speaking of Murder*. New York: Berkley Prime Crime, 1998.

King, Stephen. *On Writing: A Memoir of Craft*. New York: Scribner, 2000.

Scheier, Libby, Sarah Sheard, and Eleanor Wachtel, eds. *Language in Her Eye: Views on Writing and Gender by Canadian Women Writing in English*. Toronto: Coach House Press, 1990.

Strickland, Bill, ed. *On Being a Writer*. Cincinnati, OH: Writer's Digest Books, 1989.

Wachtel, Eleanor. *Writers & Company*. Toronto: Alfred A. Knopf, 1993.

Writers on Writing: Collected Essays from The New York Times. New York: Henry Holt and Company, 2001.

Endnotes and Credits

Unit 5

1. Kyoko Mori, quoted in Caryn Mirriam-Goldberg, *Write Where You Are; How to Use Writing to Make Sense of Your Life: A Guide for Teens*. Minneapolis, MN: Free Spirit Publishing Inc., 1999, 68.

2. Carol Shields, "The Same Ticking Clock." Reprinted by permission of Carol Shields.

3. Annie Proulx, "Inspiration? Head Down the Back Road, and Stop for the Yard Sale," in *Writers on Writing: Collected Essays from* The New York Times. New York: Times Books/Henry Holt, 2001, 185–190. Reprinted by permission of Darhansoff, Verrill, Feldman Literary Agents.

4. Ann Patchett, "Why Not Put Off Till Tomorrow the Novel You Could Begin Today?" The New York Times Web site, www.nytimes.com/2002/08/26/books/26PATC.html.

5. Raymond Obstfeld, "Maximize Your Writers' Group Experience," in *Start Writing Now!* (a *Writer's Digest* magazine). Cincinnati, OH: F& W Publications, April 2002, 53–55. Reprinted by permission of the author.

6. Andrea Griffith, "Interview with M. NourbeSe Philip," in *unherd Magazine*. Fall/Winter 2001, 14–15. Reprinted by permission of Andrea Griffith.

7. Cathleen Schine, "Dying Metaphors Take Flight" *New York Times Magazine*, August 8, 1993. Rreprinted by permission of the author.

8. Excerpts from "Fear and Loathing at the Laptop" by Sandra Martin. *The Globe and Mail*, June 29, 2002, R1. Reprinted with permission from *The Globe and Mail*.

9. Sharon Riis, "What It Means to Be a Writer," in *Telling It: Writing for Film and Television in Canada*. Edited by Anne Frank, the Academy of Canadian Cinema and Television. Toronto: Doubleday Canada, 1996, 1–4. Reprinted by permission of Sharon Riis.

10. Keith Ross, "Adapting *Lost in the Barrens* for Television," in *Telling It: Writing for Film and Television in Canada*. Edited by Anne Frank, the Academy of Canadian Cinema and Television. Toronto: Doubleday Canada Limited, 1996, pages 35–39.

11. Pegi Taylor, "Creative Nonfiction." First appeared in *The Writer* magazine, February 2002, 29–33. Reprinted by permision of the author.

12. Don McKinney, "The Big Finish," in *Writer's Digest*, February 1992, 42–45. Reprinted by permission of the author.

Index

giving information through, 121–22
narrative functions, 148–51
real speech vs., 124–26
in scriptwriting, 143–45
Dickens, Charles
Bleak House, 329
Great Expectations, 115
Dickinson, Emily, 181
Dictionary of Clichés (Kirkpatrick), 29–30
Didion, Joan, 330
Slouching Toward Bethlehem, 335–36
Dillard, Annie, 108
Pilgrim at Tinker Creek, 329
Direct address lead, 39–40
"Disappointment" (Hillabold), 191–93
Distraction, fallacies of, 70
"Do Not Go Gentle into That Good Night" (Thomas), 208
Doublet clichés, 29
Do You Sleep in the Nude? (Reed), 336–37
Drew, Elizabeth, 181
Dub poetry, 202–203

E

Echo endings, 338
Editing
with classmates, 12–14
need for, 233
peer, 9–10, 12–14
Editorials, 66–67
Eggers, Dave. *A Heartbreaking Work of Staggering Genius,* 330–31
Eliot, George. *Middlemarch,* 328
E-mail, 253–54
Emotion vs. logic, 71–72
Employment letters, 236–42
Endings, 332–39
echo, 338
poetic, 337–38
straight statements as, 338
The English Patient (Ondaatje), 114
Ephron, Nora, 61
Euphemisms, 200
as clichés, 29
Euphony, 209
Evans, Walker, 327
Examples, 46
Executive summaries, 258
Exposé features, 59

F

"A Family Supper" (Ishiguro), 121–22
Faulkner, William, 11

Fear and Loathing at the Laptop (Martin), 309–17
Feature stories
about, 57–59
angles, 63
body, 64
closings, 64
content of, 62–64
ideas for, 60–62
leads, 38–43, 63–64
researching, 62
structure, 63–64
types of, 58–59
Field, Syd. *The Screenwriter's Workbook,* 166–68
Fight Club (Palahniuk), 129
Figurative language, 216–17, 273
Filler clichés, 30
Films
action in, 145
actors, 145
acts/scenes in, 144
dialogue, 145
settings, 146
special effects, 145
viewer imagination, 146
Findley, Timothy, 148
The Piano Man's Daughter, 114
First-person narrator, 130–31
First-person point of view, 127
First-person travel writing, 89
Flashbacks, 112
Flaubert, Gustave, 290
Foreign clichés, 29
Foster, Norm
Louis and Dave, 155–58
The Visit, 163–65
Free verse poetry, 182
line breaks in, 218–22
rhythm in, 206
"Friendly Obstacles," 186
Frost, Robert, 33
Frye, Northrop. *Anatomy of Criticism,* 313

G

"Games at Twilight" (Desai), 135–36
Gardner, John, 5
Gehman, Richard, 334–35
George, Elizabeth, 115–16
Glittering generalities, 72
Going to Argentina (Vanderhaeghe), 315–16
Gordimer, Nadine. "Once Upon a Time," 110
Gould, Jan Hopaklyissumqwa. "A West Coast Woman," 110
Gowdy, Barbara, 310